A Cup of Comfort
Favorites

80 Timeless Inspirational Classic Stories

EDITED BY

COLLEEN SELL

ADAMS MEDIA
Avon, Massachusetts

A Cup of Comfort is a trademark of F+W Publications, Inc.

Published by
Adams Media, an F+W Publications Company
57 Littlefield Street, Avon, MA 02322. U.S.A.
www.adamsmedia.com and *www.cupofcomfort.com*

ISBN: 1-59337-848-3

Printed in the United States of America.

J I H G F E D C B A

Library of Congress Cataloging-in-Publication Data
A cup of comfort favorites : 75 timeless classic stories / edited by Colleen Sell.
     p.   cm.   (A cup of comfort series book)
          ISBN 1-59337-641-3
     1. Conduct of life. I. Sell, Colleen. II. Series.
          BJ1597.C86 2005
          158.1'28--dc22
                                        2005021978

This book is available at quantity discounts for bulk purchases.
For information, please call 1-800-872-5627.

 # Contents

 Introduction

"*These are the stories that never, never die, that are carried like seed into a new country, are told to you and me and make in us new and lasting strengths.*"

~Meridel Le Sueur

My husband and I recently bought a homestead that was settled in 1873, during the region's gold rush. Our farm is a hop, skip, and a jump away from what was once the Bohemia Mining District, thousands of miles of lush forest in Central Oregon's Cascade Mountains, ribboned with rivers, streams, and logging roads. Last summer while cruising through the woods on my fat-tire bicycle, I met up with two middle-aged women who were panning for gold, and we struck up a friendly conversation. I was amazed that gold was still being found only a few miles from my home and even more surprised to learn that there was probably gold in the creek running through our property. All I needed was a few simple implements, a bunch of time and patience, and a little luck.

As the lady "gold miners" gave me a quick how-to lesson, it occurred to me that gold panning is a lot like compiling an anthology. You've got to figure out where the gold might be, submerse your pan in the stream to collect a slew of material, and patiently sift through it, separating the gold from the gunk—again and again and again.

Over the course of four years, I panned near and far to collect and carefully sift through more than 30,000 stories to find the 550 "golden nuggets" published in the first 11 volumes of *A Cup of Comfort*. Each is a rare find in its own right. But certain stories have emerged as favorites not only of mine, but also of reviewers, booksellers, and most important, *Cup of Comfort* readers.

Gathered here in this special collection are some of those "24-carat gold" stories, a few each from the following books: *A Cup of Comfort: Stories That Warm Your Heart, Lift Your Spirit, and Enrich Your Life* (flagship volume), *A Cup of Comfort for Friends*, *A Cup of Comfort for Women*, *A Cup of Comfort Cookbook*, *A Cup of Comfort for Mothers & Daughters*, *A Cup of Comfort for Inspiration*, *A Cup of Comfort for Christmas*, *A Cup of Comfort for Courage*, *A Cup of Comfort for Teachers*, *A Cup of Comfort for Sisters*, and *A Cup of Comfort for Mothers & Sons*.

These are the stories that have received the most and the highest compliments from both readers and reviewers, and that have elicited the most positive audience response at readings. These are among those rare stories that strike a chord when you first read them, and stay with you long afterward. Stories so distinctive and compelling that no matter how many times you read them, they always engage, always entertain, and always move you.

We hope you enjoy them as much as we have.

—*Colleen Sell*

 Something More

The Australian summer sun beats on the thirsty bush. It burns my legs through the windscreen as I rattle over deeply corrugated dirt roads. It is mid-January in the central highlands of Tasmania, and I am here alone, recently single, recently in my thirties, and in need of physical and spiritual challenge. Over the next four weeks I will go into some of the remotest areas of the state, to walk and camp in the wilderness. In a few days I will join a handful of others on an eleven-day rafting trip down 125 kilometers (approximately 80 miles) of the Franklin River, in the inaccessible wilderness of Tasmania's southwest. But right now, this adventurer fears she may be lost. I long for the sight of a paved road.

As I drive, my thoughts collide with one another and I am uncomfortably alone with them. The last year has been hell, and I am raw from many losses. I am a pilgrim here, searching for physical hardship, for risk to plunge into. I want hard mountains, drenching rain, and big, frightening rapids to shock away my numbness. I am here to feel alive again.

After many long, hot hours, I reach the west coast. Painted with dust and melting under the late afternoon sun, I pull into the tiny coastal town of Strahan, never before so happy to see cars and buildings. Some frontier woman I am.

I check into my hostel, kick open the door to my bunk-room, and blink in the darkness of the musty room.

Then I see her. Smiling, staring directly at me as though I am expected, she is perched like a doll on the edge of a sagging bunk bed. The sight of her face stops me at the threshold for a few moments. I am very surprised to see this stranger. She is terribly old. Her tiny, frail form reminds me of my late mother. Her smile is a bit unsettling.

"My name is Vonny Helberg," she says. "But you can call me Gran Vonny. Everyone does."

Beside her on the bed lies a fractured range of odds and ends, spilling from a well-traveled vinyl suitcase. Tiny crocheted flowers, shreds of notes and papers, tubes of antiseptic cream, bandages.

"Hello," I say.

Polite conversation ensues as I search for swimming gear, uncomfortable in the presence of my unlikely roommate. I feel an overwhelming responsibility to take care of her. *What on earth is this tiny, old woman doing here in a youth hostel?*

I find my gear, smile a good-bye, and head out to explore. But I cannot shake the image of that expectant smile.

When I return later that night, she is asleep. I creep up to my bunk and ease my exhausted body into the sleeping bag, fading into sweet oblivion.

Sometime later, I am disturbed by the entry of two female backpackers. Perfumed with excesses of the local brew, they fall spectacularly over chairs and packs, swearing in German while trying to insert themselves in bed. Gran Vonny stirs.

I feel anxious. *Shut up,* I think. *Don't you know there's an elderly woman in here trying to get some sleep?*

This is absurd. Damn it. This was supposed to be a girl's own adventure. Instead, I am in a room with an old woman I feel responsible for. I don't even know her! It's all too close to the home I'm here to escape from.

I fall asleep, dreaming dreams of my mother in her final weeks, pale and aged in her hospital bed.

When I awake, the only sign of the old lady is her neat bags on the bunk. The German girls snore softly, faces crammed into pillows beneath tangled, sun-streaked locks. Their slumbering exhalation of last night's beer drives me out of the dorm and into the communal kitchen. Gran Vonny is there, writing in a small book. We smile our good mornings.

"Are you a writer?" I ask, not expecting her to be at all, but wanting to make conversation.

"Oh, yes. I'm writing about Sarah Island."

Sarah Island—one of the most brutal penal settlements in Tasmanian history, jutting from the wild waters of Macquarie Harbour, near Strahan. Convicts died in droves there, from brutal punishments, disease, and exposure. Now it's a historic site, the cells little more than crumbling ruins.

"I've always wanted to write about it, about those poor convicts. I even spent the night there a few years ago." She sips hot tea. "In a tree, as a matter of fact."

My face must be registering the thought that perhaps this lady is a bit mad. Her serene smile now suggests mischief.

"The tide came in. I went over there for a week, so I could experience a little of what they did, to help the writing.

I didn't take much with me. It rained terribly hard. Then a big flood tide came, so I climbed a tree for the night."

"When was this?"

"Oh . . . let's see . . . hmm, about ten years ago."

Oh, my God. She was in her seventies. . . .

"Do you write?" She fixes me with bright eyes.

"Ah. No. Well, I do but I . . . I'm not a writer," I stumble, feeling as though I've been caught out somehow.

She's still smiling.

"I've always wanted to be a writer." I blurt it out, like a child's confession.

"Well. You probably already are one." And still she smiles.

It is clearly time to shift the heat. I begin to ask her about herself, and a remarkable tale unfolds.

Vonny has just returned from Indonesia, where she works voluntarily in the slums, treating orphans' scratches and sores with her tubes of antiseptic cream and bandages. It's not much, she says, but the children have nothing at all. There is no support for this venture. She does it all herself, living frugally and spending everything she has to finance her mission. She has no home, no possessions. I am gob-smacked. Clearly Gran Vonny is not the frail old lady I had taken her for on first sight.

"What about family? Do you have anyone here in Tasmania?" I ask.

"No, no one. I was engaged once, many years ago. But he was killed in the war, and when you've truly loved, you don't see the point in going for anything less after that. There's been no one else."

All of this has been said so simply, as though the decision to be alone for her whole life was as simple as choosing a brand of soap. My own recently broken heart, which had reduced me to near ashes, now seems trivial when I consider what Vonny has been through. She is so alone, yet she claims not to be lonely—she has her Indonesian children. *How can anyone be this generous?*

I finish my breakfast and excuse myself, explaining that I am taking a flight over the Franklin River this morning, to see it from the air before I begin my rafting trip.

"You'll see Sarah then," says Vonny, looking wistful. "I would love to see it—and the Franklin." Her face animates. "I protested that dam you know, back in 1983."

I remembered the campaign. The Tasmanian government had planned to build a dam that would have flooded the entire valley, destroying one of the world's greatest rivers. It was a fierce fight, with "greenies" on one side, camping in the wet forests for weeks on end, enduring assaults and arrest, and the furious hydro workers on the other, enraged at the prospect of losing their jobs should the dam be stopped.

The conservation movement won, and the Franklin Dam was never built. The river was declared a World Heritage Wilderness Area, forever protected. And Vonny was part of its preservation.

As I drive to catch my flight, I imagine her among the bedraggled greenies in the forest, chatting and drinking hot tea in the rain, affixing bandages to bruised protesters. And resisting arrest. *How many more surprises does this woman have for me?*

Soon, I am soaring above the river, looking with growing excitement at the site of my impending adventure. But I am also thinking of Vonny: Giving her life to begging children in the streets of Indonesia. Writing her stories and sleeping in trees and rainforests. Devoting her life to something real. I realize that I'm here on a joyride. A week ago I had been boasting to my friends about the dangerous adventure I was about to undertake, lapping up their admiration at my courage. In reality, I am buying my adventure, paying other people to take me through it safely and making sure I get my money's worth. It is beginning to feel hollow.

I have lived completely for myself, and still I want more. More fulfillment, more experiences, more recognition, more love. Selfless acts are a rare thing in my life. I have plenty of opinions about what is right, but I have never taken those values any further than heated discussions at dinner parties.

When I first saw Vonny I felt sorry for her—a lonely old lady with nothing in her life, I'd thought. But now I admired her and felt humbled. There was no need to pity Gran Vonny.

When we land, I walk toward my car, the hollowness not quite faded. Then, on impulse, I turn and quickly go back to the wharf.

The next day Vonny and I exchange addresses. Time to drive to Hobart and meet up with my group for the Franklin trip. I hug her gently, her tiny bones feeling like bird wings in my embrace. Before I leave, I press an envelope into her hand. "Something you need to do," I say.

As I drive, I wonder what this big adventure of mine is really all about. I feel changed by the past two days, challenged. Certainly, I no longer feel like the strong, brave woman I had assumed myself to be. Not like her.

Weeks later, in my apartment in the city, I open my first letter from her. She tells me all about the flight I had surprised her with, how she had seen all the beauty and history she had loved and fought for. She saw yellow rafts far below and wondered if I was in one. I was. She congratulates me for my adventuresome spirit. But for all the rapids in that beautiful river, I never really had to be brave. I did learn something about courage in Tasmania, but from a tiny woman in her eighties, over cups of hot tea in the kitchen of a youth hostel.

That trip was years ago now. I've since moved to Tasmania. For a while, I worked in the wilderness, guiding bushwalks. I fell in love with the place and found my own beloved. I think I understand a little of what Vonny meant about true love now. Yet, in my life, I still strive to discover my own real courage. I'm still challenged to make the choice to really live for something beyond myself. I'd like to think that I am closer than I was before. I'd like to think that the strength of spirit I witnessed in that tiny, extraordinary woman will inspire me to live in true, selfless courage.

We have lost contact, and I wonder whether she has died. I wish I'd told her what she did for me, thanked her for showing me what it means to be truly courageous. But perhaps, if she is in her Heaven, the convicts of Sarah Island are sitting beside her, telling her just that.

—*Maura Bedloe*

Like a Rock

My son turns to me when the judge finally speaks.

"I'll let you take him home. Do you want custody?"

"No."

He turns pale, and I feel him trembling next to me. Hurt and fear reflect in his eyes. He is too stunned to notice tears sliding down his cheeks. At fourteen, he hears only rejection, and to him, my decision means I don't love him. I know nothing I say will help. His pain cuts through me like a knife, and my tears overflow. Then, a metal door clangs loudly, and he's gone.

What have I done? He is my youngest child. Handsome and smart, his life could be all happiness and success. Why this?

I struggle to concentrate on the reasons I'm inflicting this pain on both of us. My son is already six feet tall and 180 pounds. He's challenging authority and ignoring rules. His legal transgressions emphasize the need for supervision and professional counseling. As a single mother, I cannot offer those things while providing for him. My choices are limited.

He looks older than fourteen, and he attracts older people. He's big, daring, and confused about many things, but he's young in years and experience. The possibilities of the harm that might come to him terrify me. Mental images of my child, barely into his teens, spending his remaining youth in an adult correction facility are equally frightening. If he continues to get into trouble, he will be charged as an adult.

I know I will blame myself if he gets injured or killed, or if he does something so terrible that he ends up in prison, because I failed to take action. I must try anything and everything to change his direction.

After our day in court, I pace the floor through endless nights, asking myself the same questions over and over: Did I make the best decision? Will he ever understand and forgive me? Can I live with my decision if he never comes home?

There are no answers. No way to be sure I've made the right choices. No guarantee my decisions will help my child. No comfort as I face the possibility I've lost my youngest child by trying to help him. Right or wrong, the burden is mine alone.

My head is exploding and the ache in my chest is unbearable. I'm physically ill from worry and heartache. Though I firmly believe his welfare and his future must be my priorities, nothing prepared me for this. For months, I function robotically on the verge of total exhaustion.

Every visitation day, I spend every minute I'm allowed with my son. And every visit he asks me why I don't want him.

My only positive emotional support comes from his teachers and counselors. I cling to their encouragement and advice: He has to learn where his choices lead. He has to remember and care enough not to make poor choices again. He has to take the consequences of his decisions now; he may not get a second chance. I know they are right, but every day feels like a year and time seems to crawl. The first two months feel like an eternity.

Now, when I visit, his eyes look clear and his complexion is a healthy pink. And, he admits, he feels better. The structured, secure environment doesn't allow him to walk away from responsibilities. He makes decisions and receives instant feedback. Daily living guidelines are similar to rules and routines at home, but rules are consistently enforced with logical consequences. Regular meals, chores, personal care, study time, and recreation fill the daily schedule. He still doesn't understand, but I feel a growing conviction that my decision was right.

Finally, the day arrives for him to come home. I can barely contain my happiness. I want to believe the nightmare is over, and I work hard to fill our first few days with fun. Then, my hope for a smooth transition is crushed when I discover our relationship will not be easily mended. The little boy inside the young man carries a grudge, and he never misses an opportunity to remind me how much I hurt him. I don't blame him, but his attitude limits communication.

When his eighteenth birthday passes with no sign of change in his bitter feelings toward me, I find myself facing another dilemma. Now, he is legally responsible for himself and free to make his own decisions, no longer bound by parental rules or consequences. Will I continue to endure emotionally charged challenges, or will I get on with my life and let him make his own way? I need to be there for him, but I don't need to allow him to live in the same house. Now, I have to find a way to tell him, and I already know nothing I say will be right.

My mind replays the torment of the unknown future I've been living since that day in court. I feel I'm repeating the same scene in different movies over and over.

He is angry, but he moves. At first, he flounders, and I wonder whether I'm doing the right thing. Finally, he settles on a direction.

Our relationship smoothes out after he finds a job, rents an apartment, and starts college. The busy schedule and new responsibilities occupy his mind. He doesn't have to come to see me, but he does. Now, we laugh and talk. Our words are cautious and our emotions guarded, but I feel tremendous hope at any sign that he has not shut me out forever.

Positive changes come faster after he marries. As a young husband, he faces new responsibilities and begins to recognize my role as an adult. His attitude softens noticeably when his son is born. Witnessing his son's birth instantly adds a new dimension to his experience. The next day, he hugs me and tells me he understands a new part of my feelings as a mother.

Still, he won't talk openly about my earlier decisions and his feelings. He isn't ready to let the barrier down, but my hopes for our future rise a little higher.

During the next few years, he endures numerous challenges—divorce, losing a home, job loss, remarriage, blending families, buying a new home, and another childbirth. All add new levels of adult experiences. I also remarry during those years.

My new husband loves and accepts my family. As a result, he and my son quickly form a strong relationship. We are there for him emotionally, physically, and financially, sharing with him the joy and pain of those years, as he grows and evolves into a strong, intelligent man.

At the age of thirty-three, he is the father of three children in a blended family. As those children grow up, the parenting challenges are increasing. His two preteen boys test limits more often and more openly. Naturally, we talk about children during most phone calls.

One day, during a pause in our conversation, he says, "Thank you for not taking me home."

My first reaction is disbelief. Gradually, I realize that the subject of our conversation hit home. His nephew, a teenager nearing his fourteenth birthday, made a poor choice that almost resulted in serious legal consequences.

I'm afraid to believe he is saying what I've wanted to hear for so many years. My response is a weak attempt at a light, teasing comeback: "You mean it worked?"

"Yeah. I don't know where I would have ended up if you hadn't done that," he said.

Suddenly, the weight I've carried for nineteen years lifts. I'm glad he can't see my smile or the tears filling my eyes. "I love you, honey."

"Love you too, Ma. Good night."

—Penny J. Leisch

An American
Christmas Story

This is our Christmas story, part of the spoken history of my family. It is an urban tale, a little brassy and rough around the edges. Maybe some grandmothers live over the river and through the woods, but mine did not. Perhaps yours didn't, either.

My maternal grandparents lived on Lagonda Avenue in Springfield, Ohio, an industrial town near Dayton. Their house was a two-story frame structure that crouched next to an alley in a neighborhood of aging houses, stores, and bars. Big semi trucks rumbled through all day and all night, because Lagonda Avenue was a state route, a major thruway in those days. As far back as I can remember, we went to my grandparents' for Christmas Eve. We always arrived early on the big night. My father and grandfather relaxed with high-balls or tiny glasses of what they called "sipping whiskey" at the kitchen table, while my mother and grandmother applied finishing touches to supper.

My grandmother wore her usual spike heels and trousers, a Christmas apron tied securely around her middle, a corsage planted firmly on her ample bosom. Grandma was the center of the family universe, a woman with a steel backbone and a lap built for heavy use. My grandfather stayed in the background, in his flannel shirts and wire-rimmed spectacles. They had worked hard all their lives, both of them on rocky, played-out farms, my grandfather in iron furnaces and coal mines. After my grandfather retired, my grandmother took in renters and my grandfather worked as a security guard for one of the plants in town. Considering where they'd come from, where they were looked pretty good.

The house was festive, with spun glass snow and a crèche on top of the television set, and Christmas cards taped along the door frame. Electric candles burned in the front windows, the yellow flames staining the snow on the sills.

My brother and sister and I hovered around Grandma's shiny silver Christmas tree like moths about a flame. It had a spotlight with a colored plastic wheel that turned. The tree sparkled red, bleeding into gold, then green. We were always fascinated by the chameleon tree and by the mysterious packages piled underneath. Pajamas and clothes, for sure, but there was bound to be something from Aunt Doris, who lived in California and always seemed to know what kids liked. Maybe she'd sent *National Geographic* for my brother, who loved maps and faraway places.

As the evening wore on, the air fairly steamed with promise and impatience. We kids peered out the front windows and yanked open the door to the unheated sun porch. The Christmas Day turkey loomed in the chill semidarkness, snuggled in its roaster next to casseroles and custard pies. We paced to the front door, then back to the front windows. The watch for Aunt Hope had begun.

Hope was my mother's younger sister. She'd never had good luck with men, or maybe they'd never had good luck with her. In any event, she was the single mother of four sons by two different fathers. Hope worked at the International Harvester plant (a good union job, my grandfather said). Maybe she had to work late on Christmas Eve, or maybe it was hard to get four boys presentable. We didn't care. In the self-centered way of children, all we knew was that she was always late and that there would be no dinner and no presents until Aunt Hope arrived. When she finally did, powdered and perfumed, dressed to the nines, sons in tow and carrying a shopping bag full of presents, Santa Claus himself couldn't have been greeted with more enthusiasm.

We welcomed our cousins with the shy reserve accorded those relatives seen mostly on holidays. We pulled extra chairs around the kitchen table, fighting over who got to sit on the step stool, and our Christmas Eve supper began. There were two kinds of meat, my grandfather's special potato salad, vegetables, relishes, mysterious home-canned condiments, and two kinds of pie. Because it was a special occasion, we kids were allowed to drink Coca-Cola with dinner.

Then we settled ourselves in the living room. My grandmother pulled the presents from under the tree, one by one, examined the tags, and passed them out to the rest of us. I remember one year I bought a set of cuff links for my father (who never wore French cuffs), a quart bottle of lilac aftershave for my grandfather, and a red cut-glass ring for my grandmother (one size adjustable to fit all). Truly gifts of the Magi. All were accepted with great enthusiasm.

We passed around fudge and divinity sent by Aunt Beulah in Illinois. We sang carols in a rich chorus of related voices, "Away in a Manger" and "We Three Kings," and ending, as always, with "Silent Night." By the end of the evening, I was overwhelmed with prosperity and goodwill. As I struggled for sleep on the rollaway bed in the living room, I knew that nestled under my grandmother's silver tree were toilet water and dusting powder and a Tressy doll with hair that grows. My family slumbered around me, breathing softly while the semis thundered by outside.

Never since have I felt so wealthy.

I remember our last Christmas in Springfield. My grandmother lay confused in a nursing home, shrunken by pain and chemotherapy. She was propped up on pillows to help her breathe, her skin like aged parchment against the institutional sheets. My grandfather slumped awkwardly in the visitor's chair, trying to think of something to do with his work-roughened hands. When we arrived, Grandma brightened momentarily, greeting my sister and me.

"Well, hi, girls, where are those guitars?"

She'd always loved music, and we'd brought our guitars along to sing carols. By the time we were ready to play, she was lost again to that place she visited more and more often. The nurses suggested we sing in the lobby and they would send the music through the intercom into every room. We sang "Adeste Fidelis" and "Silent Night," tears painting our faces and dropping softly into our laps.

My grandparents are dead now, my parents also. Aunt Hope has loved and lost at least one or two more husbands. The color photographs we took on those long-ago Christmases have assumed the oddly brilliant hues typical of those times. They are snapshots, awkward, off-center, unedited—unlike my memories of those days. In my memories, my mother's face is rosy from an unaccustomed glass of wine. My grandmother presides over a groaning board, a choreographer of feasts. My father is broad-shouldered and strong again, singing tenor, the Chesterfields that killed him tucked safely in his shirt pocket. They are ghosts who come for the holidays, but they are friendly ones.

There are those whose Christmas memories are more traditional, more reverent, certainly more elegant. Never mind. This is our family's Christmas story, for what is a family but people who bring forward shared stories? My brother and sister and I still gather with our families on Christmas Eve. Children circle the tree and squirm restlessly through dinner. My sister checks the tags and passes out the presents. We sing carols in our related voices. And we keep candles in our windows for the ghosts.

—Cinda Williams Chima

Grandma and Grandpa and Karen

Although I talked to him on the phone and wrote him letters, it had been more than five years since I'd seen my grandfather. Our last meeting had been at my grandmother's funeral. When my husband, Frank, and I finally found the time and money to fly to Illinois to spend Christmas with him, I was flooded with excited anticipation.

I envisioned walking through the door of the same cozy house I remembered from my childhood visits, the one Grandpa had built himself as a young man. There would be homemade desserts beckoning from the countertops. Crunchy, undisturbed snow would blanket the front yard, just begging to be used in a snowball fight. Grandpa had even promised to buy a real Christmas tree, relenting because the little plastic one he'd been using wasn't going to cut it for his nostalgia-loving granddaughter.

I could picture every detail perfectly, except for one thing: Grandpa's new girlfriend.

I'd never met or spoken to her before, but I'd heard the news from family: Her name was Karen, and she was twenty-five years younger than my eighty-year-old grandfather—younger than my father, even. She was living with Grandpa, at least part of the time. I'd found out she'd known him for many years. In fact, before her husband had died, Karen and her husband used to spend time with my grandparents. Despite their age differences, the two couples had clicked. I would be meeting a stranger, but Karen would not; she "knew" me from years of friendship with Grandma and Grandpa.

Despite all the things that might make a granddaughter wary, I had already decided there was no reason not to like her. My grandfather had been married to my grandmother for more than fifty years before she died of cancer, and her death had been devastating to him. Grandpa deserved to be happy again, and from what I'd heard, Karen was making that happen.

When Frank and I arrived in Illinois three days before Christmas, Grandpa and Karen were waiting for us at the airport. Karen, who had fluffy blond hair and glasses, gave me a warm hug. As the four of us stood at the baggage claim area and spoke, it was immediately evident how content Karen and my grandfather were together.

Grandpa's house was just as I remembered it. In fact, it was a little spooky. My grandmother's presence was everywhere—in her pictures on the shelves, in her homemade afghan on the couch, in her handwriting on the ancient Tupperware. After spending decades in that house with my grandfather, there was no question that her memory belonged there, but it was that very fact that made it strange for me to watch Karen move comfortably among her things.

Warm-hearted and gracious, Karen did everything right. She cooked for us, cleaned, made us feel welcome, and made Grandpa smile. I genuinely liked her. Still, I couldn't help wondering how Grandma would have felt knowing her old friend had slid seamlessly into the life she had once owned. Would it have been a comfort, or a betrayal?

The question bothered me, and I thought about it on and off as I watched Karen and Grandpa together. They snuggled beside each other on the couch, their legs covered with Grandma's afghan. I thought about my own history and the times I'd felt betrayed. If Grandma could have chosen Grandpa's future girlfriend, would she have wanted him to be with a stranger, someone completely separate from the bond Grandma and Grandpa had shared, or would she have wanted him to choose a friend of hers, someone who knew everything—maybe too much—about the past?

The ability of another woman to remember and discuss Grandma could be a gift or a curse; undoubtedly, it is an element of power. Of course, I knew the question of what Grandma would want was hypothetical; Grandma was gone, and it was Grandpa who would decide what happened next. Karen was a good woman and she made him happy, and for that I was grateful. End of story.

On Christmas morning, I heard whispering, but I remained generally oblivious to anything special about to occur. Halfway through our present-opening celebration, my husband's attentive ear heard Karen mutter, "I can't wait anymore!" Abruptly, there she was, standing in front of me, looking excited, eager, and nervous. She handed me a large package and told me to open it next.

The label confused me; the present was from "Grandma and Grandpa and Karen." What did that mean? My first fleeting thought was that Karen had called herself "Grandma" and then thought better of it, but that didn't make sense. Everyone watched as I opened the gift.

As I unfolded what turned out to be a huge, colorful quilt, Karen said, "Your grandma saved the material from the dresses and outfits she sewed for you when you were little."

The quilt was amazing. Framed against a white-and-purple background were bright, cheerful squares of material representing outfits from my childhood, beginning with my birth year of 1972 and continuing through 1980. Embroidery in my grandmother's handwriting explained each square.

"Rompers, 1 year old, 1973" was a red, blue, and black plaid peppered with fuzzy white Scottie dogs. The fabric that read "Christmas 1976, blouse, age 4½" was a jumbled mass of flowers, triangles, and staircase shapes in yellow, orange, green, tan, brown, black, and white—very 1970s. One square, also from 1976, was more familiar than all the rest. It was white satin speckled with tiny turquoise dots and tiny tulips. At the top of each tulip's delicate green stem was a raised blossom of sky blue fluff. The four-year-old me had loved the blouse made of that fabric. She probably never would have believed that she'd one day give up such cheerful clothes for dark, solid colors that didn't draw attention.

Karen spoke again about my grandmother and the quilt. "She had finished all the embroidery and picked out the pattern. I just put it together." She looked at my grandfather. "Your grandpa chose the border."

I admired the border and smiled. Around the quilt's edge, Garfield smiled his sly grin while Odie let his giant tongue drool on the quilt squares. Garfield had been my favorite cartoon as a girl.

Grandpa said, "Your grandma started that before she got sick, but she never got to finish it. I was just going to throw that stuff away, but Karen offered to finish it for you."

I ran my hands over the fabrics on the quilt—silky, cottony, fuzzy, and textured—then looked up at Karen's hopeful smile. She was dying to know my reaction.

I immediately stood and hugged her, holding her tight and thanking her for the quilt. I felt many things—grateful, happy, honored—but most of all, I was shocked. What shocked me was not the quilt itself or the story of how it had come to be, but the realization that my questions had been answered. Suddenly, I thought I knew how my grandmother would have felt about Karen.

There were two very different ways to interpret Karen's gesture, but my heart knew the right answer. This was not a woman trying to show up my grandmother or take her place. Despite the fact that she now had my grandmother's husband, had my grandmother's home, and had even finished my grandmother's quilt, I realized that Karen's moving among Grandma's things showed not domination of them, but respect.

She respected my grandmother enough to let her presence remain, respected her enough not to mind when Grandpa talked about Grandma, respected her enough to know what half a century of marriage signifies. Karen had made this quilt not to outdo my grandmother, but to honor her. Her completion of the quilt that Grandma hadn't had the strength to complete was as much a gift to my grandmother as it was a gift for me.

I think Grandma would approve.

—*Alaina Smith*

Innocence and the Divine

My mother has been a teacher for as long as I can remember. Out of the many stories she has told about her life as a teacher, one in particular never fails to make me smile.

Back in the early 1960s, she taught at a small school in the country. The school served grades one through twelve, and I would be surprised if the total number of students ever reached four hundred. It was a simpler time, a time when paperwork was a minor irritation and some of the largest joys came from the smallest voices.

Though this school was not large, it did have one distinction: It was one of the first schools in the area to get an intercom system. Not a sleek, desktop model with digital displays and wireless capability like the ones today. No, indeed. Remember, this was the early sixties. We hadn't set foot on the moon yet, and color TV was still just beyond the horizon.

The intercom was powered by a huge panel that took up an entire table. The microphone was an industrial gray tabletop model that probably weighed three pounds. Each classroom had its own speaker, connected to a toggle switch on the control panel, so the principal could send messages to individual classrooms or, by throwing the master switch, to every room simultaneously, as the need arose. The teachers could respond and subsequently be heard on the large speaker mounted next to the control panel in the office.

Oh, the joys of modern technology.

My mother was teaching there when the system arrived. It was installed over the summer break so that everything would be ready when the students arrived for the new school year.

Toward the end of the summer, some of the teachers headed to school to prepare their rooms. They put fresh chalk and new erasers in the chalkboard trays, cut reams of colored paper to make bulletin board displays, checked supplies, arranged books, and took care of the hundreds of last-minute chores that precede the coming of a new school year.

During that same time, a few of the cafeteria workers came in to make their back-to-school preparations, seeing to it that the kitchen was set to start churning out peanut butter and jelly sandwiches, soup, and those lemon sheet cakes that have fed millions of students over the years. While the kitchen preparations were underway, a little girl named Mary wandered over to my mother's classroom to read while her mother sorted, scrubbed, and double-checked the supplies.

Mary's mother worked in the cafeteria, and since my mother always had shelves full of books in her room, it provided the perfect place for a little girl to sit and read while everybody finished their various chores.

About midafternoon, my mother went to the office to pick up the list of students coming to her class in the fall and to gather from the supply cabinet a few additional things she wanted for her classroom. While she was in the office, Mary's mother spotted her and came inside to say hello.

"Judy, I hope Mary hasn't been any trouble for you. It was nice of you to offer to let her stay in there with you. Lord knows there's a lot a child can get into in that kitchen."

"She was fine," my mother said. "No trouble at all. She has just been sitting in there reading, not bothering a soul. She even helped me put up one of the bulletin boards a little while ago. When I left, she was stapling the border around the edge."

They talked a while longer, and then Mary's mother said she had better go to the room and get her daughter so they could head home.

"You don't have to go down there and get her. We can just call her on the intercom, and you can wait for her here."

Both women looked around. The principal had been working with the intercom system while they were talking and he was putting the finishing touches on what would become the school's first "command center." Although it was wired and ready to use, he was still putting labels on the control panel. Each label had a number representing the corresponding classroom. There were additional labels for the cafeteria and the auditorium, and even a pair of outside speakers.

"We can do that now?" Mary's mother looked at the table full of 1960s space-age technology.

"Sure," said the principal. "We'll just switch it on, let it warm up a minute or two, and flip the switch for room two-twelve. We need to test the system, anyway, so now is as good a time as any."

He turned the large brown knob on the side of the panel, and a low-pitched hum filled the room. The amber glow visible through the seams in the panel indicated the tubes inside were heating up. After another minute, he flipped the switch for my mother's classroom, and the test was underway.

"Mary."

The principal grinned and waited for her to answer. A few seconds passed, and he flipped the toggle switch again, keyed the mike, and tried again.

"Mary."

A half-minute passed, and still there was no response. The principal asked if Mary might have left the room to go look around, and her mother assured him she would not leave the room and just wander around.

The principal flipped the switch once more, leaned close to the microphone, and increased his volume.

"Mary, are you in there?"

Five seconds passed, and then a small voice answered.

"Yes, God."

Oh, for the good old days.

—*Thomas Smith*

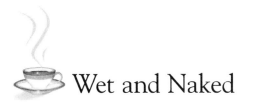 Wet and Naked

Throughout childhood my younger sister Allison and I bathed together in our parents' oversized claw-foot tub. We lathered one another's hair in mock shampoo commercials. We wrung drenched washcloths over each other, plastering hair to foreheads and laughing so hard water ran into our mouths. Once we were in the tub, Mom had trouble getting us out.

In adulthood, an autoimmune disorder robbed Allison of her health and agility. The disease transformed her from a slim, willowy dancer to an inflexible, fragile Olive Oyl.

One autumn, an odd compilation of ailments plagued her. Her left breast was infected and swollen. She had an abscess on her right buttock and a lesion on her underarm that refused to heal. The threads in the seams of her clothing tore open her fragile skin.

She arrived at my kitchen door clutching Epsom salts and a bottle of tea tree oil.

"I've come to use your tub," she said and handed me her things. "I have to soak my butt."

My parents still had their extra-long, antique tub, but as her body defied her, she chose to recline in my smaller version. Once again, we shared a tub, this time out of necessity, not for fun.

As she poured her ingredients under the steamy faucet, I adjusted the water. She looked at me with the fatigue that soldiers must feel after a long battle in the trenches.

"I want to keep this under control so they don't have to pack it," she said with a weak smile.

"Soak as long as you need," I said, forcing a return grin. But my stomach tightened.

The year before I had held her hand as she screamed and wept in the emergency room. The nurse packed the abscess on her knee, poking lengths of gauze into a hole so deep I could see beneath her skin to the smooth cartilage below.

"I'll be outside raking leaves," I said. "Just let yourself out when you're finished."

An hour later, I walked into the bathroom, smelling like leaves and cool air. I jumped when I saw Allison sprawled in the tub. She lifted her head and scowled at me as if I had put Jell-O in her bath instead of Epsom salts.

"Still here? I thought you'd be gone by now," I said, puzzled. "Isn't the water getting cold?"

"Yes, it is," she said through her clenched teeth. "In fact, it's been cool for a while now."

"Then why didn't you get out?"

"Because I can't bend my knees," she growled.

Her condition changed daily, and I hadn't considered her knees stiffening. Horrified at my thoughtlessness, I flung my shirt on the floor, plunged my arms into the tepid water, and tried to bend her knees for her. She screamed in pain, and I withdrew my arms like the pain was my own.

I slid my hands up her legs toward her bottom, to hoist her onto her feet.

"My abscess!" she screamed in warning.

"Okay," I said, yanking my hands back, holding them in the air like a surrendering soldier. "What if I lift you from behind?"

Shoes, socks, and jeans fell beside my shirt. I stepped into the cooling water. After many aborted attempts, I was soaked, the floor was covered in puddles, and Allison was still stuck.

Wiping oily drips from my face, I held my head in frustration. Buttocks, bosom, armpit—all too inflamed to touch. I slumped on the edge of the tub and looked her up and down.

"Where can I touch you?" I asked.

She looked sheepish. "I don't know."

"I'll call Mom."

When Mom arrived we mapped a strategy, listing viable body parts like inventory clerks. Somehow, as the flesh had melted from her bones, Allison had become a series of parts and afflictions: "the abscess," "the lesion," "her knees." But her whole person was stuck in my tub.

Mom stripped down, too. Her full bosom and round belly complemented the trapped stick figure.

"How did I make a daughter like you?" she asked, staring at her own plump thighs.

Mom lifted Allison's thighs, bending so low her breasts touched the water. I stood behind Allison while she braced her back against me. In an awkward dance, we lifted and rotated until Allison's long legs dangled over the tub's edge and I was flattened against the wall. Slippery flesh pressed together, I longed for the innocence and health of our youth.

As I disentangled myself from the shower curtain, Allison stood up in halting stages, like an arthritic old woman. She was twenty-nine.

Wet, naked, and now laughing, we toweled off. Three women in a tiny bathroom, the walls echoing the laughter, muffling the pain.

While Mom mopped water from her cleavage, I mopped the puddles from the floor. As children we'd left great pools after our splashing competition to see who could make the highest tidal wave. Feet flat on either side of the faucets, knees bent and full of potential energy, we'd snap our legs straight. Our tiny bodies shot through the water like torpedoes, forcing a wave up the tub's sloped back. Being bigger, I always won the contest with Allison but lost the battle with Mom. I had to mop up the overflow of our tsunami match.

Now, as I blotted the oily water with a towel, I wished it were as easy to wash the disease from my sister's body, to catch it neatly in a towel and toss it away. I'd have given all my childhood memories to wipe the disorder from her, to wring out the poison and realign her immune system like a freshly smoothed sheet.

The last puddle wiped up, I wandered into the kitchen. Allison was stretched over the kitchen counter, stark naked, bottom in the air. My mother, her bra and underwear speckled with oily water, was hunched forward and staring intently at an angry welt on the exposed posterior.

Brow wrinkled in concentration and nose inches from Allison's right cheek, Mom raised her head and looked at me. "Do you have a flashlight?" she asked.

The absurdity of the situation struck us with a tidal wave of laughter. We leaned against each other and howled, heads back, eyes closed. Allison's laugh swept me back to the days of dripping hair and mouthfuls of soapy water. Her distinct, strong guffaw defied her dwindling muscles. She was strong and whole in that laugh, and I scrunched my eyes tightly, as if clamped eyelids could keep us safe and happy in the past.

As laughter ebbed I gulped air like I'd been drowning in the memories. Hoots rolled into chuckles and came to rest in gentle smiles. Still grinning, I pulled the flashlight from the junk drawer and snapped it crisply into my mother's extended palm like an operating room nurse. She resumed her inspection.

"It's healing nicely," she said.

After saying our goodbyes, I returned to the bathroom. The oil and salts formed an uneven loop around the porcelain. The tub ring, like my family circle, was fragile but unbroken.

—*Charmian Christie*

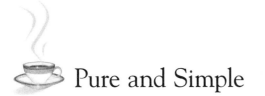 Pure and Simple

"Hey, blue eyes! You're the best part of my day, know that?" Tyrone Williams looked up at Martha Bronner and grinned.

Checking his pulse, she flushed the least bit as he placed his free hand to his chest and fluttered his eyelids in a mock swoon. Not that there was any actual flirtation between them. He was an eighteen-year-old African American with an advanced case of AIDS; she was a diminutive sixty-year-old physician, Austrian-born, with large round eyes the color of blue topaz.

After twenty-five years in the United States, she still couldn't get used to it: the easy informality of Americans, the banter and kidding that erupted at the most unexpected times, in the least likely places. Austrian men in her time greeted women with *Kuss die Hand, gnadige Frau*—"I kiss your hand, gracious lady." Overdone at times, but courtly. Here at the County Aids Hospital, she never knew how a patient might greet her: "Blue eyes," "Tiny," even "Baby," terms of endearment from men who needed an outlet for affection, a way to lighten the yoke of fear that pressed on them like a sack of stones.

"So, what do you think, doc? Am I gonna make it?" Tyrone made an effort to raise himself on one elbow, searched Martha's face. Hoarse from the cough that worsened daily, he tried to sound jocund, but there was a desperate pleading in his eyes.

"Oh, you just might," she replied with a smile, lowering her gaze, pretending to study his chart.

He was the youngest patient on the men's ward. No, he wasn't going to make it. None of them was going to make it. But Tyrone Williams would likely be the first to die. Christmas was two months away. She doubted he would last beyond the New Year. At moments like these, Martha wished she had picked another specialty, anything other than pulmonary medicine.

He fell back on the pillow. "Wonder how my mama's doing," he murmured drowsily. He closed his eyes, drifted off.

It was the first time Martha had heard him mention his mother or any family member. Other patients had visitors, especially on Sundays, when they wheeled themselves to the solarium, clean-shaven, hair carefully brushed, a little flicker of anticipation in their lackluster eyes. They sat by the windows, where the sun's rays streaked across their faces. The disease had hollowed their cheeks, left track marks on their foreheads and around their mouths, prematurely furrowed.

No one visited Tyrone Williams. On his intake, "nearest relative" was listed as a grandmother who lived in Tennessee. His father was deceased; his mother's whereabouts unknown. When questioned about siblings, he had simply shrugged. Who would mourn him, the eighteen-year-old whose life, barely lived, was slipping away? With a heavy sigh, Martha rose and continued her morning rounds.

In the corridor, patients waved to her: "Morning, doc. How you doing? Me . . ." Their voices faltered. ". . . I'm doing okay, I guess." Some of them—Haitians, Creoles, Hispanics—spoke to her in broken English. Language differences were never an impediment to Martha; she could still connect with patients. The barrier she couldn't dismantle was broken spirits. She wished she could sprinkle hope, like a priest sprinkling holy water, from room to room, in every corner—the beds where they sweated and shivered, the bathrooms where they clenched their fists and sobbed, the solarium where in the presence of visitors they put up a good front.

Winter blustered in with scarcely a backward glance at the last autumn leaf that shuddered and fell to the ground. It was a week to Christmas, the holiday that each year Martha wished would hurry and be done with. The star-shaped cookies dusted with red and green sugar, the holiday punch, the roast turkey dinner, all left a bitter aftertaste. Dreading the new year, patients clung to the familiar one, clutched it for dear life. They feigned merriment, tossing jokes at one another across the corridor like Ping-Pong balls. Frightened children in the husks of grown men, they played "let's pretend." At Christmas Eve mass, their veneer cracked and they unashamedly wept. Visits and gifts from family and friends cheered them a little: crisp, smartly tailored pajamas; hand-knit slippers; soft robes of every color and design—grim reminders of the fixed perimeters of their lives.

"Go ahead, put it on. No point in having it lay in a box forever," a stout woman said to a blond, fair-skinned man who was smoothing the folds of a plaid robe. His face turned ashen. There was no right thing to say at an AIDS hospital.

On Christmas morning, a line formed at the telephone booth. Martha knew that, even if Tyrone Williams had had the strength to sit up in a wheelchair and wait his turn, since no one ever called or came to see him, whom would he call? The hourglass of his life was rapidly emptying. She remembered his words, "I wonder how my mama's doing." His mother must be alive, then.

Martha went to his room, sat at his bedside. "Mr. Williams," she began gently, stroking his hand, the parchment-like skin purple-blotched from all the needles that had jabbed his veins. She never called patients by their first names, an American custom she thought disrespectful. "Mr. Williams, when was the last time you saw your mamma?"

He thought for a moment. "Four, five years ago, maybe." His voice trembled. "Before I messed up." He turned his face to the wall.

"Where did you see her?"

"Where? . . . Tennessee."

"Where your grandmother lives?"

"Where my mamma lives."

"But it states on your intake that you don't know where your mother lives."

He turned to face her. His expression was uncomprehending.

Martha was puzzled. After a moment, it dawned on her. She leaned forward. "Your grandmother . . . she's the person you call 'mamma'? She raised you?"

He nodded slowly.

Martha paused, then softly said, "She must love you very much."

He struggled against tears.

"What's her name, your mamma?"

"Stephens. Cora Mae Stephens."

She patted his hand and rose. "Don't let me hear that you haven't touched your dinner tray," she said, affecting a stern tone.

"Okay, baby," he murmured thickly, managing a feeble smile.

Later in her office, she pulled his file. His grandmother's name was on the intake: Cora Mae Stephens, Knoxville, Tennessee. There was a phone number. Martha jotted it down, tucked it into the pocket of her white coat.

Shortly after dinner she returned to his room, a phone in her hand. He was sleeping. Bending over him, she said, "Someone is waiting for a special Christmas gift from you, Mr. Williams."

Bewildered, he looked from Martha to the phone to the scrap of paper in her hand. She had begun to dial.

At the sound of a woman's voice at the other end, Martha tentatively asked, "Mrs. Stephens? Will you hold please?"

She placed the phone in his hand, folded his thin fingers over it. He held it as if he didn't know what to do with it.

"Tell me what I should say!" his eyes pleaded. His forehead glistened with beads of perspiration; his hand trembled.

Martha nodded at him with a reassuring smile, and then left the room. She shut the door behind her and stood outside. He wouldn't be long. He hadn't the strength.

When she came to his room on New Year's Day, Martha knew that he was moribund. Leaning over him, she placed the stethoscope to his chest. He groped for her free hand. She was glad she was there for him to hold on to in his last moments.

In a gesture that took her back a quarter of a century, a gesture that spanned two disparate cultures, two generations, two skin colors, he slowly brought her hand to his lips. There was nothing courtly about it, no flourishes, no bows. There was only love, pure and simple.

—*Bluma Schwarz*

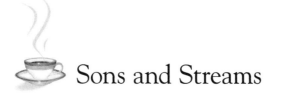# Sons and Streams

I have three sons. And in my dreams we are on the Queets
River, fishing, casting out long, crystal lines into the water.
The lines drift down clear rivulets and bump against smooth
gray rocks slick with moss. The forest of cedar and spruce at
the river's edge is deep and wild. The boys are young, and
they gather at their father's wading boots like goslings under
gander wings.

I sit on the mossy bank and sketch, shaded by massive
spruce as old as Time. At night, I read *The Lord of the Rings*
to the boys by flashlight and firelight. The sparks rise up like
fireflies and disappear into the star-splashed sky above the
sleeping firs and pines.

We are together, and we are whole.

Someone once wrote that the mother of three sons has a
special place in heaven. I have never felt such a burden, but
rather, have relished each individual life as it came to me at
birth. Their personalities were as telling as when they first
suckled: one had to figure it out, one was ready to go, and one
held my finger in his tiny hand.

My nana had three sons. Well, actually four. Her firstborn died a baby boy after eating green corn on a summer day long ago. I see her now in her Gibson Girl skirt and shirtwaist, casting out her line into a river in Colorado. She is wearing a hat more fashionable than a sun stopper. The water's edge is flat and bare with few trees. The sun beats down from the cloudless sky. She is looking upriver at my grandfather, who is fishing in tweeds with his hand on his hip. At her feet, my knickers-wearing uncles tie their bait to their Spanish gut lines on bamboo poles. They are young and full of adventure, ready to do more than throw a line into the low-riding river, but Nana is patient. She fishes and waits.

What is a mother to a bevy of boys? A gaggle of guys?

I dreamed of a girl. There was a tradition in my side of the family of women handing down their stories and treasures. At my mother's house, there is a box with a ship made of gesso on top; handmade lace spun from homegrown flax; Nana's china dolls with exquisite silk dresses and tiny brass buttons, thimbles from 150 years ago, and letters and poems. We named our girl Robin Lynn each time I was pregnant, but when the doctor told me that my third child would most likely be a boy, I put aside that dream and looked to the ease of hand-me-downs and the familiarity of raising boys.

From the time they could walk or ride in a backpack, we fished, camped, and hiked in the deep forests of the North Cascades, finding our way on fish trails to alpine lakes tucked under craggy peaks. Or we went to the Queets and the Hoh on the Olympic Peninsula, where the salmon flung their way upstream to their end. Their father was always there, his fishing and camping wisdom the backbone of their education. I showed them history in the occasional ruined cabin, the springboard notch in the ancient cedar stump; sang songs and told stories.

The year we crossed the Queets, my youngest was tall enough to ford it, the water coming up just below his small backpack. We hiked north through dense Pacific Northwest rainforest. I took pictures with a cheap camera, and the images, though bright with the reds and blues of the boys' rain jackets and deep greens of woods, blurred. But memory is stronger and brings each image back as sharp as when they were first shot. The boys perched on a huge beached drift- wood tree. My oldest, with his Swedish blond hair cut into a fifties crew cut, proudly holding up a salmon as tall as he is. My middle son with his first salmon cradled in his arms like a treasured puppy—just as the ranger arrived to check on fishing licenses. He didn't have one, but it was his first, and his joy turned the official's other cheek. Later, my youngest caught one, too. With his dad's catches, we carried out nearly fifty-eight pounds of fish.

Three sons, as solid as a triangle. Three has always been my favorite number.

And then my husband suddenly died.

At first, we huddled together like harried sheep, numbly going through the paces of grief and braving the holiday season so lacking in cheer. But in time each son had to make his way back to his own life, two in other towns. There, they grieved in different ways. One thought of quitting college. Another rolled up in his blankets and avoided work. The third began to implode. The triangle could not hold.

Losing your father can be devastating to a young man in his early twenties. It is a time when he is finally beginning to figure things out and step into true manhood. A time when he is ready to listen to his father's advice.

What is a mother to sons without a father? How do you lead when your own heart mourns?

I went forward, encouraging them each to move forward and go for their dreams, and I set out toward some dreams of my own. By Thanksgiving the year after my husband died, we were gathered at the table with friends and working hard at creating happiness. We laughed, played Scrabble, and went en masse to see *Harry Potter*, though we were restless, waiting for *The Lord of the Rings: The Two Towers*.

New Year's came. Hopes were raised. One son had finished school and was engaged to be married. Another had chosen to leave work for grad school. The third slept, and we didn't recognize the storm that was to come. Two months later, his raging grief of months literally exploded in a shattering of glass when he threw himself out a window. The triangle was broken.

Dealing with a serious crisis with a child is difficult enough as a parent. The grief of facing it alone is even worse, especially when the parent is a mother and the child a son. Society dictates that the relationship should grow less influential as the boy matures into manhood. He should turn to his father. Moms are for Mother's Day.

After my husband died, I grieved for what I had lost. But I also grieved out of fear that somehow I would lose my sons as well, as they went off on their own paths in their lives.

But the days and nights of just being there for my troubled young-adult son—at the emergency room, by the hospital bed, on the phone—has brought me better understanding and wisdom of what it is to be a mother to sons. It takes courage I did not know I had. It means listening, staying silent when nothing more needs to be said, to provide a foundation of support without enabling when all else fails for that person; to let go.

My nana knew grief. The grief for a precious baby who died so young from an illness cured easily today with salt and sugar water; for a young son with appendicitis sent off on a Pocatello train, thinking she'd never see him again; and for sons gone off to fight in trenches in World War I. And when she, nearly ninety-five years old and most in need, lived beyond them.

I see her on the river, the boys crouched at her feet. The future is ahead of her, and she is looking with pole in hand.

Sons and streams.

That is something I know, and she gives me strength. Is not our whole life a stream on which we drift?

I have three sons.

And in my dreams we are together again, battered but together on the Queets. We may not fish. The poles and tackle boxes are in my garage, and the water rushing down at high water keeps us from going across. But we will put some of their father's ashes there and watch the eagles in the trees as they welcome him. I do not know the future, but I hope for forgiveness and healing. I hope for wholeness. And my three sons gathering around.

—Janet L. Oakley

 Snow Angel

Lillian and Mom came late to their friendship. Both widowed, they met and their relationship bloomed when Lillian moved to Lafayette, about a block away from Mom's house. When arthritis ended Mom's daily walks to the post office, Lillian, who loved to walk, volunteered to pick up her mail and bring it right to the house.

Thus began their daily chats over coffee.

Very few days passed during the next ten years that Lillian didn't walk up the back alley and across Mom's yard to her back door. Watching through the kitchen window, Mom set the mugs out the moment she spotted her friend. Lillian laid the mail on the table, pulled Mom into a hug, then sat at the kitchen table to tell the news she had heard at the post office. Mom filled in the background stories.

Lillian spoke in awe of how Mom knew everyone in the township. A fifth-generation native, Mom knew just about everyone, their family histories and secrets.

Lillian had always been an "outsider." Having moved to the area during World War II, as a working mother, battered wife, and then a divorcee, she was out of step with the conservative farming community.

The two friends would sip and talk a while. Looking at the clock, they would start making plans for lunch. Usually they called a couple of other widows in town. Everyone would pile into Mom's car to head for a favorite restaurant. Eventually Lillian took over the driving, since she was younger, seventy-something to Mom's eighty-something.

They plotted back-road routes that were free of traffic and didn't require the left turns Lillian dreaded. It never failed that Mom met someone at the restaurant she hadn't seen for a long time, and Lillian would add a new acquaintance to her growing list.

Over the years, Lillian, a flighty, small-boned, birdlike woman, shrunk even smaller. Mom baked and cooked and offered her special treats.

"I made some of those cookies you like," Mom would say as she accepted her morning mail. "They'll taste good with the coffee."

Lillian would usually take a bite and say, "Oh, Gladys, you'll have to give me the recipe."

They both knew she wouldn't bake any cookies, and they knew that Lillian would take only one bite, never two.

One cold November day, Mom worried and paced. Lillian had been rushed to the hospital. They talked on the phone, and friends took her to visit, but she knew that Lillian's "thin" had turned to frail.

Several friends and family members began bringing Mom's mail. But two weeks later when Lillian came home from the hospital, she phoned to say, "I'll be there tomorrow with your mail. Just so you know and don't let anyone else get it."

Mom protested. "It's cold out. The ground is covered with snow, and there are icy patches, and, well, I just don't want you to do it."

"I'm fine. What's a little snow? Now, Gladys, don't you worry. Just get that coffee on in the morning."

The next morning Mom and I stood by her kitchen window. Mom was afraid she'd see her friend and afraid she wouldn't.

"Lillian shouldn't be out in this," she fretted, as the wind whipped past the house.

Mom's bent and arthritis-damaged body shivered with a frisson of fear as she saw the figure swathed in a heavy winter coat, wool scarf wound around her head, and big heavy mittens clutching a plastic grocery sack filled with mail.

We watched Lillian place one foot in front of the other, then struggle to do it again. She'd stop every couple of steps, bend and press forward, head down against the wind. Slowly she traveled up the alley's incline and into Mom's yard, past the little cement-block garage and into the grassy area, which was now covered with almost a foot of snow.

Lillian turned her face toward the kitchen window and saw her friend peering out. She smiled. Suddenly, she dropped the mail bag and flung her arms wide. She fell backward onto the ground.

"My God, she's fallen! I've got to help her!" Mom panicked, cursed her walker for keeping her from her friend, and sent me rushing to the back door.

She looked out of the window and yelled and motioned me to look. Tears mingled with laughter as we watched Lillian flap her arms and legs, producing a perfect snow angel.

Mom crept out of the kitchen, slowly moved her walker across the back porch and out into the yard. I ran ahead to help Lillian up and dust the snow off.

Lillian saw Mom and shouted, "You stay right there, missy! Don't you come out here!"

She laughed as Mom yelled, "You scared me half to death! Get in here and get warm."

In the doorway, they grasped each other in a hug that death could not defy. They clung to each other for another six months before Lillian slipped away.

Now, Mom makes coffee for her son, the neighbor man, and the woman down the street as they take turns bringing her mail. Someone inevitably mentions Lillian's snow angel.

Mom always smiles and nods.

Recently she said, "You know, Lillian always thanked me for being her friend, for introducing her to people and including her. But she was the one who gave me so much more."

I smiled, remembering Lillian, who always had something nice to say.

Mom continued. "She gave me a reason to get up every morning. Every morning."

Again she paused, looked out of the window to where Lillian had made the snow angel.

"I never knew what a real friend was, until she came to my house. . . . Wasn't that snow angel something?"

—*Dawn Goldsmith*

Steady as She Rises

The plane left Boston's Logan Airport right on schedule, lifting off over the deep blue waters of the Atlantic before banking and heading west into pure radiance. It was a picture-perfect day for flying—unless you had a terrible, secret phobia.

"Mommy," my ten-year-old niece Jo whispered. "The man next to me is crying deep inside, like a puppy."

Her mother, Mary, tried not to stare at the well-dressed man in the aisle seat. Leaning down until her ear was right next to her daughter's lips, she whispered, "What do you mean, Jo?"

Usually when Mary flew to Indiana to visit her parents, her own little family occupied the seats six across. She had been filled with trepidation at the thought of leaving her husband, Chuck, in charge of Tim, eight, Max, seven, and Will, five. At the same time, she wanted this outing to be special for Jo, who had just recovered from a long bout of pneumonia that had hospitalized her for four excruciatingly frightening nights.

It had worried her when Jo had passed on the window seat, saying that she'd probably sleep the whole way anyway and her Mom would get to see the landscape for once. Now, with the thought of a weird, whimpering man sitting inches away from her exhausted daughter, Mary felt her heartbeat accelerate uncomfortably.

Yet, the stranger looked perfectly sane, conservatively and neatly dressed in a navy suit, white shirt, and navy tie with fine red and white diagonal stripes, his sandy hair a little gray at the temples. His eyes were closed, as if he had decided the most practical thing to do was to catch up on his sleep during the flight, even though he had a wafer-thin computer case balanced on his lap.

"I don't hear anything, sweetheart," Mary whispered into Jo's ear, afraid that her little girl might still be sicker than anybody had realized. What if Jo were hallucinating, imagining strange sounds coming from the dignified businessman beside her?

"Mommy, look." Jo jerked her head a little toward the man.

Mary looked and felt a surge of relief mixed with pity for the stranger. His hands were clutching the armrests with fingers so white she thought the knuckles could pop through the taut skin at any moment. She relaxed. "Let's just let him sleep."

Jo nodded a little and shut her own eyes. Mary watched her for a moment and then rested her own weary head against the seat. She fought off the temptation to call home, where Chuck's mother would be bustling around the house preparing dinner, or to call her husband at his office. Instead, she dozed off, but when the plane hit a pocket of turbulence, her eyes flew open and she heard herself gasp, "Chuck!"

"It's okay, Mom," Jo said. "It's just air."

Mary felt the reverberation of metal all the way up her spine, jiggling her senses and shattering her sense of peace. "I know." She sat back, resisting the temptation to grab Jo's small hand. "You relax, honey. It's nothing."

Another bounce sent all the passengers scrambling for their seat belts even before the captain's calm voice reassured them that everything was fine.

"Buckle up, honey," Mary said to Jo, trying to keep her voice from trembling.

But Jo was leaning over the man in the aisle seat, asking, "Mister? Mister, are you okay?"

Even Mary heard the groan escaping from the poor man's pale lips. "Jo, let the flight attendants handle this," she said, watching his eyelids flutter. "Just let him be, honey."

"Mom, he's scared," Jo whispered in the same tone of voice she used to reprimand Max for teasing Will. Then, in the tone she used to comfort her baby brother, Jo said softly, "It's just a little air wave. It's over now, see?"

The man's eyes opened warily as Jo's warm, little hand patted his. "What do you know about airplanes, young lady?" he managed to ask.

Although Mary immediately took offense, her daughter just laughed. "Not too much," she admitted.

The white lips curved upward a little. "You're an honest kid, anyway."

"My name's Jo." Before Mary could stop her, her daughter said, "And this is my mom. You can call her Mrs. Clark."

Both the man and Mary laughed. "I'm Mary," my sister-in-law said reluctantly. "And don't feel you have to talk."

The man frowned a little and introduced himself merely as Dale, adding, "I never talk on flights. Too busy praying."

"I know what you mean," Mary said. "We don't talk to strangers, anyway, do we, Jo?" she added for good measure and turned her face toward the window to prove it.

"He's not a stranger," Jo piped up. "At least, not now." She swiveled in her seat a little. "So, Dale, want to know why I'm not afraid to fly?"

Mary heard him grunt. "He's not feeling well, Jo," she warned. "Why don't you read your book?"

"What are you reading?" Dale asked.

Picking up on the genuine interest in his voice, Jo started to tell him all about old Hepzibah's penny shop in the ancient house with its seven gables. "I love Nathaniel Hawthorne," she confided. "He lived just a few miles down the coast from where we live. We go to Salem all the time."

The color was coming back into Dale's face, Mary noticed. Almost absentmindedly he released his grip on the armrests. "That's pretty advanced reading for you. What are you, nine, ten?"

When Jo emphasized that she was ten, Dale shook his head a little. "That's great," he said almost to himself.

"So, anyway," my niece said with the determination that had brought her through such a frightening illness, "the reason I'm not afraid to fly is because I know how to sail."

Dale laughed. "I suppose that's kind of a riddle, right, Jo?"

Jo shook her head. "No, it's the same principle," she expounded, not a bit self-conscious. "That's why early airplanes were called airships. It's because the air is just like water and can hold up objects the same way the ocean holds up a boat." She leaned toward Dale a little more. "I don't get scared every time my dad's sailboat bobs a little, so why would I be afraid when the plane does the same thing?"

Dale was flipping open his laptop, and Mary thought Jo

had worn out his patience. "Jo, honey, why don't you read a little?" she repeated.

"I'm going to write that down," Dale said. He looked at Jo, and I can imagine what he was thinking, since I've had the experience myself of looking at Jo's shiny brown hair and marveling at the busy brain beneath. "Better yet, why don't you?"

Jo put down her tray, and Dale deposited the laptop on it. "What should I write?" Jo asked.

"Just what you told me," Dale said, and watched as Jo's fingers tapped out the letters. "And you know how to use a computer, too. Amazing."

"Don't you have kids?" Jo asked.

Mary sat up straight, afraid Jo had gone too far.

"They're older," Dale explained. "Twice your age and then some."

As Mary relaxed again, the plane jittered a little. While Dale let out his breath, he didn't grab the armrest. Instead, he watched my niece write down her explanation of the physics of flight.

When she stopped, he asked, "What do you know about lightning? Or fireflies? Or blenders?"

Jo stopped writing only when the plane landed smoothly on the tarmac, surprising all three of them.

"It's been the best flight I've ever had," Dale said. "Jo, do you think your mom would give me your address and phone number?"

Mary let Jo give him both, and then they both shook hands with him.

"I hope you never get scared in a plane again," Jo said solemnly.

"I don't know about that," Dale was honest enough to say, "but I do know one thing for sure. Whenever I do, I'll think of one brave little girl."

Mary and Jo forgot all about Dale during their visit and only remembered him on their flight home, but he wasn't on the plane. Once they were back in the little town of Rockport, Jo went back to school and Mary resumed her duties as a full-time mom.

About a month after their trip to Indiana, Mary got an excited phone call from the director of the town's public library. She had received a letter and a current catalogue from a senior editor at one of the country's largest publishers of children's books, telling her that she could select $1,000 worth of books as a donation to the children's room in Jo's name. Of course, the editor was Dale.

The local newspaper did a story about the gift, and Jo sent the clipping to her airborne friend with a thank-you note. When Dale wrote back, he said that he planned to give Jo credit in the introduction of a new science book he was planning for very young children, with her parents' permission.

"You are a remarkable young lady," his letter concluded. "I'm sure I'll never meet anybody else five miles up in the clouds with her feet planted so firmly on the ground."

As usual, Jo had a scientific observation on the tip of her tongue. With a wrinkle of her nose and a shake of her head, she sighed, "That's impossible."

—*Nan B. Clark*

The Beaded Bag

Mame, the mother of ten children, sat in the old rocker in the kitchen, her beaded bag in her lap. Hours before, she'd bathed the younger children and tucked them into bed, helped her husband candle and clean eggs to be sold the next morning, and churned a tub of butter. The smell of fresh bread baking in the oven pleased her. She sighed. After a busy day on the farm, these midnight hours were her own.

The clock chimed. Mame looked up at Lenora, her eldest daughter living at home, standing in the doorway. "Nora," she said, "I thought you'd be asleep, after helping with the milking and catching up on your studies."

Lenora smiled. "You know I can't sleep while you're still up."

"I know how that is." She strung three or four shiny cobalt blue beads onto her needle and stitched them into place. "It's good to have company."

"The beading is taking a long time, Mama."

Mame laughed. "Can't work long before falling asleep," she said, smoothing her apron so she could see all the beads lying in her lap. "If I start to doze, read me some of that *Huck Finn* you're studying, will you? I always did favor Mark Twain."

"You and Daddy's sister, Aunt Vilate. Remember when I was nine, and she gave me *Tom Sawyer* for my birthday?"

Mame nodded. "Such a dear she is," Mame said, threading more beads. "Each year Vilate invites me to her luxurious home in Salt Lake City for a two-day stay. Old as we are, we still giggle like schoolgirls, reminiscing about those early days."

"She's like a sister, isn't she?"

"Oh, yes." Mame gazed wistfully at the pastel blues, greens, yellows, and violets in Vilate's floral painting hanging above the kitchen table. "She's an accomplished artist, you know. Paints like the masters." Mame paused. "But, even more important, Vilate has a kind heart that takes joy in making others happy." She pulled out the handkerchief tucked beneath her sleeve and wiped her eyes.

"Check the bread for me, will you please, Nora? I could use a hot heel of bread slathered with butter and honey."

"And a cold cup of milk?"

"Exactly."

Later, as her worn hands continued threading the shiny beads and working them onto the bag, Mame smiled as she remembered her last visit with Vilate.

"Come with me," Vilate had said, grabbing Mame's hand.

"Where are we going?"

"Downtown."

Mame caught her breath. "But I can't afford . . ."

Vilate hugged her hard. "Don't worry. You're my guest, and I've arranged for a special surprise!"

In the beauty parlor, the beautician coiffed Mame's beautiful dark auburn hair into a stylish 'do, a luxury indeed.

A little while later, Mame's dark eyes sparkled as she caught her reflection in the department store mirror. What a gorgeous blue brocade dress! From the meager income of the Kimball farm, she knew she could never have had one so beautiful.

"You look regal, like a queen," Vilate said, circling Mame again and again. "Now for the final touch."

"The final touch?"

Vilate nodded. "A beaded bag will add that exquisite final touch to your new outfit," she said. "You choose the beads, and I'll show you how to make the bag."

The next day, with their heads together next to Vilate's blazing fireplace, Mame had received her beading instructions.

Remembering, Mame smiled and sighed. Wouldn't Vilate be surprised, she thought, if she knew that I was making the bag for her? If only I can finish it in time for Christmas.

In and out, in and out went her needle, as the blue beads glimmered from the raised pattern on the bag. All was silent, except for the *tick, tick, tick* of the grandfather clock. Her eyes felt heavy.

"Mama?" Lenora tapped her on the shoulder. "You should go to bed. Here, I'll help you."

A month passed, then two, then three. Bouts of chicken pox worked their way through first one child, then the next, causing unimaginable worry and distress. Between baking soda baths to stop the itching and cool cloths to stop the fever, little time remained—not even in the midnight hours; yet, night after night, Mame worked on her beaded bag. Often, she and the rooster greeted the morning together.

"Goodness, Nora," Mame said one evening, "I never dreamed so many beads could fit onto one bag." She chuckled. "Well, I've hand-stitched the floral taffeta lining and made a pocket for the mirror." She handed Lenora the open bag. "What do you think? Shall I add a small ruffle around the top of the lining?"

"That would look smart," Lenora said. "Are you going to cover the mirror?"

"I thought I would—with a piece of matching taffeta."

"An elegant beaded bag for an elegant lady," Lenora said, hugging Mame.

"My thoughts exactly. But remember," Mame said, putting her finger to her lips and winking, "It's our secret."

Lenora grinned. "You'll get it done by Christmas, I know."

"I believe I will. After I finish the lining, I want to add seven rows of beaded tassels at the bottom."

"Wish I didn't have to leave for college next week," Lenora said, running her fingers over the tiny flowers carved in the silver frame at the top of the bag. "After all your work, I'd love to see the finished product."

"You'll see it on Christmas day, when Aunt Vilate comes for dinner." Mame kissed her daughter's cheek. "Thank you for your company and for keeping me awake."

In bed that night, Mame was awakened by a raspy sound, followed by a fit of coughing.

"Crozier, what is it?" she cried, raising her husband's head.

"C-c-can't . . . breathe . . . get . . . the doctor." He lay motionless in her arms, his face as white as death.

"Nora!" she screamed. "Come quickly! It's your father!"

Mame thumped his chest, rolled him over, massaged his

back. He gasped. Rattling sounds escaped from his chest and seemed to catch in his throat.

"Call Doctor Whiting, Nora! Tell him to hurry!"

Mame helped Crozier to the overstuffed chair, covered him with an afghan, and sat beside him, holding his hand. An eternity seemed to pass before she heard the *chug, chug* of the doctor's car coming up the dirt driveway.

"Bronchial pneumonia," Dr. Whiting said. "Keep him warm and in bed. He's feverish. A shot of whiskey wouldn't hurt. If he gets worse, call me."

Despite her vigilant care, Crozier's condition did get worse.

"Maybe I should wait to start college, Mama," Lenora said. "You could use some help with the younger kids, and—"

"Your father and I won't hear of it," Mame interrupted. "The good Lord will give me the strength I need to bear this burden." She drew a cool bowl of water from the bathroom faucet and bathed Crozier's face. "Pack up your things, Nora. Your brother will be here to pick you up before you know it."

After Lenora left the room, Crozier wheezed, "Where are we going to get the money to pay for the rest of her tuition at Utah State?"

"The Lord will provide," Mame answered.

Later that evening, she finished the last remaining tassel on the beaded bag and held it up to the light. The beads glimmered and glistened. Mame hugged the bag to her chest as tears rolled down her cheeks.

"I know how much you would have loved it, Vilate," she said out loud. "It was to be my thanks to you for all you've done for me over the years. But Nora needs her education. I know you'd understand."

Sitting at the table, she wrote to her eldest son, Eddie:

Since your father has been ill, money has been scarce. Lenora has her college tuition for Utah State with the exception of fifteen dollars. Will you please take this beaded bag to the Catholic Carnival and have them raffle it off. Surely it is worth fifteen dollars!
    Love,
    Mother

She tucked the note inside the bag, found a suitable box, and lovingly wrapped her gift in butcher paper. Tying it securely with string, she set the package on the table, where Reid would not forget to mail it on his way to school. In due time, the fifteen dollars arrived.

Three months later, Crozier had recovered and the family was celebrating Christmas. As Mame opened her special gift, tears fell upon the wrapping. She tried to speak, but no words came.

"We couldn't do it, Mama," Eddie said, wiping his eyes. "Nora told us about you, Aunt Vilate, and the beaded bag—how you worked on it night after night during the wee hours."

"All of us gave what we could," Reid explained, "even the younger ones."

Mame hugged each of her children in turn. "Thank you," she whispered to each of them. "Thank you."

That afternoon, Mame and her family watched as someone else's eyes filled with tears.

"Oh, Mame!" Vilate said, holding up the beaded bag. "This is my all-time favorite Christmas gift! How can I ever thank you?"

Mame's heart felt as though it would burst. Her eyes scanned the faces of her ten children, her dear husband, and her beloved Vilate. "You just did," she whispered.

—*Mary Chandler*

"The Beaded Bag" was first published in *GRIT* magazine, December 13, 1998.

 Dad's Belt

Of all the things my dad left me when he died, a piece of an old combine belt was the most valuable. It was the belt his father had used to beat him with, and it always hung over the door to our bathroom as a reminder of how things had been but would never be again.

My father grew up poor in the remote Canadian province of New Brunswick. He worked the coal mines from an early age, and his young life was filled with hardship, hard work, and harsh discipline. The man he called his father was actually his stepfather, but he wasn't told of this fact until after the brutal man had died.

Throughout his youth, the daily routine of work and turmoil was broken only by visits from his Uncle Buck from Winnipeg. Buck was a large bear of a man, who came twice a year, like clockwork, to visit his sister and her children. My dad said he was the kindest man he'd ever met, and I guess it was his influence on my father that helped him break the cycle of abuse and forbid it from entering his own home when he became a husband and father.

We couldn't have asked for a kinder, gentler man than my dad, and we all trusted and loved him deeply. When he talked of his childhood and the beatings he'd received, his eyes would slowly slide over to the belt hanging on the wall and his whole demeanor would change. The power of those beatings must have been terrible. After these stories, I always went to bed with a heavy heart, thinking of the childhood that had been robbed from this kind and loving man.

My father taught us that no matter what happened in our lives, we would always be welcome home anytime. And we knew that we could always count on a smile and a tender word of advice to soothe us when we got there.

Time continued her dance, and we all grew up and moved out. Still, we continued to receive guidance and love from our father until the day he died. It hit us all hard. As we gathered on the old farm, tears flowed freely for this man who'd had a miserable childhood but had filled ours with affection and beauty.

In the days immediately after my father's memorial service, the lawyers came and the last wishes were stated and passed on. Although the estate was meager, we all received one gift beyond value and explanation.

In his last days, our father had taken the belt down from the wall and cut it into four pieces. We all received a piece of the belt that had hurt our father so terribly. That night, we sat around crying and discussing what he could have been thinking when he did this. As the night wore on, it began to dawn on us.

The belt symbolized everything he'd taught us not to be.

It was his trophy. He had lived through the abuse. Instead of abandoning life, like so many others might have, he'd embraced it, and in so doing, he'd turned a legacy of hate and hurt into a legacy of love and happiness.

Now, I keep that belt on my wall. We all do. It hangs as a reminder of the obstacles we can all overcome, with grace and kindness. And when my daughter is crying because she's lost her Pokémon cards or skinned her knee, I hold her close, look at that old belt, and think of a man she will never know. A man I am honored to call Dad.

—*John Gaudet*

 # Little Big Woman

I had just poured myself a cup of coffee and dropped into a chair at the kitchen table. My daughters, Carla and Elaina Marie, were off to school, and my husband, Carl, was off to work. Each morning, the woodsy scene on Caney Mountain came alive as the sun crept down the side, chasing the dark with a cheery shade of raspberry. I always took time to enjoy the drama before beginning the day's chores on our small farm.

Then I saw it. Thick, black smoke billowed into the sky from Caney Mountain. Sparks spit through the treetops in the early morning mist.

"Miss Natalie's house is on fire!"

In a panic I slammed down my cup, spilling coffee, and flew out the door. I raced down the hill past the wide-eyed cattle. Seeing me coming, they had lined up like soldiers to watch. I scrambled over the hog-wire fence and galloped across the road that snaked along the valley floor.

"No time to take the driveway!" I puffed, and plunged into the woods leading straight to Miss Natalie's house. My mind raced. "Poor Miss Natalie. She's probably still asleep. Overcome with smoke by now. The whole sky looks black from here!"

Mountain laurel brushed at my face; blackberry briars scratched my arms and snared my clothing. "Almost there!" I wheezed. The smoke pressed in, limiting my vision. Suddenly, an ear-splitting roar vibrated through the sooty shadows. I pulled up short and stared. Miss Natalie was sawing a downed jack pine into stove-wood lengths. A brush pile burned farther uphill. Open-mouthed, I watched, too relieved to be annoyed that my legs felt like oatmeal and my heart boomed in my ears.

At that moment, Miss Natalie discovered my haggard figure and jumped back, startled. "Goodness, Joyce, you scared me. You okay? You look awful. Why are you wearing your robe and pajamas?"

"I, uh . . . thought, uh . . ." I stopped and sucked in a breath. "I thought your house was on fire!"

"Goodness, no!" She giggled. "I'm just burning a little brush. How do you like my new chainsaw? I bought it so I could clear out some of these old jack pines. The woods are cluttered with them, don't you think?"

"Yeah, I guess so." My flushed face began to cool, and my pounding heart to slow. I flung out my arms and turned toward home, stumbling over fallen logs I must have jumped over on my way up. I forced my unwilling legs to carry me back across the road and up the hill. The chainsaw roared to life again.

"None of your business!" I hissed at Sweet Pea, our milk cow, who was still rooted to the ground, gawking. "Come to the barn, you old witch! I have to milk. Now!"

Warm milk streamed into the bucket. "A chainsaw! At her age! Sixty-eight if she's a day; maybe seventy!" I leaned my head into Sweet Pea's flank, trying to relax. I really shouldn't have been surprised. Carl, who's known Miss Natalie all his life, takes her wild and stormy nature in stride. To those who don't know her well, she's a frail little lady with angel wings who could persuade anyone to bungee-jump from a cloud. To me, she's a never-ending source of amazement.

Miss Natalie's neighbors love her, even after two of them wrestled her new 300-pound Buck stove into her tiny house. Even after others had installed her new sink and cabinets from Lowe's. Even after poor young Greg inched her new organ from the truck bed, across the porch, and through the door. "Fine boy," she commented. "Good neighbors in this community. I'm proud to live here."

Carl and I had decided to build our own house after discovering how much interest was tacked onto a loan.

"Good," said Miss Natalie. "I'll help."

Two days before construction was to begin, her red Jeep truck bounced up the driveway and slid to a halt, barely missing the split-rail fence and the kids' pet rooster, Roho.

"Where do I start?" she asked, tying on a Harris Hardware apron and taking up her favorite blue-handled hammer. Every day, Miss Natalie hammered, sawed, sanded, peeled logs, and planed lumber. When work slowed, she swept up sawdust and burned debris. When it came time to finish the kitchen, she said, "You go on now, Joyce, and do something else. I'll handle this." Two days later she had sized and nailed up more than a hundred pieces of four-inch poplar board paneling.

One morning, I was stacking lumber when Miss Natalie's bespectacled face appeared over the edge of the roof, forty feet up. "Bring me those roofing tacks, Joyce. I need to fill my apron."

"Not on your life," I gasped, getting dizzy just looking up.

Carl shouldered the box of nails and climbed the ladder. Together they threw row after row of shingles into place. In two days, the job was done. Miss Natalie nailed the last one down.

"There!" she declared.

A fire blazed in the fireplace of our new house. Miss Natalie and I relaxed in comfortable silence, but I was aware of the wheels turning in her head.

"Do you think Carl could find a cow for me? A nice little Jersey? They give lots of cream. I could churn and make butter. I'll build a little barn and clear some brush for an electric fence."

I stared at her. "A cow?" When would I stop being surprised?

"Cow!" Carl yelled when he heard. "How can she milk a cow with her arthritic hands?"

"She'll manage," I stated. "She always does."

"Yeah, I guess," he said.

"She still has the pioneer spirit," I offered.

"Hmm! All she needs is a musket and a coonskin cap."

Blam! Blam! Gunshots echoed across the valley. "Uh, oh, what now?"

I finished hanging clothes on the line and hurried to answer the phone.

"Joyce, want to come for lunch?"

"Don't tell me . . . It's squirrel season?"

"Right. Nice and fat."

"I'd love to," I said. "Did you wear your coonskin cap?"

"Pardon?"

"Never mind. I'll be over at noon. Thanks."

The fried squirrel was delicious. Watching Miss Natalie scurry around the kitchen flinging things on the table, I realized why all young folks like her so much. While other people her age grow old, Miss Natalie remains young.

My husband, two children, and I hurried into our best clothing one Sunday morning and headed off to church. As we drove down our driveway, we saw Miss Natalie—stretching to see over the dashboard—drive by in a cloud of dust. Her new Buick with its plush sheepskin seat covers flashed by, hardly more than a red streak against the gray pavement.

"What a transformation!" I said. "On Sundays, she lays aside all work and dresses like the Queen of Sheba, all bejeweled and made up."

"I want to be just like her when I grow up," declared Carla from the backseat.

"Me too!" piped little Elaina Marie.

I understood why. She spills over with hope and wonder and finds secrets everywhere. Her yard preens itself in a profuse array of flowers. She is a woman of farm, earth, and work. Her brain brims with knowledge of herbs and healing and of wisdom born of communication with Creation. She tries her hand at watercolor art, too, and would fly with it if she had an ounce of patience.

The Bible speaks of the light of the Lord's smile on certain people. I think He laughs outright when He observes Miss

Natalie. Goodness knows God Almighty is the only one she listens to. She is steered by a star, with a faith that rises higher than Caney's summit—right up to heaven.

As I write this story about my mother-in-law, Natalie Matilda Barnett ("Granny" to the kids), I wonder if the names and places should be changed. The neighbors are growing curious about the identity of the little old lady in shorts, Nike sneakers, and sunglasses speeding up and down the road on a flashy new ten-speed bike. It's red.

"We can't imagine who she is," we declare.

—*Joyce Lance Barnett*

A Bike with Pink Ribbons

The summer heat was taking its toll on me. I'd recently been diagnosed with multiple sclerosis, and heat aggravates MS. A debilitating fatigue had kept me under self-imposed house arrest—just my air-conditioner, big-screen TV, dogs, and me—day in and day out, the entire summer. I was bored, lonely, and depressed. My whole life depressed me. On top of feeling lousy and being unable to do the activities I normally enjoyed, I had been forced to give up a high-power executive position and, along with it, my company car.

I thought about going to the air-conditioned mall but nixed that idea. My closets and several bureaus were already stuffed to the max. The thought of my designer suits getting lumps on the shoulders from hangers, the dust on my silk blouses, and the array of matching shoes, purses, and accessories, painful reminders of who I used to be, just colored my mood a darker shade of blue. I certainly didn't need to wear Gucci anything to the supermarket. Besides, I had already attempted to shop through my depression on the Internet. I counted fifty-three purses, dozens of pairs of shoes, and a host of other things I didn't really need. What I needed was to get out of the house.

So, I got into my brand-new red mustang convertible (also purchased online) and just started driving. Of course, because of the heat, I couldn't even put down the top on my fabulous new convertible. With the air-conditioning blasting, I drove around town and out of town, going nowhere in particular. I passed a sign that said "Indoor Flea Market" and, figuring the building would be air-conditioned, decided to turn around and check it out. I'd never been to a flea market—had never purchased anything that wasn't new, wasn't a brand name, and didn't have at least a double-digit price tag. So, there was no temptation of adding to my overstocked wardrobe, or to my house, for that matter, and a flea market seemed like a safe way to distract me from my boredom and depression.

I felt like an alien who had landed on a different planet—a world lined with tables and tables of junk: an ancient toaster, mismatched dishes, raggedy clothes, and assorted other discards. Why would anyone buy this stuff? Who would have the nerve to sell it? Then I noticed an old man selling used and torn paperback books for a quarter apiece. Clearly, he must need those quarters, I thought. I filled my arms with books and gave him five dollars. His bright smile of thanks was disproportionate to the purchase. My emotions wavered between wonder and depression, but his smile did seem to lift my spirits, if only slightly. I put my books in the car and went back into the flea market.

I walked and looked, as much at the people as at the wares they were buying and selling, fascinated by both the bargain hunters and the peddlers. At one stall, I noticed a little girl's bike with worn pink ribbons—and a $10 price tag—hanging from the handlebars. It looked as if it had been pulled from a dumpster. I just shook my head and started to move on. Just then, a woman and a little girl stopped to look at the bike. The child was about ten years old, and the pink bows in her long blond pigtails matched the pink ribbons on the bike. Her eyes opened wide with excitement. The woman's face lit up, too, for the briefest second, and she almost smiled, but it quickly passed. She looked to be about my age, yet she seemed twenty years older. Dark circles surrounded her eyes, and her cloths hung loosely on her thin frame, as if held up by the memory of her former figure. The child reached into her pocket and pulled out coins and a few crumpled bills.

"Please, Mommy, please?" she said. "Do I have enough money?"

"Honey, we need so many other things. I don't think there's enough for a bike, too. Let's look for the other stuff we need first, and then we'll see. Okay, sweetie?"

The little girl's face fell, and then a silent understanding passed between mother and child. She took her mother's hand, and they continued their search for other, more important necessities. My heart was in my throat. I walked up to the man at the booth, prepared to give him a piece of my mind. Why hadn't he sold the bike to the little girl for a dollar or two, or just given it to her? Luckily, I realized the answer before I had the chance to say a word. The seller was an old man dressed in rags, and even though he, too, looked like his heart was in his throat, he clearly needed those ten dollars.

I handed him a ten-dollar bill and asked him to please give the little girl the bike when she and her mother passed by on their way out.

"What's your name, miss, so I can tell the lady who gave her the bike?"

"Just tell her it was a present from a grateful woman."

"Will do," he said. "But do you mind me asking what you're grateful to her for?"

"Everything," I said.

I hid around the corner and watched, half expecting the old guy to just pocket the money. When the mother and daughter approached the table, the vendor flagged them down and wheeled the bike over to the child. The little girl's face glowed, and the mother smiled a full smile that time, tears glistening in her eyes. The mom wrote something down on a piece of paper and gave it to the old man. After they left, I approached the vendor.

"I did as you said, miss, and they were real grateful. She asked me to give this to the anonymous woman," he said, handing me the slip of paper.

The note said that she and her daughter had just moved into town with just the shirts on their back. She said they were starting a new life here, and I had made their day. She signed her name and wrote down the name of the motel where they were staying temporarily "until we get on our feet."

"Seems like they're running away from something," the vendor said sadly. Or to somewhere, I thought.

When I arrived home, my house no longer seemed like a prison. It seemed comfy and safe, and as luxurious as any five-star hotel. I was as happy to see my dogs as they always are to see me, and I chatted to them happily as I went into the basement and gathered up some boxes. Whistling, I went to my closet and filled the boxes with designer suits and matching shoes and handbags, and pulled piles of clothes from my dresser drawers. I put a note in the box, wishing the mom good luck with her new life and the little girl much joy with her new bike—and thanking them for the gift they'd given me. I wrote that if she had the courage to start over, then so could I.

That miserable hot summer day, I spent ten dollars for a new lease on life. Now, that's what I call a bargain!

—*Beth Ambler*

 Little Black Cat

They live in nursing homes on opposite sides of the country. They used to write to each other, but now neither can remember if the other is still living or whether they are young or old. They live mostly in a time gone by, when they were young and happy.

Irene, the older sister, is nearing ninety. When she was a young widow, she drove her nine-year-old daughter to Northern California to make a new life. The trip took four days. Now, she can no longer live alone. She has fallen and broken bones and is often confused. The last time I saw her, she held a pile of unopened birthday cards on her lap. She was sitting in her wheelchair in the garden of the nursing home, fingering the envelopes she had received a week ago. She had forgotten her own birthday.

Lucille, the younger one, is my mother. She has lived all her life in the mill town where they were born. She worked hard in factories, weaving carpets, sewing uniforms, or stitching basketballs. In those years her hands were rough and red. Now they are soft as she fingers the edges of her blanket. I wheel her chair to the sunroom on the fourth floor. She is examining the blanket's stitching, looking for mistakes, as though she were back at work. I tell her I have seen Irene, and she smiles. I know what's coming, and I sit back and listen as she tells the story.

In the 1920s, they were little girls, the daughters of parents who had left Poland at the dawn of the twentieth century to come to America. Grandma and Grandpa Smitka made their way by train from Ellis Island to a crowded factory town on the Mohawk River in northern New York State. Their first child, a daughter born when Grandma was only a girl herself at seventeen, died in infancy from influenza. Irene was born a few years later, in 1911, and Lucille came along three years after that. Four more children quickly followed, and though all were well loved, their parents' time was hard to come by. Grandpa worked in a broom factory and later a butcher shop. There was no automatic washing machine or dishwasher, no self-cleaning oven or even hot running water. Grandma had her hands full, and Irene and Lucille often took care of the little ones. Irene, the oldest and, according to Lucille, the bossiest, held authority over the other children, but most of the chores fell to Lucille.

When Irene was a toddler, a bout with polio left her "crippled." She limped in her heavy brown shoes, and she often fell when she tried to run. She was very smart, but Grandma didn't have the time or patience to teach her housekeeping skills. So her second-in-line sister, Lucille, was the one who wheeled the babies in their carriage, fed them, and washed their little dresses. She was the one Grandma sent to the store for a last-minute loaf of bread or a bottle of milk. Sometimes, in that busy household, Irene felt she was in the way, with nothing to contribute. Since she was excused from most of the work, she had lots of time to read and study, and so she became "the clever one" in the family. On the day of Mom's never-forgotten story, Irene performed a bit of the magic that only big sisters can.

Lucille was at the kitchen table working on a school project, a pen-and-ink drawing. Her dark brown eyes concentrated on the precious sheet of white paper. There was only one piece and no extra for mistakes. She worked for hours, creating an outdoor scene like the ones near the creek where all the children played. Just as she was finishing the painstaking job, a drop of ink fell from her pen and landed at the bottom of her drawing.

Heartbroken, Lucille began to cry so loudly she alarmed her big sister, who was reading in the next room. Irene couldn't run like the others, but she could get around fast enough when she wanted to. Her heavy leg thumped on the wooden floor as she hurried to the kitchen table.

"Luca, what's the matter?" she asked, using her pet name for her sister.

Lucille wiped her wet face with her sleeve. She sniffed and moved away from the table, so that Irene could see what had happened.

"Give me the pen," was all Irene said.

Irene's dark brown curls fell over her face as she bent over the drawing. Holding her locks back with one hand, with her other she carefully dipped the pen into the blob of ink. Using the sharp point, Irene slowly pulled out a pair of tiny feet, then a head with two pointy ears, and finally, as Lucille watched spellbound, a long and curving tail. Irene had transformed the ugly ink spot into a perky black cat!

More than seventy years have come and gone, but Lucille, my mother, still remembers. Mom doesn't stay long in the present anymore, and she may not recall your name. But ask her about Irene and her eyes sparkle.

"It was like magic," she says, her eyes shining as she tells the tale.

Then she smiles to herself with the smile of the girl she was, warmed by the memory of a sister's love and the magic that turned tears into laughter.

—*Linda C. Wisniewski*

This story was published in *Mocha Memoirs*, Volume 5, Issue 8.

A Christmas to Remember

He toddled around the corner and into the living room, where he stopped cold. His little mouth dropped open, and the light in Ryan's eyes rivaled the glow of the lights on the Christmas tree. What he saw there were two big shiny Tonka toys, a tractor and a fire truck with a ladder. There were other packages, too, mostly from his grandparents and one or two small ones from me. But those would have to wait. He only had eyes for those trucks.

I looked at Mike, who was looking at Ryan. I couldn't tell whose eyes were brighter.

"Those are for you, Ry," I said.

That was all the encouragement he needed. He ran to the fire truck, climbed on, and rode three laps around the living room on top of the truck. Then he hopped off and lay down on his belly, pushing the tractor and making engine noises.

He's such a boy, I thought. Looking at Mike, I could visualize him doing the same thing when he was a kid.

Before long, Ryan had both Tonkas upside down, examining every inch. Ryan wanted to know every detail of every toy he had. If the Tonkas hadn't been welded, he would've surely taken them apart to have a better look. He was Mike's son all right. In fact, in only a few minutes, Mike was right down there with him.

At two and a half, Ryan was the perfect age for Tonka trucks. At thirty-three, Mike was the perfect age to enjoy them with his son. I'm not sure which of the two of them had the most fun.

Eventually, we had to remind Ryan that he had other presents to open. With each one, he seemed happy and excited. What he really wanted, though, was to just play trucks.

But there was something unusual about those Tonkas that Ryan didn't notice. Tonka is famous for using standard colors on its toys, mostly school bus yellow. Ryan's tractor was navy blue, and his fire truck was wine-colored with a silver ladder. These weren't the Tonkas you buy in the store now. They were the good old hard metal ones no longer produced. For weeks, Mike had sat in his lonely little trailer in the evenings, cleaning, repairing, and sanding those trucks to make them good as new. Then he had painted them. Now he was getting the payoff for his labor of love. Ryan was in kid heaven.

It had been a hard year for Mike, Ryan, and me. Only a few months earlier, I'd asked Mike to move out of our home permanently. We still cared for each other, but his alcoholism and all the bad things that came with it had finally succeeded in beating the life out of our marriage, and I'd given up trying. After the initial bitterness, we became friendly again. Though our marriage was definitely over, because of Ryan, there would always be tender bonds between us.

The breakup left both of us financially drained. I felt dismal after Thanksgiving, when I realized that Christmas was coming soon and I had no money. I could manage to get a small tree and maybe after that, if I really squeezed, I could come up with five dollars to buy Ryan a few Hot Wheels. That was it. But compared to Mike, I was practically rolling in the dough. Of course, he would spend Christmas Day with us and share our tree. But I knew that he would be hard-pressed to have even one extra dollar to buy Ryan anything at all.

It was depressing at best. I wanted so much to make a wonderful Christmas for Ryan. Not that he needed the toys, and not that gifts are the heart of Christmas. Ryan would be surrounded by love and celebration and the recognition of the true meaning of Christmas with or without presents. But I'd waited a long time to have a child. And I was anxious to experience the joy that parents feel when they put things under the tree that they know will delight their children.

One afternoon in early December I was on my way home when I heard a man on the radio say that he had a yard full of old Tonka trucks that he was selling for two to three dollars each. They needed some TLC, but they were sturdy and fixable. Ryan had played with Tonkas at a friend's house and adored them. It was the perfect gift for him, and I knew the perfect guy to do the fixing up.

I was so excited, I didn't even stop to call Mike and ask what he thought. He was still at work, anyway. I went straight to the address the man on the radio had given. It was just as he'd said: he had dozens of trucks, but they all needed lots of attention. I scoured the yard looking for the best of the bunch. Some of them had rubber parts that were broken, and I wasn't sure how those could be fixed. Finally, I found two that were well worn but still had all their parts intact. I paid the guy four dollars and fifty cents, almost my total allotment for Christmas. He loaded the metal trucks into the trunk of my car, and I drove to the auto body and paint shop where Mike worked.

Just as he was getting ready to leave, I pulled up next to his car and told him my idea: We could give Ryan a joint present. I bought the trucks, and he could fix them up like new. I was sure Mike had sandpaper and tools, though I wasn't sure about paint. When I opened the trunk and showed him the trucks, he caught my enthusiasm—partly because he would have a great gift for Ryan, one that took Mike back to his own childhood and boyish delights, and partly because he would have a cool project to fill his lonely evenings. I expected him to be interested. But he was more than that. He was thrilled.

As we stood there with the trunk open, Mike's boss came out to see what the excitement was about. Mel had become a family friend, and he loved Ryan. He was about sixty, but I guess guys of any age still love toy trucks, because he had to pick them up and examine them right along with Mike.

"What a great idea," he said, turning the tractor around in his hands. "Real metal . . . how about that! Tell ya what, Mike. Feel free to use any tools or sandpaper in the shop. You can even take some home this weekend. And when you're ready to paint, you can use whatever we have leftover from spray jobs. Ryan's gonna love these."

He was right. Ryan loved them at age two and a half, and he loves them now, at eighteen. He still has those two Tonkas. When he was old enough to understand, I explained to him how his dad had spent hours upon hours turning old trucks into new ones, just for him. Ryan no longer plays with his trucks, and his dad is gone. But he can pick them up at any time, look them over, and run his hands over their smooth surfaces. Someday, he might pass them on to his own children. For now, they serve as solid-metal proof that he was the target of a whole lot of love.

—*Teresa Ambord*

 # The Comforter

"I've made you at least five comforters, Liz. And there's not a one in sight when I'm chilly." Mother feigns sternness, but her voice is shaky, the cruelty of body parts carrying no lifetime guarantee.

"Ah, but there's never one far away." I laugh and head for the den. I return, arms full of cornflower blue and mauve patches, and tuck the quilt around her knees. "To make up for the inconvenience, I'll include a cup of coffee absolutely free of charge."

"That's more like it," Mom says and chuckles.

I bring each of us a steaming mug. She grasps hers with both hands, attempting to get cup to lips before tremors betray her.

At that instant, the thought strikes me: I've just tucked her in and brought her a drink. When did we switch roles? When did I become mother, and mother become child? Did it happen gradually or as suddenly as it seems?

A cascade of memories floods my mind: When new skates throw me to the sidewalk, Mom is immediately there, applying kisses and tape to my scraped knees and soothing words and hugs to my damaged pride. Sitting tucked beside Mom on our old flow-ered sofa as she drilled me on words from the third-grade speller. Mom loosening my braids and guiding my awkward hands as I attempted to wind reluctant locks around a plastic curler. Mom admonishing me through a mouthful of pins to hold still while I fidgeted and twirled in my first formal dress.

"Your white daisies are lovely." Mom reaches out to touch a bright yellow flower, part of an arrangement on the coffee table.

"They're yellow daisies, Mom, not white," I say in a low voice, not sure I want her to hear. Not sure I want her to realize that the girl who once blushed in her first long dress is now correcting the creator of that dress in identifying the color of a flower. It is, after all, an unimportant detail that cataract-glazed eyes can no longer discern.

"They look as though they could use a little water." Mother dips one finger into the vase and pulls it back dry.

I set down my coffee cup. Over the knot in my throat, I manage, "I've been so involved at the school's Clothes Closet, sorting donations for the fall sale." I pick up the vase and escape to the kitchen.

"You and your projects," Mom calls after me with another chuckle.

Old memories gurgle up like the fresh water bubbling to the top of the vase. . . .

As I piled bulging suitcases and a one-eyed teddy bear into the family car, Mother stood in the doorway with my younger brother and sister. I waved, and already missing my room's yellow-flowered wallpaper and Mom's goodnight kisses, I ran back for one more teary farewell hug, while Dad waited in the car. Her return hug was followed by a gentle swat on the seat of my jeans. "Go on," she'd said, "I've spent too much money on foot-lockers and popcorn poppers to have you back out of college now."

Suddenly, I picture in my mind's eye the red-white-and-blue quilt. While I wrote heady letters home expounding on my all-important causes, my newly acquired knowledge, and my freshly formulated opinions, Mother sent praise and encouragement. One such letter was tucked among the folds of a lap-size red-white-and-blue quilt of her own creation.

A few years later, the red-white-and-blue quilt and I moved into our own apartment, furnished with a love seat and kitchen table bought on credit. Mother congratulated, lined shelves—and co-signed.

Then came that special Fourth of July when fireworks exploded—between Christopher and me. I rushed home with my husband-to-be in tow. Did I see Mom's shoulders droop slightly? Did a hint of a wrinkle cross her face? But the wrinkle quickly rearranged into a smile. The shoulders squared. And Mom's arms enfolded us, as she rejoiced with me, her child in love.

The water spills over the top of the vase and across my hands. I turn off the faucet, grab a towel, wipe down the green ceramic, and return to the living room to set the flowers on the table.

"Mom, remember when I used to call home sniffling about marital spats and strained budgets?" I suddenly realize I speak to her in louder tones these days.

"Yes, yes." She smiles. "I think I threatened to lock the door if you tried to come home."

"No, you didn't. But you placed a hand on each of my shoulders, like you always did when you were about to say something profound, and said, 'Liz, making a marriage is like making a comforter.' I thought, wow, she's flipped for sure. Then you said something I've never forgotten. You said, 'You and Christopher are beginning with a collection of separate pieces of cloth, all different colors and shapes. You must arrange them into a pattern. You'll try them one way, and if that doesn't work, you must try another. With patience, eventually you'll come up with a whole new pattern, a unique design all your own, that has never before existed.' You were absolutely right!"

"Well, wasn't I quite the guru, though?" she laughs.

I stand, give her a hug, and pick up our empty cups. At the kitchen doorway, I stop and turn to say, "I'll tell you this, guru, there were some days when that design was a little too unique. Days when I was ready to throw out the whole damn bag of scraps."

I leave her laughing and go to the coffeemaker.

As I refill our coffee cups, I think about the good laughs and good times that came after those early marriage-making days. Was I still the child when I went to Mom on sun-drenched summer days, babies in tow? Together, she and I had giggled at the antics of toddlers and at my belated introduction to the real art of quilting. We exchanged favorite books and secret hopes. We hadn't yet exchanged places.

And there was the tissue thing. Like some intuitive wizard,

Mother always magically produced a tissue from a sleeve or a pocket when tears erupted or a nose dripped. But then there was that day she and I were huddled in a hospital room, dreading the sound of the gurney that would whisk her away for surgery. That time, it was I who offered Mom a hankie and assurance. Was it then that we traded places?

Or was it much later, when her aching back or her swollen, arthritic knees kept her on the couch all day? I presented her with my first comforter about that time, an imperfect burgundy and rose reproduction of one of her masterpieces. It was also during that period that often, over her protests, I'd tidy up the stacked dishes in her kitchen.

"Liz, dear, you do too much. You have a family to see to. Just leave the dishes. I'll be fine in the morning."

I chose not to notice that things wouldn't always be fine in the morning. I glided through the days, the years, careful not to look too closely at the toll that time was taking on my mother, willing life to remain the same. Mom would always be there, I assured myself, to teach, to sew, to tend, to make my boo-boos better.

But the mother who once shooed me off to college now clings to a farewell hug, though I live just blocks away. Now, I'm the one who drives the car, opens the door, and carries the packages; who advises and encourages, soothes and pampers, supports and praises.

How did this transformation come about? Perhaps it is the work of a makeup artist—a jokester flaunting a sober sense of humor who has sprayed her chestnut hair silver, perched eyeglasses on a smooth face made corrugated, stuffed cotton in unsuspecting ears.

"Liz," Mom calls.

My daydreams scatter, and I return to set down cups of fresh coffee.

"Someone is coming to the door, dear." She wears a mysterious smile.

I catch a glimpse of movement through the window. It's Sara, my daughter, running up the walk, clutching the hand of a young man. Pausing at the hall mirror, I brush back a straying gray curl, square drooping shoulders, and reach for the door.

—B. J. Bateman

All Creatures Great and Small

y daughter, Jill, paused halfway down our front steps. She turned and said, "Mom, will you sing to me? Will you hold me and sing like you used to when I was a little girl?"

Her husband and two little stepdaughters stopped on the sidewalk and looked back.

I always sang to my kids when they were young. Jill and her older brother shared a bedroom, and I knelt between them, holding one's hand and stroking the blond head of the other. And I sang. I crooned through "Dona, Dona" and "Kumbaya." I swayed in rhythm to "Swing Low, Sweet Chariot." I never missed a verse of "Hush Little Baby." I made up songs, too, a habit that drove my husband crazy. On nights I was out, the kids begged, "Sing 'The Horse Broke the Fence,' Daddy," or "No, we want 'The Big Wheel' song." And they didn't mean "Proud Mary," which he might have managed, although he really couldn't carry a tune even when he knew the words.

The kids and I always finished with "All Things Bright and Beautiful," and I watched their active bodies quiet and their eyes grow dreamy as they imagined the purple-headed mountains and the ripe fruit in the garden of the old hymn.

By the time I warbled my way through the refrain for the last time, one of them had usually twitched and fallen asleep.

As Jill grew from child to adult, it became apparent that she had inherited her father's trouble carrying a melody. She cuddles with her girls every night and reads to them, but she just can't sing to them.

I baby-sat for our granddaughters not long ago. After I tucked them into our king-size bed, I sang "Dona, Dona," "Kumbaya," and all the others. Hannah, the six-year-old, lay still as a stone, gazing at the ceiling. Four-year-old Brianna came forward on hands and knees, staring into my eyes from so close that her features blurred. In the dim light drifting through the open door, I saw her lips half open, glistening. Trancelike, she held perfectly still, listening as if she wanted to inhale the songs directly from my mouth.

It was a few days later that Jill asked me to sing to her. She said, "The girls talked about your singing, Mom, and it brought back all the memories. I remember my cool pillow and your hand on my hair. I remember my nightgown with the sunbonnet dolls on it and the pink ice cream cone quilt you made. And the fish mobile and my toy puppy with the music box. Sometimes I woke up when you kissed me one last time."

That's when she turned and asked, "Mom, will you sing to me again?"

Her husband stood beneath the street lamp with a child balanced on each hip. Her father and brothers stood behind me, illuminated by the porch light.

She's very tall, this girl of mine. Standing on the step below me, she still had to stoop to put her head against my chest. I wrapped my fingers in her long hair, and she wound her arms around my waist.

"What shall I sing, Jill?" I asked.

"You know, Mom," she said, looking up and smiling.

"'All Things Bright and Beautiful'?"

"Of course." She snuggled closer. "All the verses."

I kissed the top of her head and began to sing.

All things bright and beautiful,
*All creatures great and small . . .**

I swallowed a lump in my throat and stroked her back as I continued through the verses. Off-key, she joined in.

Jill began to cry, and so did I, but the words still flowed as my mind traveled back over the years. I remembered her birth, how ecstatic I'd been to have a daughter, what an easy child she was, her habit of rescuing small animals, championing the underdog, and befriending the outcast. I remembered how she loved to please others—and still does.

This girl of mine who married young and took on the daunting task of raising another woman's children is no longer under my wing. She's a young woman now, and I can no longer tuck the ice cream cone quilt around her shoulders each night. I cannot protect her from pain, from hurt, from mature responsibilities. I can't make growing up any easier for her.

Jill's tears soaked through my T-shirt and mine dropped to her bowed head. She clung tightly, and then looked up into my face.

"The purple headed mountains. Don't forget the purple headed mountains," she whispered, staring at me through the dim light just as Brianna had a few nights earlier, drinking in the words, the memories, and the song. Drinking in my love.

The purple headed mountains,
*The river running by . . .**

My voice cracked, and I could sing no more. We stood locked together on the stairs.

I know the enormity of the task she's taken on is sometimes almost more than she can handle. I know how hard she's working to create a home of the house she now lives in. Cradling her in maternal love, allowing her to remember falling asleep to a mother's singing—it was the best I could offer her that night.

Jill squeezed me tightly and then turned toward her husband and stepdaughters. Her dad hugged me as I watched her settle the girls into the backseat of their car. Then I heard the hymn again. I strained my ears, listening. Jill was humming the refrain. As they pulled away from the curb, Brianna's thin, childish voice burbled from the open car window:

All things wise and wonderful,
*The Lord God made them all.**

—Peggy Vincent

*"All Things Bright and Beautiful," Cecil F. Alexander, *Hymns for Children,* 1848.

 Rockn Da Nose

I am fortunate to be the mother of three wonderful sons. I adore my boys, but if I said I completely understood them, I would be lying. At times I've found it best just to accept them for who they are, no matter how confusing that might be. And believe me, there are aspects of their personalities that leave me bewildered—yet oddly proud. Take, for instance, the drive they all seem to have had, at some point, to shove things up their noses.

The other day as I cleared the breakfast table, my two-year-old, Raphael, walked up to me, sniffing vigorously.

"Rockn da nose," he stated.

"What, honey?"

"Rockn da nose." Sniff, sniff.

I looked at him, puzzled. *Did he just say he has a rock in his nose?*

I picked him up and stood him on the table—much to his delight. He's not allowed to stand on the table, although he's often convinced that he has a good reason to do that very thing. He looked around, pleased. He was probably wondering if this meant the unreasonable "no throwing things at your brothers" rule would also be repealed.

I tilted his head back and peered up his nose. I couldn't see anything, so I scrounged up a flashlight. The only flashlight I could find was Raphael's cow flashlight, which moos when you turn it on. So the cow and I had a look up Raphael's little snub nose. Sure enough. Rockn da nose. A little bright white rock was glistening from within the depths of his nose.

The cow mooed.

I sighed.

Last week he had put a sticker up his nose. Tomorrow . . . I don't know, probably the cat or something. For some reason when my boys are two they seem to have a compulsion to put things up their noses. When my middle son, Max, was two, I glanced at him one day and was startled to see him looking . . . strange.

Closer inspection revealed that he had wedged two pennies in his nose, one in each nostril. They were perpendicular from his face, causing his nose to jut out unnaturally.

"Owie," he said matter-of-factly.

Indeed. What I couldn't understand is why he would have worked so hard to achieve this look. It can't have been a comfortable process. There seems to be something in a little boy's brain that spies small objects and thinks, "Hey, I know just the place to put those! My nose!"

I remember when my oldest son, Tre, was two. One day my mom was watching him while I was out. When I came home, Mom was sitting on the floor next to Tre, with a stricken look on her face. It seems they had been playing with dried beans. I don't know why. I've found my children have a bizarre effect on my parents. Pretty much anything they ask for, my parents seriously consider giving them. So, say I walk into the room and discover Mom giving one of the boys a marshmallow 4.5 seconds before dinner; I'll give her the raised eyebrow of questioning, and she'll look back at me helplessly and protest, "But he wanted it!"

Anyhow, apparently Tre wanted to play with beans that day, and what Tre wants, Grandma delivers. Together they'd sorted beans, poured beans from cup to cup, run their fingers through great piles of beans, and generally had a grand old bean time. By the time they were done, the beans were all over the floor. So Mom had gotten out the vacuum, only to discover that our vacuum mainly just flung the beans all over the living room, with great clatters and pings.

"It was like shrapnel," she said. She started hand-collecting beans, and at one point she looked at Tre, who was "helping," and said, "Now, don't put one of these up your nose."

So, she was sort of right when she said it was her fault Tre had a bean wedged in his nostril. She was fretting that we might have to take him to the emergency room to get it out before it started to swell and cause damage to his sinuses, or something like that.

I walked up to Tre, plugged his unobstructed nostril, and said, "Blow, honey."

Well, it worked six years ago, and it still works today. Just as his big brother shot the bean out of his nose way back then, so did Raphael shoot the rock out of his nose.

I'm so proud.

I don't understand, but I'm proud.

—*Kira Hardison*

 # King David

Dave took a swipe at his headdress and looked at the clock. The headdress was itchy and he felt squeezed, like a used tube of toothpaste. He loosened the cord of Dad's old bathrobe a notch and hoped he wouldn't trip over it. At least his old Nikes didn't show, except when he had to pull up the robe to walk onstage.

He looked at the clock again. He tried not to look at it, but his head kept swiveling around. They were really busy at the store, but she'd work it out. She said so.

Dave didn't want to be in the program, didn't want to be a king. Kings had singing parts. Miss Hixson went right on with it, anyway, and the first thing you knew, you were singing. That was the way she operated—on everything—on the whole fifth grade.

"I don't believe it!" Mom had said when she read the invitation. "I've never heard you sing a note in your whole life. This I've got to hear!"

Dave didn't know he could sing, but Miss Hixson knew. She said he did fine with his verse—she said that to all the kings—but it was a relief when all three of them zoomed in on the chorus.

Miss Hixson spoke to Mom and Dad at PTA and told them, "I do hope you'll be able to come. David does so well. You'll be proud of him."

Dad looked in his book and shook his head. "It's our last sales meeting of the year. I have to be there. I'm sorry."

Mom said she'd try . . . was the busiest time of the year at the store . . . same day as the company Christmas party . . . she was helping with the arrangements . . . she sure would try.

Dad told him that Mom would be named sales associate of the year, with a bonus. It was supposed to be a secret, but she knew.

Dave looked at the door, which was opening. It was just Rob's mom. Rob was only Joseph. He didn't sing or talk or anything—just stood around up there trying to look holy.

It was almost time. He was breathing a lot, which wasn't easy, with his heart crowded up there in his throat. He hoped he'd be okay when he got started. He swallowed.

Miss Hixson got up and welcomed everybody: mostly mothers, a few grandmothers, and a couple of fathers—people like that, who didn't work—and announced the program. Then she sat down at the piano and played, "Oh, Little Town of Bethlehem," while Steve and Chris pulled the curtains open, real jerky.

The shepherds were there, kneeling by the crib, Keith scrounging around on his knees, knocking into Rob, who forgot he was holy and jabbed him one. The kids laughed.

Miss Hixson glared and shook her head. Then, nodding to the bathrobes, she launched into "We Three Kings" and they all stood up—like robots.

"Remember, you are kings. Be proud!"

Who was there to be proud for? Just that morning, she'd said she planned to be there.

Kevin started up and tripped over his bathrobe cord. He yanked it away from Dave's foot, hissing. "Watch yourself!"

Kev grabbed up his robe and charged up the steps to the stage. Scott gave Dave a shove from behind.

When they got up there, Miss Hixson played the last stanza and started over at the beginning, with Kev, Scott, and Dave kind of straggling in after her. By "Oh-oh, star of wonder," they were together and sounding better. Louder, anyway.

"Let it spill right out," Miss Hixson said. "Sing from a full heart. From joy."

Yeah, right.

Kev had the first solo. "Born a king . . ." And he was off, eyes pinned on Miss Hixson, who nodded and smiled her PTA smile. Kev's mother was mouthing the words and nodding, but not smiling. Then they were into "Oh-ohh" again.

The door opened again. Mom! It wasn't.

Scott was next, blaring out, "Worship him, God on high." Scott's mom let her breath out on the "Ohh-ohhh."

The door stayed closed. And it was Dave's turn. He swallowed and started, a little late, but pretty much on key, anyhow: "Myrrh is mine . . ." His voice way off somewhere and shaky. Miss Hixson gave him one of those "Don't-blow-it-now" looks, and he gulped and quivered out, "Breathes a life of gathering gloom. . . ."

Miss Hixson nodded and smiled as he hustled on through "Sorrowing, sighing, bleeding, dying, sealed in the stone-cold tomb." Another "Ohhh-ohhhh," the last verse, the last big "Ohhhh-ohhhhh," and they'd made it!

Kev and Scott looked at their mothers, who were grinning like cats. Miss H. gave the guys the "get lost" nod, and Dave hitched up his robe and dove for the steps, the other guys stumbling after him.

He slumped in his seat. His heart floundered against the lump in his throat. She'd get to her Christmas party for sure. Guess she couldn't do both. All he wanted now was to get out of the stupid robe, get that scratchy thing off his head, and just forget about kings, Christmas, the whole thing. Anyway, he wouldn't have to see this place again for two weeks.

After school Dave took out the trash and rode over to Scott's on his old three-speed. He wanted a ten-speed, like Scott had. No use rushing home. Mom would be at her party. He was supposed to be home by six, when his father came, but why should he? Other people didn't show up when they were supposed to.

At 6:15, the phone rang and Scott told him it was his father, asking for him.

"Lucky you. I don't even know where my dad is."

"But the ten-speed—he gave it to you?"

"Musta been drunk." His lower lip stuck out.

Tonight, he and Dad made sandwiches.

"How was the program? Was Mom able to get there?"

Dave shook his head.

"I know she'd have come if she could."

Dave nodded, trying to get the sandwich down—it didn't

want to go—and said he guessed he'd go lie down a while.

His father gave him a funny look and nodded. Dave lay down on his bed with a comic book, turned the pages for a bit; and then he was being held prisoner by robots—only he and he alone knew help was coming. He could hear the secret code. Tapping, tapping.

It went tappy-tap-tap again. The door opened a crack, and his mom's voice whispered, "David . . . David."

He turned over with his back to her, faking sleep, and after a while the door closed. Now he was wide awake. Hungry. He thought about starving. Maybe dying. Then she'd be sorry. He wondered how long it would take him to starve. Too long, he decided, and tiptoed out to the kitchen. He could hear her talking in the living room.

". . . rat race today, but Joan said she'd handle it. I was in the restroom getting ready to leave when she got sick. I didn't know she was pregnant. I had to stay."

"Don't cry, darling, you couldn't help it. Dave will understand."

"When I . . . I . . . tried . . . just now . . . he turned his back. I came home the minute I could get away."

Her voice sounded hiccupy.

"Your Christmas party. You didn't go? You'd been so looking forward to it, and your award . . ."

"I couldn't face it, just wanted to get home, to explain, so he'd know. . . . Oh, Jim! He sang. And I missed it!" She choked.

Dave found himself standing there, hand on the refrigerator door, filled with an urge that, for the moment, had nothing to do with food.

"Oh-ohh, star of wonder, star of night . . ."

He gave it the royal treatment. Not like a robot. Proud. Like a king. He gave it his all. From a full heart. From joy. Just spilled right out.

They clapped when he finished. Rushed in to hug him. Dave turned on the light and opened the fridge.

"What's to eat around here, Mom? I'm starving!"

—*Mary Helen Straker*

Ninety-Day Wonder

When I dream about my father, as I often do, he is usually teaching me something. His voice is firm, bellowing through the room like a drill sergeant with a new recruit. Sometimes, his hand flies up to gesture and I flinch, duck my head, afraid he might rap me for having let my attention wander.

A few months after my birth, in 1944, the U.S. Navy sent my father to Officer's Candidate School at Cornell University. He was among a select group of men chosen to complete the equivalent of a college education in just three months. The Navy called them "ninety-day wonders." In his mostly ordinary life, this hailed as an extraordinary achievement, and it was probably why he expected nothing less than academic excellence from his children. To my father, second best was a close cousin to failure.

Now, while visiting my parents' Florida home, I watch my father proudly show me racks of golf slacks hung meticulously and arranged by color in his closet. He lifts the bamboo shade and gestures toward the sun, gloating, as if he were responsible for its being there. It's a great day for the driving range. At last, he can hit that little white ball again. I agree, reluctantly, to let him give me a golf lesson today.

Just a year ago, the choice of what to wear seemed insignificant, almost banal, among decisions of what stocks to buy or sell or where to travel during his comfortable state of semi-retirement. Then, like a flash tropical storm, his life changed dramatically. Two days after elective bypass surgery at the age of seventy-two, he suffered a massive stroke. He had decided on the surgery after several consultations and opinions, the consensus being it could add ten, maybe twenty, years to his life.

The operation was a clinical success. He said post-op that he'd felt minimal pain and discomfort. So, on the second day, he became a little stubborn, insisted on a trip to the bathroom over the indignity of using a bedpan. It may have been the mistake of his life. It caused a blood clot to travel and lodge in the left portion of his brain, the part that controls patterns of speech, communication, and the memory bank of learning. The stroke paralyzed his right side. All his words and thoughts lay trapped inside him.

I flew to Florida immediately, not knowing what to expect, shocked at the sudden change in his condition.

My mother begged me not to become emotional when I saw him. She instructed me to talk very slowly. Then she said, "The man in that room is not your father."

Those words echoed in my mind as I'd walked down the endless corridor to his room. He was propped in a huge vinyl chair with support bars. Twisted tubes connected him to a machine that made loud pumping sounds, like an aquarium.

His left arm was bent, the hand pressed against his cheek, holding up his head. He looked 100 years old. I gulped hard, choking back tears, while I stood frozen at his right side.

"Hi, Daddy," I said, the endearment startling me; I hadn't uttered it in years.

He groaned, and I bent over to kiss him, chatting nervously, trying to avoid his sad liquid eyes. But they searched my face, looking for answers to all the questions he could not ask.

"Don't worry," I said. "Everything will be all right."

In the days that followed, doctors rotated into and out of his room, looking for hints of improvement. They did not recognize this new patient as the vibrant man who had marched into their office just weeks before, methodically gathering information, captain of his own destiny. Now, they seemed to press him too hard, asking for the names of his children and his wife. He looked at them with disgust, annoyed at this test. They dangled simple familiar objects in front of his face: a comb, a ball, a cup. When he shoved the rubber ball into his mouth, I threw myself over his chest and squeezed his cheeks until he released it. He could name nothing.

But once in utter frustration, he screamed, "Get out of here, all of you!" Involuntary speech caused by pure anger.

After further testing, the speech pathologist reported that his impairment was severe. There was a chance he could endanger himself, mistake or misuse a razor, a fork, a knife. Recovery would be an uphill battle. It would depend on his willingness to relearn the simplest of concepts and on loads of sheer luck.

Within a few days, in the same hospital, he began his rehabilitation. Although he suffered bouts of depression, he waited anxiously for his daily speech and physical therapy. He sat staring at his watch, always ready for someone, anyone, to knock on his door. *Could he really know the time,* I wondered, *or was it just habit?* Like a toddler, he struggled trying to feed himself with a spoon. He insisted on trying to walk, grunting loudly if you dared stop him. He developed a new vocabulary of four-letter words, commonplace for stroke victims. The staff cheered him on as he marched tentatively down the long hospital halls in his first pair of Nike high-tops. He responded like Rocky, with arms raised and garbled words that sounded like, "I'll do it. You'll see."

In less than three weeks, my father walked unassisted and went home. He continued speech therapy at home on a computer. He sat for hours, mesmerized by the images on the screen. The therapist used simple preschool programs designed to help him link sounds with words that suddenly appeared new, as if never learned. He was starting over.

I told his therapist he would work harder than anyone. I told her of his passion for knowledge, about the Navy and Cornell. I told her how he was constantly sending us, his children, articles to read; words of advice and concern substituted for words of love. She listened but turned from me, from my pleading eyes. She already knew what I was afraid to hear: My father was no longer the man I'd known; she would not dare forecast his future.

Dad's emotions have taken the place of much of his language. Yet, while watching him through this struggle, I am learning from him still.

His little notebook lists addresses and our names, names he might never again say. He gives out business cards describing his disability to anyone who looks at him with trepidation. Sometimes when our family gathers around the dinner table, his head darts back and forth as he desperately tries to take in the nuances of our conversation, determined to be an active participant no matter what. He laughs when we laugh, leans in when we whisper. As I watch him struggling to understand, my heart pounds and I urge everyone to please slow down. When they don't, his eyes often meet mine. "Oh, God," I might hear him whisper.

Today, I'm startled when my father walks out of his bedroom modeling lime-green golf slacks and, smiling broadly, says, "Good, huh?"

What can I possibly say to this wondrous man, who's fought far longer than ninety days to perform these simple and momentous tasks, to utter the simplest of phrases? What else, but . . .

"Perfect!"

—*Sande Boritz Berger*

Till Death Do Us Part

With the first snip I knew I had made a terrible mistake. If my sister Maureen was preparing to enter the life of a fourteenth-century monk or if she wanted to look like St. Francis of Assisi, then the haircut was well on its way to perfection. Considering she wanted to look like a seventh-grade Farrah Fawcett, the damage was beyond repair. Scissors in sweaty hand, I worked desperately, slicing random layers and angles into my younger sister's treasured mane. When I finally stopped long enough to breathe and admire my handiwork, I knew instantly that she'd never live down the horror just inflicted on her by her ninth-grade sister.

My only hope of salvaging this catastrophe, and saving my skin, was my gift of gab. Usually, I could talk myself out of anything and talk anyone, especially Maureen, into anything. Now, I needed to convince her that her new "do" looked just fine—great even. I'd have to rely on the same powers of persuasion that had swayed her to let me cut her hair in the first place.

For days, I'd pleaded with Maureen to let me "feather" her hair. "I can do it!" I proclaimed boldly. "You'll look great!"

Always the thinker, always the play-it-safe sister, she thought about it for what seemed like centuries before agreeing to let me take the orange-handled weapon to the hair she had spent thirteen years growing.

Her pondering drove me wild. Why think when you can act? That was my unspoken motto. My modus operandi was to jump on the sled and fly down the hill like a banshee, then deal with the stitches in the emergency room after knocking out the Stop sign with my forehead. My ever-cautious li'l sis, on the other hand, actually stopped to consider what would happen if she rode a sled with a broken steering column down a steep hill with a steel post planted at the bottom. She recognized the inherent danger of that joyride just like she knew that letting her amateur hairstylist sister have a whack at her hair was probably not a good idea.

You'd think that having a just-do-it older sister might have had something to do with Maureen's being the cautious creature she was, but she had been that way even as a toddler. Once, as we sat on the edge of the ironing board with a steamy iron nearby, I urged her to "touch it with one finger."

"C'mon, it's no big deal. Just do it."

"Mommy said no," she said matter-of-factly.

"Just touch it and see what happens," I coaxed. Couldn't she see the fun she was missing? The thrill of the risk? The allure of the danger?

It took several precious minutes to convince her that worlds of joy awaited her if only she would touch the darn thing before Mom got back. Her scream of pain did bring our mother back, in a flash, like a lightening bolt. And just as swiftly I was picked up, spanked, and returned to my seat before I knew what had hit me.

At the tender age of two and ever after, Maureen could be left in a room of outlets and forks, boiling pots, and matches and never risk harm to person, herself or anyone else, or property. She had an uncanny ability not only to learn things but also to apply them to life. I, on the other hand, was always looking for a new hot iron.

Several years after the iron incident, the two of us sat bored and idle in the stifling July heat that only a High Plains desert can produce. One of us decided it was a perfect day for a lemonade stand. Buoyed by the idea of making some quick cash, which was always in short supply, I jumped to my feet and dragged Maureen, whose motivation was no doubt to offer cool relief to our heat-oppressed neighbors, into the house. We scurried around mixing up a gallon pitcher of overly sweet honey water with a faint lemon flavor, grabbing a stack of Dixie cups from Mom's picnic supplies, and making a crude sign that read, "Lemonade: 10¢ A Cup."

All day we waited in the sun's heat, all the while sipping our own sticky tonic to cool off. It didn't take long to near the end of our supply—and without one customer passing our remote rural route that dead-ended nearby. We were close to calling the whole thing a bust when I heard the faint roar of an engine. Our expectations soared as we strained to listen to the approaching vehicle, peering over the hill leading to our small business on the verge of bankruptcy. We jumped up and down, waving our sign, and then the miraculous happened. The car stopped.

We leaned in the open passenger window. "Do you want lemonade?"

"Sure," the man replied.

We hastily filled the cup to the top with sun-warmed lemonade and thrust it in the window.

"Bring it to my side," he said. "I have the dime right here." He displayed the silver coin in his palm.

"Okay," I said and headed to the other side of the car.

"No, Marla." Maureen grabbed my arm as she backed away from the car.

Couldn't she see there was a dime for the taking? It would make this whole useless day worthwhile. Why was she holding me back? I broke free and started moving toward the man, who kept urging me forward.

"No, don't do it," Maureen said repeatedly.

Only her determined warnings made me hesitate. Suddenly, I felt afraid. I didn't know why I was afraid; I just knew I should be.

At that moment, one of our older sisters appeared, and the man sped off with his dime. If Maureen hadn't slowed me down, the rest of my life's history, if I would have had one, might have been rewritten.

It wasn't just danger that Maureen could sense. On the rare occasion that our sugar-fighting mother would allow us to have ice cream, I would swallow the icy crystals with superhero reflexes. Maureen would sit quietly, lick her cone, pause to savor the taste, take another lick, pause to savor, and so on. As I'd come out of a brain-freeze that had thrown me on the ground in agony, I would watch her take one small taste and another, one after the other, slowly, reflectively, careful not to miss a drip. It had a hypnotic effect. The clock's ticking grew louder in my ears. My whole head seemed to be on fire. Only a taste of her ice cream could quench the flames of desire that had me prostrated before her.

"Maureen?" I'd say, as pathetically as possible. "Could I please have a really small lick of your ice cream?"

"No."

"Please," I'd beg, on my knees. "Just one teeny-tiny, itty-bitty, smallest-bite-ever-recorded-in-the-history-of-the-world?"

"No," she'd say adamantly. "Last time you promised to take only one tiny lick you took a really big bite."

Last time? What in the world did last time have to do with right now? Why didn't she just bring up the caste system in India for all it had to do with the present situation?

So, I would persist. "I promise on the Bible, on a stack of Bibles, I'll only take a little bite . . . Please, Maureen? . . . Just one small lick?"

Before long, she'd make a plea to my mother or father, who would intervene and demand I stop kissing my sister's shoes.

Although born less than fifteen months apart, our personalities were worlds apart. She pressed the clothes of her Sunshine family dolls. I cut off all my Barbie's hair and chewed most of their hands and feet. My clothes could be found on the floor or, if it was cleaning day, behind any piece of furniture; hers were always mysteriously hung up in the closet and neatly folded in drawers.

Yet, despite the fact that our brains operated on two completely different frequencies, we were sisters through and through, with all that entailed. We shared marathon Barbie sessions, baby doll extravaganzas, hours of acting out self-scripted plays, late-night giggles, clothes, and the understanding that family was everything. We grew, we changed, we moved out, and we moved on with our individual lives.

As we made our separate ways in the world, we never really stopped to examine our influence or dependence on one another. Our relationship was comfortable, reliable, and totally uncontemplated.

One day when our two budding families were together, her husband, Scott, and I were engaged in our usual exchange of brilliance. He was teaching his small children to "moo" whenever they saw me, and I was trying to get them to say, "What's that smell?" every time he walked by.

My husband, Kevin, and Maureen watched us. They were used to Scott's and my banter, but that day, they were also comparing notes about how Scott and I did certain things the same way, about our similar annoying habits and quirks. Okay, so maybe Scott and I did have a few things in common—but, I suddenly realized, we certainly weren't alone.

Case in point: A few years earlier I returned home exhausted from a full day of undergraduate classes and a part-time job. I was looking forward to my date that night with Kevin, whom I had been seeing for only a few weeks. A girlfriend was with me when I came home and found the envelope on my apartment door. In it was a note from Kevin, explaining that the martial arts school where he studied was having a demonstration that night and at the last minute had asked him to help. He wrote that he'd love it if I could come, admission was five dollars, and he thought I might want to bring a friend. Also in the envelope were directions to the show and ten dollars.

My girlfriend's mouth dropped open. "You are so lucky!"

Kevin had thought the whole thing through. He understood that I was a broke student who didn't have five extra dollars, much less ten, and that girls prefer to travel in packs when going somewhere unfamiliar to see someone we don't know well. That day, that minute, I knew there was something about Kevin that I needed in my life—something familiar and very comforting.

I have five sisters, all of whom I could write long essays about. Each is amazing and loony in her own ways. Each is essential to my life. But Maureen is different . . . she's the one I married.

—*Marla Kiley*

A Dittle Code

Have you ever noticed that colds don't command much respect? My family, for instance, has a great deal of difficulty recognizing that the common cold is an illness. Take last Monday.

"Mom, why are you in bed?" my daughter, who is fifteen-going-on-thirty-five, asked. "Are you sick?"

Before answering, I grabbed a tissue from the nightstand and honked into it. "I have a dittle code," I managed to say.

"A what?"

"A dittle code, c-o-l-d."

"Oh." She leaned over me with obvious suspicion. "Are you sure it's not strep throat?" She tickled my chin. "Come on, open up, let me see."

I opened my mouth and said, "aahh." I have always been a good patient.

"It's red all right," she informed me. "But I don't see any of that white yukky stuff like I had."

"It'th jutht a dittle code," I admitted in a rather apologetic tone. "All I need ith a dittle retht."

I grew up in a time when a cold was a perfectly respectable

ailment. At the first cough or sneeze, my mother would press her lips against my forehead to assess my temperature. If I was hotter than her lips, I had a fever. She'd change my bedding, smoothing the fresh linens with her hands so no wrinkles could irritate my feverish body. I never knew what medicinal value clean sheets had, but they felt wonderful against my aching muscles, and the coolness of the pillowcase eased the fever in my cheek. Next, she'd throw together the ingredients of her special potato soup, a recipe brought with her from Germany.

I would snuggle down in my bed, knowing the warm soup, which I actually couldn't taste because of my congestion, would be wonderful. I could hear my mom outside my darkened room, whispering, "Shh, she has a cold, let her rest," to the other members of the family. As I got better, each person would tiptoe to my bedside to see how I felt, leaving a little something—a book, tissues, an orange.

But that was another time. Last Monday, no sooner had my daughter inspected my throat than my six-year-old slipped in to check on me.

"Let me see, Mom," he commanded. With brisk efficiency, he climbed up next to me, drew my head down, and puckered his lips against my forehead.

"A thousand degrees," he said with authority. He pulled down my lower eyelashes and inspected my eyeball. "And your blood is low," he concluded.

"You can't have a fever with a virus, and the common cold is caused by a virus," said my thirteen-year-old son, who had joined us at bedside. Evidently, he'd heard about the thousand-degree fever. "Therefore, you can't have a cold."

"Who thays?" I retorted. "I do tho have a code."

"I say it's type-B flu," said my husband, who came in next.

"I'll bet it's a sinus infection." This was from my oldest son.

"Has to be tonsillitis." My daughter would not be outdone.

"Iron-poor blood," said my youngest.

"Why can't I be thick with a plain ode code!" I wailed.

My family, or paramedical team, contemplated me for one long quiet moment.

Okay, so maybe I was being a little childish at that point. But I couldn't help it. After all, where was my cool, clean pillow? Where was my potato soup? I broke the silence by sneezing violently into a tissue.

"Shhh," said my husband. "Let's give her some rest."

"Here, Mom, I'll turn over your pillow," said one child.

"How about some vitamin C and antihistamines?" asked another.

"I'll read you a story later if you want," said the third.

Then, one by one they tiptoed out. My husband paused at the door. "How about some soup?" he asked.

Soup? My heart gave a little lurch. "You're going to make me potato soup?" I ventured.

A look of confusion came over his face. "Potato soup? You must be feverish. Sweetheart, it's either a can of chicken with rice or split pea with ham."

"Thicken thounds nice," I said and answered the phone on the first ring. "Heddo."

"Hello? Who is this?"

"Me . . . your thisther."

"How come you don't sound like my sister?"

"I have a dittle code."

"Come on. Are you sure it's just a cold? Sounds more serious."

"I do tho have a co—," I started to protest hotly. Then I took a deep breath. There comes a time in everyone's life when the will to fight for the truth is weak. "Actually, thith, there'th a very good chance I have a thinuth infection or tonthillithith with iron-poor blood."

Colds command such little respect these days.

—*Kristl Volk Franklin, The Woodlands, Texas*

What Dreams Are Made Of

"Luuuuuke!" my daughter Allie exclaims loudly from the living room. "Mama, Mama, he here! Luke here now!" She runs unsteadily toward the front door, her shiny black shoes clattering loudly on the tile floor. She pauses to tug at her new red velvet dress, patting the logo as if to make sure Winnie the Pooh is still there. Crowing with excitement, she struggles briefly with the front-door latch, and when it gives way, she claps her hands, proud that she has mastered the troublesome latch at last. Surging forward onto the wooden deck, she strains on tiptoe to catch sight of her friend. Peeking coyly through the wooden railing, she catches sight of Luke waving excitedly from his seat in the Aerostar van parked in the driveway below. Luke, grinning from ear to ear, opens the window to respond, "Here I am, Allie, here I am!"

Luke bounces impatiently inside the van until his mother slides open the door to free him. Fifty pounds of exuberant energy, he bounds up the steps to our deck, waving merrily at Allie the whole time. Together at last, Allie and Luke hug excitedly and chatter about the activities planned for the day. Catching sight of me in the doorway, Luke makes a running leap into my arms. "Ice cream, Allie-Mom," he signs. I pretend not to understand, asking if he wants a glass of water. "No, Allie-Mom," he signs, "I want ice cream cone. Cold ice cream." I laugh and promise him a delicious treat after he's had his dinner. Reassured, he kisses my hand like a courtier before turning to wave good-bye to his mother.

Allie and Luke first met eight years ago, coming face to face on a patchwork quilt placed on the floor of a busy classroom in the foothills of the Sierra Nevada Mountains. Allie had been attending the special program for infants with developmental disabilities for two years; Luke was a year younger and had just moved from southern California. They were immediately attracted to one another and spent the next hour happily exploring each other's face with inquisitive fingers. Born with Down's syndrome, Luke and Allie had not yet learned to walk or talk. But they communicated easily with one another, rolling happily around on the blanket in coy games of hide-and-go-seek and steal-the-pacifier. Smiling, gurgling, and crowing, they brought smiles to the faces of teachers and parents alike. When the class was over, they would cry miserably and strain toward each other as they were carried out the door and tucked into car seats.

Today, Luke is the muscular one, the athletic busybody who likes baseball and hockey. He runs, jumps, and swings a bat with intense concentration and great vigor. An unabashed show-off, Luke likes nothing better than a stage and an appreciative audience. He bursts into song at every opportunity, clutching an imaginary microphone and waving his arms dramatically in the air. There are no strangers in Luke's life; he greets newcomers with a firm handshake and a big smile.

Allie is more subdued, preferring to watch new people and scenes for a while before joining in the fun. She loves to read and shares her newfound information with Luke by reading aloud from road signs. She injects a note of caution into their games. Climbing and jumping are not for her; she prefers a more studied approach, hanging onto the handrail as Luke leaps up the stairs.

Over the past eight years, Luke and Allie have forged bonds of friendship that transcend their disabilities and limitations. They interact easily, using a combination of body language, spoken speech, and sign language. Luke has a hearing impairment and wears specially made hearing aids. Knowing that he removes them frequently when they "buzz" in his ear, Allie checks carefully to see if he is listening when she has something important to say. Although both children can speak, they struggle to get out the right words. Both have used sign language since infancy to allow them to communicate without frustration. Allie's speech is more garbled, complicated by a stroke during an operation to correct a congenital heart problem. Out in public, she steps back while Luke strides forward to plunge into new situations.

Today, the two conspirators head for the large wooden toy box in the playroom. Their blond hair shines in the sun, and their blue eyes sparkle with the anticipation of shared games and mischief. Together, they construct elaborate fantasies peopled with cats, dogs, alligators, and gorillas. Luke puts on a long black fright wig and poses like a runway model, while Allie growls from behind her tiger mask. Luke grabs his Peter Pan hat and brandishes his sword to fight off Captain Hook. Allie laughs appreciatively, dons her silken butterfly wings, and joins him in a flight across the imaginary sky. Suddenly, they both shed their disguises and drop onto all fours. Allie is a small gray kitten, and Luke loudly barks his way toward her. Squeaking in mock fright, she crawls up onto the sofa. Luke joins her, and they laugh uproariously at their own daring.

"Food now, Allie-Mom, then ice cream," Luke communicates hopefully in a combination of sign and speech. Allie seconds his request with a gleeful cheer and hops around in excitement. They run to the bathroom to use the toilet and wash their hands. Faces gleaming and hands still dripping water, they come back and sit side by side at the dining room table. Companionably, they munch on grilled cheese sandwiches and French fries. Luke passionately urges Allie to try his chocolate soymilk; Allie solemnly signs "Yucky" and sips daintily from her glass of nonfat milk. "White is better," she signs. After eating their long-awaited ice cream, the two stack their dishes precariously and carry the piles to the kitchen sink.

Then they race back to Allie's bedroom to change into their swimsuits and head for the inflatable pool in the backyard. Reaching the wooden steps leading up to the pool, they discover that Allie has forgotten her sandals. Luke gallantly offers his arm, and they return to the house, signing "No shoes" when I ask them what they need. Five minutes later, they come out of Allie's bedroom with armloads of towels, sunscreen, plastic toys, goggles, flippers, and assorted paraphernalia. They stagger up the wooden steps to the pool once more, dropping their burdens onto the soft grass. Carefully and conscientiously, they arrange their towels side by side before slathering each other with sunscreen. Then and only then do they jump joyfully into the pool, sending waves of water sloshing over the side. I rest on a lawn chair in the shade near the fence, watching as they maneuver their flotilla of plastic boats and make imaginary milkshakes in the water. Luke tosses a foam rubber ball, which splashes water up into Allie's face. She grimaces in distaste, then grins and tosses the ball back at his chest.

Forty minutes later, both shout "Done" at the top of their lungs, while signing to me as if I just might be hard of hearing. I wrap each shivering body in a colorful beach towel and point them toward the blanket on the grass in a patch of sunshine. They head gratefully for the blanket, stepping gingerly across the prickly grass. Lying side by side, they laugh at some shared joke and kick their legs with joy. Then Luke jumps up, unable to be still for more than five minutes. "Come on, Allie," he says. "Let's have a bath!" They gather up their armloads of treasures and head down the wooden steps to the house.

An hour later, bathed and dressed in their soft cotton pajamas, they watch *Annie* on video as I read the newspaper. Luke sings along merrily, until Allie pokes him with an elbow and frowns at his intrusion. Subdued, Luke yawns widely and comes to sit beside me on the couch for a cuddle. Soon, Allie joins us, and I have a warm little body tucked under each arm.

"How about we go to my bed and read?" I ask. Instantly, the two buddies hop up and pull me by the arms to the bedroom. We climb up into my bed, where I am completely surrounded by a huge pile of books and two drowsy children. We read about all their old friends: Madeline, Clifford, Curious George, Peter Pan, and Captain Hook. Luke and Allie adamantly express their desire to try all the fun adventures in the books, although Allie isn't too sure she wants to join in the sword fight. Luke, however, vows to whip all of the pirates single-handedly. We read for another twenty minutes before Luke drops off to sleep; Allie hangs on for another ten, but then gives in and closes her eyes. Silently, I work my way free of their arms and legs and climb out of bed. Tonight, the two friends are together in the land of dreams. I kiss each sweet face and tiptoe out of the room.

—*Sandy Keefe*

 Placid Drive

When I was five years old my family moved to Placid Drive, smack in the middle of what my sister called "Nowhere, America." There were only a few houses along our dirt road—rusty farm homes with needle-straight grass and scratchy fences. My sister and I rode past these houses every day, ringing our bicycle bells with loud *brrrrringsss*, popping wheelies with a jerk of our handlebars, and taunting each other back and forth with, "I'm gonna beat you." We raced to the finish, a yellow construction sign that read "No Outlet." She usually did beat me—her ten-speed over my banana seat—and she would laugh smugly all the way to the end of Placid, the only road that led to the Ulmstead barn, where the neighborhood horses lived.

From the first time she heard the sound of hooves clomping, my sister vowed to have a horse of her own. She spent weeks wallpapering her bedroom walls with pictures of ponies, and she doodled stick-figure drawings on notebooks. She placed monthly *Horse Lover* magazines in the bathroom reading rack, where my parents couldn't miss them. When Mom and Dad pretended not to notice, she threw a fit, begging and pleading, promising and praying, warming and buttering, until somehow, my parents bit. After her tantrums and tears, Jean Renee got her pony. She named it "Bunny."

The Ulmstead barn with its neat red trim looked like a picture in one of those home and garden magazines my mother read. But instead of being shiny white with a fresh slap of paint and a green garden backdrop, this barn was the color of sawdust souring in the sun. From the outside, it looked barely tended to, with weeds winding around the silo and ivy choking at the roof. The paddock doors outside the barn creaked open and slammed shut, over and over again all day long, the whim of whatever humid breeze happened to pass. On the inside, the barn was dark and damp and smelled like leather.

Walking into the barn was entering a world unseen. No matter the time of day, it took a few moments before my eyes adjusted to the dimness. The first time I went in, I barely made out the long hallway of hidden stalls and ceiling rafters. As the doors slammed shut, a flourish of fly-paper strips waved in the wind, textured with tiny winged corpses frozen on sticky film. Oily white paint peeled from the walls and doorways, curling in ways that called to me.

The passageway was always still and soundless except for the scuff of my shoes. To my side were silhouettes of discarded saddles and rusty tack, and bright blue brushes tangled with hair. Barn cats slinked out from their hiding places, gray and matted and mice-fed, covered in mites and crying. Pellets of grain scattered the floor, and horse shoes donned doorways—always face up, for luck.

The hollow hallway led to the loft. While my sister hauled grain and pitched manure, I hid upstairs among straw bales and squirrel droppings. I imagined I was a runaway, storing supplies of carrots and trough water to make it through the winter. They'll never find me, I would think, smiling to myself. I can live here forever.

The hayloft wasn't the only secret place in the barn, as I soon discovered. I stole away to shadowy horse stalls and clanged steel gates behind me. Once inside the stall, I fantasized about being in a carnival or the circus. Here, I could be a clown on stilts or, my favorite, one of those long-legged, high-diving beauties.

Standing tall on an overturned water bucket—my twenty-story diving board—I peered through the steel rails and clicked my tongue. "Ladies and gentleman, horses everywhere . . ." I grinned into the dusty stall, delighting in echoes railing above me. Horses shuffled in their shoes with brown egg-eyes blinking and dumbstruck. I lifted my arms wide and rounded my chest, and with one last look, I plunged—leaping forward, landing headfirst into my hay mountain, luckily missing buried manure below.

"She did it, everybody!" I marveled to the horses around me. Rolling in the scratchy bale, I basked in my death-defying feat and listened to echoes of the barn: floors creaking, voices muffling, beasts clamoring inside steel cages.

I stared up into the dimness of the barn—no lights except what filtered in from a few faraway windows. Yellow dust floated down and up and all around, lifting and spinning inside a current of air made visible by the light. There was no sound except for horses chewing, grinding their teeth. Dust caught in my throat, and my eyes began to itch. Inside my box, inside my head, I was behind closed doors, but free.

Then I heard that voice. My sister's voice.

"Come on!" Irritated at my existence, at her responsibility.

I waited, quiet, wondering if she would find me.

"*Now!*" She spoke through clenched teeth, startling me. "I said come *on!*"

I sighed, knowing I could no longer be a trapeze artist, a runaway, a long-legged anyone. As soon as I heard her calling, kid sister was all I was. "Kiddo," she called me.

It was time to go.

Back at home, when my parents told my sister and me to "play nicely," we pretended we were in the movies. She loved Clint Eastwood westerns and strutted around in a cowboy hat and chaps. Between our kitchen and foyer swung two white-paneled saloon doors, just like the Old West. One lazy afternoon, my sister stormed through the doors with both hands on her guns and sauntered up to the breakfast bar, spurs clicking at each step.

"Barkeep," she snarled with a side grin, "fix me a stiff one."

I poured us two shots of lemonade in Dixie cups, which we downed in one gulp, wincing like we were drinking the hard stuff. We nodded at each other with squinty eyes and whispered, "Smooth." This was the funniest thing we'd ever heard. We fell over ourselves laughing at one another, as we launched into an unspoken game of who could make the goofiest face and the best Western wisecrack.

This went on for a good while, but then my sister got serious.

"This town ain't big enough for the both of us," she growled.

I giggled again, but she didn't laugh. She pulled the water guns from her pockets and started firing at me, square in the eyes.

"Aw, no," I screamed and turned to run, but in my haste I tripped, smacking hard onto linoleum. Pain pulsed on the inside of my bottom lip. I put my hand to my mouth and felt my chin wet. When I saw the blood, I started to cry, gasping for my breath as she stood over me.

"You wait till Mom gets home," I threatened her through my tears.

Then I'd see her squirm with fear. She knew that if I told on her, she would be in big trouble.

I always told on her.

Days when we didn't go to the barn, I ran away without going anywhere. I hid in closets or under beds, in corners and behind doors. Sometimes I snuck around like a secret agent spy, collecting clues to some unknown mystery.

I crept inside my sister's room and searched for her diary or other concealed goods. This was dangerous work and took daring on my part. It could be done only when she was home, because she locked her door behind her when she left. I had to wait until just the right moment—right before she was about to leave the house, when she scurried between her room and the bathroom, arm-deep in curling irons and eyeliner and makeup mirrors. Her distraction was my opportunity.

As soon as her head was in a fog of Aqua Net hairspray, I slipped inside her door and dove underneath the bed. Safe! I lay there on the cool hardwood floor, making my mark in the frosting of dust babies, and waited. Sometimes more than an hour would pass before she finally left, clicking the door behind her. Once my mom called for me, but, of course, I couldn't come out. I remained at my post until the enemy left and I was free to start my assignment.

When she did leave, her room was mine. I searched through her notebooks; I thrashed through her clothes. I was an expert spy, a secret agent who had infiltrated unknown territory. Every five minutes or so, I darted my eyes back and forth and spoke into my wristwatch: "Agent M here. Mission under way." I kept my voice low, clearing my throat a couple of times for effect. "Subject has left the building. Over." I continued my search, humming the music from television's *Get Smart*.

I learned a lot about my sister through these spy efforts. I found stashed Parliament cigarettes. Empty Bartles and James bottles. Juicy letters to boys I didn't know. Diary entries about losing virginity.

Virginity?

I wondered about that one. I didn't know she had virginity in the first place. Later, I asked my mom about it.

"Hey, Mom, what's virginity?"

She paused in picking out shell fragments from a bowl of backfin crabmeat and wiped her mealy hands on a paper towel. "Where did you hear that word?" She looked me square in the eyes beyond her glasses, scowling.

"Um, a magazine," I stammered. Suddenly realizing this might be bad, I covered, "*Seventeen* magazine."

"Oh," she said and looked away. Long pause. "Well, what it means is . . ." She went back to picking crab, fingers buried deep in stringy white meat. "A virgin," she said, clearing her throat, "is . . . someone . . . who isn't . . . married."

I was thoroughly confused.

"A virgin means not married?" I got the feeling I should drop it, but couldn't. Not until I got to the bottom of this. "So, then, if you lose virginity, it means you're married? Like, to a husband?"

"Sort of, yeah." My mom sighed. "Go play now."

And with that I guessed that my sister must be secretly married. I couldn't believe it. First, she shaves her legs and now this. Did my parents know? They couldn't. Surely I would have heard about it before now. Shocked by my expert spy work, I breathed into my mood ring, low and slow and sure of myself.

Mission accomplished.

When my sister left home, we sold the horse. She was eighteen, after all. She had a boyfriend (who, according to what I had learned, was actually her husband, for all I knew), and she no longer needed a horse.

We drove down to the barn—the four of us, the last time as a family—to say goodbye to Bunny. While my parents talked to the new owners, I wandered around the Ulmstead barn, picking up stones, kicking at driveway dirt. I knew I wouldn't have reason to come there again. My hayloft was gone, all of my hiding places exposed. In its place was a fancy reception hall where they held weddings and Super Bowl parties. I knew I would never see an invitation.

I felt sorry for myself until I saw my sister petting Bunny for the last time and crying. Her shoulders sank silently, her back turned to my parents so they wouldn't see. She looked small to me for the first time, small for being a big sister. Small and alone and afraid to move on—not just from the barn and Bunny. But from us—her family, her childhood. I walked over to her and stood quietly, just slightly behind her. She never turned around to look at me, but I remained close enough so she would know I was there. Close enough so she would know that's where I would always be.

—*Elaine C. Gast*

The Educated Dude

Of all my students in eleven years of teaching, Mac holds a special place in my memory. Mac was in my second period English class. He sat in the fourth seat of the third row behind a larger boy who completely hid him from my view. Mac was small for his age. I can picture him now in his standard outfit of faded blue jeans and a plaid shirt with several pencils in the pocket, his sandy brown hair uncombed, his blue eyes twinkling. He had plenty of friends and fit smoothly into the group.

Mac seemed to be attentive and to work during class, so I was surprised to discover after the first few weeks of school that he had not handed in even one assignment. And, even though he wasn't doing his assignments, he wasn't causing trouble, so he was the kind of kid I might easily have overlooked.

Something about Mac, however, drew my attention and made me curious to know more about him. Perhaps it was his independent spirit, the nonchalant way he walked into the class each day, greeting his friends and bouncing into the seat behind his desk. Still, I did not act on my inclination until the guidance counselor asked me to complete a progress report on Mac.

"His parents have asked for a team meeting," she said. "They think Mac is learning disabled or emotionally disturbed or lazy. They aren't sure what, but they think there is something wrong with him. What can you tell me?"

I couldn't give the guidance counselor much information about Mac. "He's not all that interested in English. He doesn't turn his work in very often," I said.

"But," I hastened to add, "he's not disruptive and he seems like a happy kid. Quite cheerful, in fact. I could be wrong, but I don't see any signs that Mac has a serious problem. I like him."

When I checked in my grade book, I was surprised and embarrassed to find that I did not have a single grade recorded for him. Mac had not even turned in weekly spelling tests that the whole class did together. Somehow, he was slipping through the cracks. *From now on*, I thought, *I need to pay closer attention to Mac.*

The process of getting to know Mac began the next day. I was sitting at my desk grading the weekly spelling tests while the class worked on a vocabulary assignment. I noted that, once again, there was no paper from Mac in the stack. Out of the corner of my eye I watched Mac casually sauntering down the aisle so that he could toss a wadded-up piece of notebook paper into the trashcan.

"Having trouble, Mac?" I asked.

"Naw," he muttered cheerfully and ambled back to his seat, pausing for a word here and there with his classmates.

The following day I assigned the class a short essay in which the students were told to describe an activity they enjoyed. After they began working, I wandered down the rows of desks, encouraging the students, chatting with them about their ideas for the essay, making my way as unobtrusively as possible toward Mac. When I reached his desk, I saw his arm ease over to cover his paper so that I couldn't see what was on it, a behavior that I had grown accustomed to over the years.

"Any problems?" I asked.

"No." He smiled in his usual happy-go-lucky way.

"Make sure you finish something by the end of the period," I said.

"By the way, class," I announced, "I'm collecting whatever you are able to complete today."

"Why can't we finish it for homework?" one student asked.

"Today, I want to see what you've done in class. I'll hand your papers back tomorrow, and you can work on them some more, if you'd like."

A few students made the standard moans and groans, but no one appeared to be especially disturbed by my announcement, least of all Mac, who continued to hover over his paper until I had passed by and out of range. I continued my maneuvering around the classroom for a while and then went back to my desk and sat down, watching Mac as much as possible without being obvious.

Until then, I had not taken a close look at Mac's work habits. Now, I saw that he was inattentive to his assignment, spending most of his time chatting quietly with other students around him. I saw him ask a girl for a better pencil. Then he went up to the pencil sharpener, stopping now and then to check on what his friends were doing. Once back in his seat, he wrote for a few minutes and then gazed out the window.

"Well, I know he has written something," I thought to myself.

Near the end of the period I announced that it was time to turn in the day's work. "Okay, class, time is almost up. Finish the sentence you are working on and get ready to pass in your papers. Be sure to put your name on the paper," I added.

My announcement was the signal Mac was waiting for. He got up and walked toward the trashcan, wadding up his paper as he went. I moved quickly to stop his mission.

"Not today, Mac," I said, cutting him off. "I want you to turn in whatever you finished."

"It's no good," he said with his likable boyish grin still in place.

"I don't care," I told him. "I want to see what you've done so far."

Mac looked at me curiously, considered rebellion, and then decided to humor me. Reluctantly, he handed me his paper.

"Thanks," I said, smoothing out the wrinkles. "I'm looking forward to reading this." I spoke matter-of-factly and immediately turned away to speak to the class. "Please pass in your papers right now. The bell is going to ring any minute. Please don't leave without giving me your work," I emphasized for Mac's benefit, to ensure he didn't think I was singling him out for special attention.

The next hour was my planning period. I eagerly flipped through the papers to find Mac's crinkled one. He had written two or three short sentences about going hunting with his father in ordinary looking, legible handwriting. I could find no reason why he would throw it away rather than hand it in.

I smoothed out the paper and circled one misspelled word and wrote the correct spelling on the paper. I thought for several minutes about the kind of comment to write. Finally I wrote, "Good start. Tell me more about hunting." After more deliberation, I wrote C– at the top of the paper. So that Mac would not be suspicious, I wrote a comment on all of the other students' essays as well.

The next day I passed out the papers at the beginning of the period and told the students to read my comments and to continue working on their essays. As soon as I had a chance, I walked near Mac's desk and struck up a conversation with the boy who sat next to him. Just as I hoped, Mac quickly became interested in what I was saying and I was able to draw him into the conversation. Casually, I mentioned that Mac had written about a topic that I found interesting—going hunting.

Mac gave me a quick, suspicious look and then decided that my comment was genuine. I left him and his classmate engaged in a conversation about Mac's topic. A few minutes later I cautioned both of them to get back to work.

"Let's get those ideas down on paper," I said encouragingly.

At the end of the period, Mac turned in the revised paper, which now had two more sentences. I was jubilant with this small success. I wrote "Much better!" in the margin, and gave it a grade of C+.

From then on, Mac became the focus of as much subtle, special attention as I could give him. My moves were carefully planned, but my goal was simple. By the end of the year, Mac was going to have enough confidence in himself to hand in his assignments and he would begin to value his education.

After the evaluation and team meeting Mac's parents had requested, the guidance counselor stopped by to tell me that the staff had advised the parents to relax. Everyone concurred that Mac was normal but perhaps slightly immature. His parents were persuaded not to make any major decisions about their son, and the counselor promised to keep them informed of any changes in his behavior.

During the next few weeks I chatted with Mac whenever an opportunity presented itself. If he turned in his work, I commented favorably. If he did not turn in an assignment, I expressed disappointment. Slowly but surely, the papers started to come in regularly.

One day I suggested that he pay closer attention to spelling and punctuation. "Otherwise," I said, "your writing is quite good."

The flattery and added pressure were too much for Mac.

"Hey, Mrs. Walker." He looked me directly in the eye, unsmiling and speaking seriously for the first time since I'd known him. "I don't want to be no educated dude."

He had me there. Making him into an educated dude was my plan exactly. Perhaps I had no right to try to change Mac's self-image or to make him become someone he didn't want to be, even if it was, in my opinion, for his own good.

"Well, Mac," I responded after reflecting on his comment, "there may be some advantages to being an educated dude that you haven't considered."

I turned away and walked toward another student who was standing at my desk with a question. Out of the corner of my eye, I saw Mac give me a small, unwilling smile. He and I both knew that we were engaged in a struggle and that I was, at that point, winning.

The campaign to increase Mac's confidence in his academic ability continued day by day as I made occasional calculated comments to him. One day when I thought he was ready, I wrote "Excellent work!" on a particularly interesting composition he'd written and gave it a B, his first one. When I handed back the papers, I saw Mac show his to the student who sat next to him. He was pointing with pride at the grade. I knew then that I had won more than just a skirmish.

On his next report card, Mac got a C in English for the semester. The guidance counselor told me that he'd been doing better in his other classes, too. Mac himself confided to me that his parents were happy with his grades for the first time in his life.

"If I keep doing good, I'm supposed to get a dirt bike for my birthday."

As the year went by, Mac and I continued our quiet friendship. He wasn't the type to come by after school to see me or to give me a Christmas card. But once or twice when we passed in the hall, Mac acknowledged me by saying, "Hi!"

It was a lot from Mac, and it was enough for me.

—*Bonnie L. Walker*

An earlier version of this story was published under the title "Mac Wore a Mask of Indifference" in the March/April issue of *Learning 92*.

My Enemy, My Friend

The first time I saw him, he was pointing a machine gun at us. It was early spring of 1945, and my grandparents and I had just emerged from a bunker, where we had spent a terror-filled night.

I was nine years old and living in Hungary with my grandparents, who were raising me. World War II raged around us, playing havoc with our lives. We had been on the road for many months, traveling in our horse-drawn wagon, searching for a safe place. We'd fled the village of our births in the Bacska region when Tito and his Communist Partisans (guerillas) began closing in. By day we'd move swiftly, ready to jump out and take cover in a ditch if warplanes approached. By night we camped along the roadside with other refugees. I usually lay bundled up in my feather bed in the back of the wagon, cradling my orange tabby cat, Paprika. War was almost all I had known my whole childhood. There seemed to be no safe place to be found.

After the Christmas of 1944 when we were almost killed in the bombing of the city we were in at the time, Grandfather decided that a rural area would be safer. So we moved to the country in upper Hungary and settled in a small house that had an old cemetery as its neighbor. There, Grandfather, with the help of some distant neighbors, built a bunker in the ground a short distance from the house.

On the eve of that early spring day in 1945, we'd spent the entire night in the bunker. Warplanes buzzed, tanks thundered, and bombs exploded all around throughout that sleepless night. Finally, at daybreak, everything grew deathly still. Grandfather decided it was safe to go back to our house. Cautiously we crept out into the light of early dawn and headed toward the house. The brush crackled under our feet as we walked past the cemetery. The monuments, separated by tall, dry weeds, looked lonely. I shivered, holding Paprika tightly in my arms.

Suddenly there was a rustle in the bushes just ahead. Two men jumped out and pointed machine guns directly at us.

"*Stoi!*" one of the men shouted. Since we were from an area where both Serbian and Hungarian had been spoken, we knew the word meant, "Stop!"

"Russians!" Grandfather whispered. "Stand very still and keep quiet."

But I was already running after my cat. She had leapt out of my arms when the soldier shouted, so I darted between the soldiers and scooped her up. The younger of the two soldiers, tall and dark-haired, approached me. I cringed, holding Paprika against my chest. The soldier reached out and petted her.

"I have a little girl about your age back in Russia, and she has a cat just like this one," he said. Then he gently tugged one of my blond braids. "And she has long braids, too, just like you." I looked up into his kind brown eyes, and my fear vanished. Grandfather and Grandmother sighed with relief.

Well, both soldiers came back to the house with us and shared in our meager breakfast. From them we learned that the Soviet occupation of Hungary was in progress.

In the following months, many atrocities occurred in our area and throughout our country, but because the young Russian soldier had taken a liking to me, we were spared. He came to visit often, bringing little treats along for Paprika and me, and he always talked longingly of his own little girl. I was terrified of the Russians in general, but I loved his visits. Then one day, almost a year later, he had some disturbing news.

"I've been transferred to another area, *malka* ("little one"), so I won't be able to come and visit anymore. But I have a gift for you," he said, taking something out of his pocket. It was a necklace with a beautiful turquoise Russian Orthodox cross on it. He placed it around my neck. "You wear this at all times, *malka*. God will protect you from harm." I hugged him tightly, and then watched him drive away, tears welling in my eyes.

World War II was over, but for the people of Hungary a life of bondage had begun. Many men who had been involved in politics or deemed undesirable were rounded up by the secret police, never to be seen again. Not long after, the knock on the door we dreaded came: They'd come to take away my grandfather. Fortunately, he managed to sneak out a window. Grandfather went into hiding, leaving Grandma and me to survive the best we could. Not long after, my cat died, and life truly seemed unbearable. Sometimes, I would finger the cross the soldier had given me and wonder where he was. Was he back home with his daughter? Did he remember me?

The time passed in a haze of anxiety and depression. Then, in the fall of 1947, a man came to get us in the middle of the night. He would take us to the Austrian border, where we'd be reunited with my grandfather, who had obtained counterfeit papers so we could all cross the border to freedom. We traveled all that night to a place where the ethnic Germans of Hungary were being loaded into transport trucks and expelled from Hungary. When we arrived, a weary-looking man with a thick, scraggly beard and a knit cap pulled low over his forehead was waiting for us.

"Grandpa!" I cried out, rushing into his arms, so happy to see him again. Together, my grandparents and I moved toward the transport truck loaded with dozens of people and got on, fake papers in hand. I knew if we were found out, Grandpa would get hauled off to prison, and worse, he might be executed. I watched as the Russian soldiers drew closer, and I prayed to God to keep us safe.

One of the guards boarded the truck, and I caught my breath. "Grandpa," I whispered. "Look, it's my soldier, Ivan! He is checking this truck." I wanted to jump up and run to him, but Grandpa shushed me. "Maybe he won't recognize us," he whispered, pulling the knit hat further down his forehead.

In minutes, Ivan stood before us. My grandfather handed over our papers without looking up. I leaned closer and put my hand protectively on Grandfather's shoulder as I peered cautiously at Ivan, searching for the old kind sparkle in his eyes. But he was intent upon the papers, his expression grave. I didn't dare breathe. At last he handed the papers back to Grandpa.

"Everything is in order in this vehicle," he finally said. Then, stealing a wink at me, he walked away and got off the truck. Seconds later, the truck began to move forward. I looked over my shoulder and caught his eye. "Thank you," I silently mouthed, lifting the cross hanging around my neck. He nodded discreetly, and then quickly turned away. As we crossed the border to safety, we all said a prayer of thanks to the Lord.

Although we suffered greatly during the war, the memory of a kind soldier who befriended me and turned my fear to faith will always stay with me. He demonstrated to me that friendship and compassion can be found anywhere, even in the heart of an enemy.

—*Renie Burghardt*

The Favor

It's hot—summer, humid, Maryland-in-late-July, sticky hot. My three sisters and I share a room, two to a bed, a jumbled mix of limbs and tossed sheets. All four of us hang over the mattress edges, trying to catch some semblance of a breeze from the small, round, putty-colored fan set smack in the middle of the room between the two beds. It barely manages to slice through the molasses-thick air.

I can't sleep. I feel unsettled from the heat, and my legs are jittery and jumpy, "growing pains" as Omi would say. I spot Barbara's foot on my side of the bed. We'd argued earlier, a disagreement of great importance, depth, and merit: She had played with *my* Barbie doll. So, I lean down and pinch up her sweaty big toe and move her foot over to her side. She doesn't even awaken, not a grunt out of her, but I am satisfied that the gross infringement is rectified. This is my right, of course—to punish her—because I am older, which is a right and a lesson handed down to me from my two older sisters, Sandi and Ann.

Ray, our only brother, is *the* oldest. He gets to sleep across the hall in the roomy, one-person-occupancy bedroom. He is leaving for Vietnam soon, and then it will be Ann's turn for the big room. I'm jealous, of course, but also maybe a little sad, not only because of Ray's departure from home but also because of Ann's departure from our shared room, although I would not, could not ever admit it. You see, I don't really mind sharing a room. We all fight, for sure, but less rather than more, and I like the activity.

I see Ann rise and head toward the bathroom. I watch her, spying. She turned sixteen in January, practically a grown-up, and she always bossed us around now, acting all moody or weird without rhyme or reason. The bathroom light casts a soft triangular glow into the bedroom. Highlighted in its light on the wall across from me I see the plaque, its shiny varnished finish casting a wet sheen in the heat. For a brief moment in my sleepy haze, I think the angel on the plaque is perspiring as well; she's working too hard to help the little girl across the bridge. Sometimes the picture scares me and I question it: Why only one child? Where are the rest of us? Where's Ray? Why is the angel helping only one girl, one sister, cross over? Where are Mom, Dad, Omi? Ann always reassures me that the others are already safely across, that this last little girl is crossing to meet everybody, that the beautiful angel has made sure all are safe.

Ann comes out of the bathroom, the light behind her silhouetting her shape. I see the glass of water shimmering in her hand as she walks over to Sandi. She dips two fingers in the glass and slowly flicks droplets of water, showering them across Sandi's face, then her upper body, then her lower body, and then, last, she dips four or five times into the glass, letting each rivulet fall puddlelike onto Sandi's pillow.

Ann moves to me next. I keep my eyes closed, letting the water bless my body. It feels cool and refreshing. The jitteriness in my legs begins to calm, and the heat momentarily dissipates. For the first time that night, I feel the wind from the fan sail across my body like a lilting, elusive breeze, escorting me to sleep.

Barbara is last. Like Sandi, she doesn't wake. Like me, she doesn't stir. And all of us sleep more peacefully.

Now, thirty years later, I stare down at Ann, the small hospital bed made larger by her thinned body. The bed is a necessary intrusion, a bulky, clumsy invader. Her real bed is pushed to the side. We—Sandi, Barbara, and I—take turns trying to sleep there, the bedspread and sheets in a continuous rumple.

We use wet towels to cool her down. Her temperature remains dangerously high, her body so hot it is surely boiling her blood. Sandi goes into the adjacent bathroom to fill the syringe with the Adavan and morphine cocktail. The light from the bathroom filters out across Ann's bed and halos her head.

The seizures started two days ago, making Ann's arms and legs flail about. We can do nothing to stop them, nothing to stop the painful dance of cancer eating away at her body, but we try. Barbara kneels at the foot of the bed rubbing Ann's feet, while Sandi and I gently hold her arms that kink rigid from the spasms. We hear the bones snap from the poison that has spread to her marrow. We whisper to her, sharing stories from our childhood, offering prayers of peace and calm, but nothing seems to work, for cancer knows no religion or peace. Ann, always the boss, always the organizer, has already told us her wishes, down to picking out her own tombstone and the songs she wants sung at the funeral.

I see the old plaque from our childhood bedroom hanging on her wall above her bed. I realize with a pang that the child in the picture is Ann, that she is moving across the bridge from earth to heaven and that we are not waiting on the other side for her, but she will be waiting up there for us. I hope the angel helps her across. Surely her God will ease her pain and suffering soon. I cannot fathom the reason why Ann, so devout and so trusting of God's will, must suffer so, and I have long stopped waiting for an answer. While her deep faith has helped her through this, her suffering has accelerated the abandonment of mine.

At the sink, I dampen more washcloths. With one, I will wash her face; her teeth have bit down again onto her lips, causing them to bleed. As I re-enter the bedroom, Sandi and Barbara look up at me and reach out for a cloth. We cool her papery skin with the damp cloths, grateful to return the favor from so long ago, hoping with silent prayers that it is enough, wishing her a peaceful sleep before her walk across the bridge.

—*Rebecca Christensen*

Reglar Feller

Jimmie Joe Thomas was a reglar feller, he used to assure me, just like you and me. But I could see differences. For one, I dressed better than he did. For another, he had more money than I could ever hope to have. But he never patronized me. When we went out drinking, we took turns paying for drinks. He gave my opinions, when I offered them, the same weight as those from his lawyer or his banker—probably more weight than those of his lawyer, because he had no abiding love for those "bottom fishers," as he called them.

Out-of-towners who saw him in his bib overalls and denim shirt as he walked the railroad right-of-way usually mistook him for a gandy dancer checking the tracks. Locals all knew he owned the railroad. A time had come a while back when shipping rates threatened to destroy Jimmie Joe's ability to meet competitors' prices on the furniture produced at his factory. Not one for long hassles and prolonged haggling, he up and bought the railroad. After that, he used the railway to bring in raw materials as well as to carry out finished furniture. The increase in business brought down the costs at his furniture plant enough to where he added more workers and also brought down his shipping rates to where rival furniture makers starting shipping on his train line.

Jimmie Joe soon discovered that a railroad consumes large quantities of coal, which costs large amounts of money to buy. So when the local coal yard was on its last legs and ready to lay off workers, he stepped in and bought it, too. Of course, his trains not only hauled in coal for both his railroad and his furniture factory—but also for other businesses and homes in the area.

"I ain't got nothin agin book larning," Jimmie Joe once told me. "There just warn't enough money coming in to keep us, so I quit school and got a job. I kin hire college boys now, so I just cain't see the need to go back fur any edjication."

He started in the furniture factory as a floor sweeper and moved up the ladder quickly. With his fast mind and analytic ability, he worked out better ways to do things—things that had been done the same way for years. When he started to earn a more comfortable wage, he married the factory owner's daughter.

Sara Jane, his love light, fitted well into his life. She gave him three home-cooked meals a day as well as the love and encouragement that make the difference between a successful man and a happy-as-a-king successful man. Better educated than her husband, Sara Jane could talk intelligently about books, music, and philosophy—but never in front of Jimmie Joe. People around them always saw her in a stiffly starched house dress, scented slightly with bath soap and wisteria, taking freshly baked cookies to a schoolroom or home-cooked meals to shut-ins. Not once did anyone ever hear her advise her husband on any subject; still, her presence could be seen in all his enterprises.

Jimmie Joe frequently contributed articles to *Furniture South*, the regional magazine of the industry. It was my job to clean up his writing and correct his grammar. Some other "self-made" men in his position resented a single change to their work. "Do whatever it needs to make it fitten to print," Jimmie would say.

When the union sent in organizers to organize the plant, they found little support from the workers. A few, those who had been let go after many unsuccessful tries to help them fit in, did join the cause. When Jimmie Joe looked out his office window and saw the picketers in front of the plant, he exploded, "That's a damn shame!"—whereupon, he had a trailer pulled into the parking lot stocked with sandwiches and hot coffee for the picketers. Union management called it "unfair labor practices." The picketers, tired of freezing off their rumps in the bitter cold, called it a might friendly thing to do. The vote went against the union, and things went back to normal—except for the head of the organizing crew, whom the union promptly fired.

"That young feller worked purty hard, even iffen he wuz on the wrong side," Jimmie Joe told his foreman. "See if you cain't give him a job in shipping."

One of the reasons the union had been unsuccessful had to do with the peculiar, for its time, wage program in force in the plant.

"You give em a raise every year when things are good, then they ain't about to give any back when hard times come," Jimmie Joe contended. So he fixed his pay rates at just below the prevailing wage. Then he set up a plan to share plant earnings with the workers in the form of an annual bonus.

When things were good, all the workers got a bonus. When they knew things weren't going well, they didn't expect it.

There was no gender differential in the pay scale. And blacks, whom Jimmie Joe never learned to call anything other than "colored people," had the same color-blind opportunity as any other person.

Death came, as it must to all men, to Jimmie Joe Thomas. Though he looked in the pink of health, a massive coronary finished him off at seventy-nine. He was mourned by his wife, his employees, and the townspeople. In his will, he'd set up a trust that would take care of Sara Jane for the rest of her life. He gave to the usual charities and furnished new uniforms for the local ball team. The balance of his estate went to the workers, in shares proportionate to their years of service in his holdings.

Yes, Jimmie Joe Thomas was a reglar feller—who lived a remarkable life of simple grace.

—*Charles Langley*

The First Day

Dozens of eyes stared at me. A sea of unfamiliar faces loomed large and forbidding. My teaching career was off to a nerve-wracking start. Terrified, I summoned the courage to smile. The appearance of several eager grins reassured me. Eyes and grins turned, expectant, and I knew I had to speak.

"Hello, boys and girls," I said, and introduced myself to the group of children standing in front of me. "I'm so glad you all came today."

My words sounded weak and small. *Project your voice,* I thought.

"This is such a special and exciting day—your first day of grade one."

Several children straightened their shoulders as if suddenly aware of their importance.

I directed my next comments to the intimidating row of parents lining the back of the room. Nothing in my education courses at university had prepared me for the folded arms, the candid looks of appraisal, and the eyes narrowed with suspicion. I was twenty years old, and I looked about fifteen. My shaky voice and nervous mannerisms had betrayed me. No wonder the parents were less than enthusiastic.

"Of course, the moms and dads are welcome to spend the morning with us," I said. "However, I'm sure some of you have other things you need to do."

Go home, I thought. *Please go home and leave me alone. I don't know about you, but I have the feeling I'm in the wrong place.*

No one moved. No one spoke.

"I'd be happy to answer any questions you might have," I said.

More silence.

I took a deep breath. "Perhaps we should get started."

I picked up a list of the students' names from my desk and began to read. "Tommy Adams. Are you here?"

A tentative hand went up, and I felt a flicker of relief.

"Tommy," I said. "Can you tell me your address and phone number?" In a moment of optimistic inspiration earlier that morning, I had decided not only to call the roll but also to check whether each child knew his home contact information.

Tommy frowned. "No," he said.

The flicker of relief I felt a moment earlier sputtered and died. I nodded.

"That's perfectly all right," I said, as Tommy's head drooped in defeat.

Great, I thought. *I ask the poor kid his first question, and he doesn't know the answer. Forget the phone numbers and addresses.* I glanced at the wrinkled paper clutched in my sweaty hand.

"David Allen, are you here?"

Another hand went up. His eyes glittered with excitement.

"I know my address and phone number," he announced with a triumphant glance at Tommy.

Tommy's eyes widened with indignation. "I know my phone number and address, too, David. I'm just not going to tell her," he said, pointing at me. "She's a stranger, and my mom told me never to tell a stranger my phone number or address."

Oh, God, I thought, *what ever made me believe I could be a teacher?*

There were mutters and whispers from the parents brigade at the back, and several mothers, after saying good-bye to their children, left the room.

Like rats leaving a sinking ship, I thought.

I gestured toward the rows of desks in front of me. "I'd like everyone to find their seat now. You'll find your name taped to the top right-hand corner. I'll take the roll after you're all seated." *And just before I run screaming from the room.*

A few more mothers kissed their children good-bye, glanced my way as if to say, "My kid had better be in one piece when I get back," and departed.

The room came to life with excited chatter and the sounds of wooden chairs being pulled across the floor. Then, a child's mournful wail filled the room. In the corner, clinging to his mother's coat like a baby orangutan, was Tommy Adams.

"I want to go home," he sobbed. "I want to go home."

The room fell silent as everyone stopped to watch the drama. I reached out to touch Tommy's shoulder, and he flinched.

An apologetic look appeared on his mother's face. "He doesn't like new things, but he's never made a fuss like this."

I knelt down. In a soft, low voice, I attempted to comfort him. "It's all right, Tommy. Please don't cry. Everything's going to be okay."

I suppose I was consoling myself, too. This was not how I had pictured my first day of teaching, and a part of me wanted to howl and cry just like Tommy.

I tried bribing him. "Tommy, would you like to be in charge of picking out a story for me to read to the class?" I asked.

His face buried in his mother's leg, he shook his head.

"Would you like to be my helper and collect the milk money?"

He hesitated for a moment this time, but after a few seconds, he shook his head again.

I glanced up at his mother. Her eyes and voice pleaded with me. "I have to get to work." This announcement provoked more crying from Tommy, this time louder and more desperate.

"Can I tell you a secret, Tommy?" I whispered.

I held my breath and waited. He stopped crying. He was listening.

"This is my first day, too," I said. "I'm new, and I'm kind of nervous and scared."

He turned around and stared at me, his red and swollen eyes full of incredulity. "You're scared?"

I shrugged and nodded. "A little. I've never been a teacher before, but you were in kindergarten, right?"

"Yes, I was. I used to get a sticker almost every day."

"I can tell just by looking at you that you're the kind of boy who would get a sticker almost every day." I reached out and held his hand. This time he didn't pull away. "I need your help," I said. "I could really use a friend. Someone who knows all about school. Someone like you."

A thoughtful look appeared on his face, and I gently squeezed the tiny hand. "Would you please stay and help me out?"

He sniffed, wiped at his eyes with one hand, and nodded. With a silent prayer of gratitude, I stood up and led Tommy to his desk. When I glanced back at his mother, she smiled and nodded. I gave Tommy a gentle nudge. "Tell your mom you'll see her in a little while."

I held my breath as the little body stiffened, but then he turned around and waved. "Bye, Mom. See you after school."

I exhaled with relief and looked up at the clock. It was 9:30. Only two hours to go until lunch. I might just make it.

—*Susan B. Townsend*

A Five-Dollar Bill

It was the third week in December, and I was writing out my charity checks. I had intended to write fewer checks that year, because I wasn't working and had definitely decided that charity begins at home—my home.

However, when I counted up the number of checks, I was shocked. Instead of fewer, there were more. For a moment, I was tempted to tear up a couple of envelopes, but I couldn't. Once I'd sealed the envelope, it was as if I had given my word, and I don't like to go back on my word. So, I mailed them all and patted myself on the back for being such a "charitable" person.

But I didn't feel charitable. I felt grumpy. Why? Maybe because I do it all at once, so it feels like a lot of money. Maybe because the amount grows every year, because more people are in need. Or maybe it's simply because my back hurts after sitting in one position for such a long time. Whatever the reason, I walked around for a few days like a bear that has been woken up in the middle of winter. Definitely not someone you wanted to tangle with.

Then something happened that opened my eyes and gave me the swift kick in the pants I needed. While I complain about donating to charity, the truth is, I can afford to. Even though I wasn't working that year, I had been able to save money over the years and certainly wasn't destitute. If things got bad, I knew I would be able to go back to work, at least part time.

In the meantime, although I buy a lot of my clothes secondhand and may not go out to fancy restaurants, I live in a house and I always have money to put food on the table and to pay the heating bill. Giving to charity means fewer frills for me, but that's what they really are—frills.

I can afford to give to charity and I do, but not until it hurts. Then I met a woman who did give until it hurt. And I felt ashamed of myself. She didn't set out to shame me, any more than she set out to be a knight in shining armor to a homeless man.

All she wanted was a hamburger.

I discovered her on a Web site we were both writing for. I was a veteran, which in cyber-time meant I had been there for several months; she was a newbie. I had read a few of her stories and liked their humor and honesty.

But when I saw one of her stories, "That Time of Month," I almost passed it by. My first reaction was that she was writing about . . . well, a time of month all women are familiar with.

For some reason, I decided to read it, anyway. That's when I found out "that time of month" is when the money from one disability check is gone and the month still has a few days left. When lunch is watery tea, a few crackers, and maybe half a can of bargain-basement tuna fish when you hate tuna fish.

And when dinner is the other half of the can without the crackers.

Then you remember the five-dollar bill you managed to save for just such a time, when the thought of eating tuna fish makes you gag. Feeling incredibly rich, you decide to splurge on dinner out. Not at a four-star restaurant, but at McDonald's. Forget the truffles; all you want is a hamburger with all the fixings. If you don't order fries and a drink, you'll even have some change to put away for another month, another hamburger.

Instead of taking your purse, you just slip the money in a book you got at the Salvation Army store for a quarter and will now return so someone else can enjoy it, though not before you take out the money, of course. Then you get dressed and, clutching the book, painfully walk down the stairs and begin the slow, two-block trip to McDonald's.

As you cut through an alley, you notice a bundle of rags. You peer closer. The rags turn into a man huddled against a building. He looks at you and half smiles. You clutch the book a little tighter, but he doesn't look that frightening.

You smile back a little tentatively but continue walking. Your thoughts are on that burger, now just a short block away.

Then you stop. Suddenly, the burger, the same burger that just a minute ago meant everything to you, doesn't seem important now. You turn around and hand the book, complete with your last five dollars, to the raggedy man, telling him you hope he enjoys it. He looks at you for a moment, and then quietly thanks you.

You return home, trying to convince yourself that tuna isn't that bad, not when you can eat it inside a warm apartment, knowing you will have a bed to sleep in that night.

The story was told matter-of-factly, just another day in the life of someone. There was no patting herself on the back for being such a good person. No complaining about the hard life she was living.

I was so impressed, I did two things. One, I put a link in one of my articles so anyone who read it would know about her story and could easily click on it. Since we got paid a couple of pennies per click, I hoped the extra readers would translate into another burger to make up for the one she'd lost. And two, I e-mailed her to tell her how much I had enjoyed her article.

A day later she e-mailed me to thank me for the link. I e-mailed her to tell her she was welcome. Then she e-mailed me to comment on one of my stories. I e-mailed her to comment on one of hers.

Since then, we've moved from talking about writing to talking about ourselves. Through little snippets she's told me and stories she's written about her experiences, I've come to realize what a remarkable woman she truly is. Not that she would ever say that about herself. So I'll say it for her.

Having battled, and continuing to battle, major medical problems and depression, she has somehow found the strength to reach out to others. She has learned to find joy in small things and to teach others to do the same. If you're stuck in a wheelchair, decorate it. If you've lost a breast to cancer, write a story about your parrot eating the prosthesis, so others can smile. If you have only five dollars, give it away and enrich two lives—yours and that of the person who receives it.

I would like to say that knowing her has made me a better, more generous person, another Mother Theresa, and that I, too, would give away my last five dollars. But I know myself better than that. I know I'd hang on to my last five dollars with every ounce of strength I had.

Still, though I'm certainly no saint, I've begun to take one or two tentative steps toward being that better, more generous person. These days, if I give spare change to street people a little more often or don't grumble quite as much when I write charity checks, I know why. It all started when a woman gave her last five dollars to someone she didn't know and created a ripple effect ending hundreds of miles away—with me.

—*Harriet Cooper*

Lessons from a Four-Year-Old

"Okay, time out," I tell Katie, fed up with the little power struggle we're having over bedtime.

She protests, but resigns herself to a corner for the four minutes. Forgetting it's dark in there, I pull the door almost closed. She cries and says she's scared.

"Be scared," I suggest, obviously in need of a time-out myself.

The four minutes are tough on me. Katie hardly ever needs discipline, and it's foreign territory. When it's over, we hug, and talk. Since I yelled at her, we decide, maybe I need a time-out, too. Her eyes light up. A little order is restored to her kid universe.

"Four minutes!" she announces, with great relish. I congratulate myself on the creative parenting, while she pauses at the door. Her eyes are wet. "I won't close it," she says. "I don't want you to be scared."

I think I'll spend my time in the corner crying, too.

Giving birth to Katie was like taking on a personal trainer—for life. I supply the breastmilk, training pants, and

Barbie dolls. She provides a moment-by-moment reminder of what's important.

The hair salon is always noisy, but Katie silences it on her first visit.

"I love you, Gloria!" she exclaims, settling into her chair for a trim.

She's known her only ten minutes, but in that time Gloria has washed her hair without getting soap in her eyes, massaged her scalp, and given her a sucker to help her sit still. What's not to love? The words hang in the air, though. No one knows how to react. We're not used to saying "I love you" to one another, not to people we barely know, not at ten o'clock in the morning. At least one of us is wondering what kind of world it would be if we were.

"Hi, sweetheart!" a bank teller greets Katie, handing her another sucker.

"Hi, cutie!" Katie fires back.

From the look on the woman's face, it's been a while since anyone has called her "cutie." My smile confirms it: You heard her right. "What the heck?" she tells Katie, and gives her stickers, too.

Katie's exuberance is occasionally interrupted by a little meltdown when she's tired. She is a kid, after all, and the world ends when things go wrong. My husband is uncomfortable when she cries. He swoops down and tries to solve the problem, but in the process creates a new one: Even though the problems may be fixed, she needs to feel badly and cry a while longer, but she knows he disapproves.

I almost love it when she cries. She sits on my lap, and we chat. "What happened?" I ask. She tells me. "That sucks," I agree. "That really sucks." We wax poetic on how cleansing a good cry can be. Maybe she feels better or maybe she gets bored, but the tears subside.

Now that she's ready, Katie and her dad, who is still anxious to help, tackle the problem together.

"Hearts are popping out of me!" she tells him.

"Huh?"

"Like in the cartoons," she explains.

Before Katie came along, grocery shopping was a painfully boring chore. Now I make sure we never get through our list, so that we have a reason to come back in a day or two. She wants me to admire her reflection in the mirror above the produce, negotiates for still another sample, reminds me that girls live for chocolate and wants reassurance there's plenty at home.

By the time we reach the checkout I ask her, as I have before, "Do you ever stop talking?"

"Never!" she says, proudly.

"Yackety-shmackety!" I tease her with a nickname one of my girlfriends assigned her because of her chattiness.

"Yackety-yack, don't talk back!" she whispers in a silly voice.

I tickle her. She giggles.

The line is moving slowly, and we're going to be there a while. Not a problem.

"Yackety-yack, don't talk back!" Katie whispers in my ear again, and waits to be tickled.

The giggles build to a crescendo, and soon everyone around us is infected. We can't stop laughing. I try to remember what was boring about grocery shopping. You can have your trips to the Bahamas and weekends in New York City. Just send me back to the store with my preschooler for more milk and bread.

When I was a teenager, my little sister got hamsters and continuously pestered our dad to watch them play.

"Kids have the secret to life," he told my mom and me. "I watch the hamsters, but I'm thinking of all the other things I should be doing. To a kid, that hamster is the only thing in the world."

I was lucky, growing up, to have so many of the adults in my life tell me that their biggest regret was not appreciating their kids more when they were little. Determined to keep that from happening, I did everything right. I nursed Katie around the clock for two years, designed my work so she's almost always in tow, and when she asks me to play I almost always say yes.

But time is a formidable opponent, as I learn one summer evening when the local newspaper arrives. School officials are pushing for all-day kindergarten, and when Katie is five she'll likely be in it. There is a hole inside where my stomach used to be. I feel as if a half year of her life has been ripped away from me. Next fall, kindergarten. Then it's off to college. Or so it will seem. I can't even breathe, I'm crying so hard—but Katie knows what to do.

She crawls up on my lap, hugs me, and doesn't let go.

—Maureen Anderson

Ah, Fruitcake!

I stood at the kitchen counter chopping pecans while my sister rifled through the lower cabinets between my legs in search of her industrial-sized baking sheets.

"Oh, this will be fun," she chattered, "baking our Thanksgiving fruitcake cookies together for the first time in years."

I spread my legs a little wider and looked down at her. "What are you talking about? I hate fruitcake."

If I had been a man I would have been castrated with one sharp blow. Her head came up so fast and with such force I barely had time to step back and out of the way. Her mouth gaped and her hands agitated the air from her position on the floor.

"Hush your mouth. Baking fruitcake cookies is a family tradition. We will do it and we will do it with the respect our foremothers set down for us many years ago."

I couldn't respond for a few moments. Finally, I said, "What planet are you from? I've never made fruitcake cookies. We made cocoon wedding cookies, Santa-shaped sugar cookies, and Daddy's favorite, oatmeal with red and green

M&Ms. But Mother never baked cookies with disgusting lumps of candied fruit."

Sissie's palm caught her scream. She bowed to the ground, almost weeping, like a female Dalai Lama doing penance for a horrible sin.

"Mother failed you, pure and simple," she managed to gasp. "I got married too young and left you to be raised by a meno-pausal wreck. She had me as a child and you as an old hag."

"What are you talking about?"

"You are my little sister and you know nothing about cookie tradition. What else did she fail to teach you? Do you have good dental hygiene? Do you have a clue how to bake bread? How many pickles do you put up each year? Did you breast-feed Mary Kate or was she a bottle baby? Oh, Lord, I think I might fall out right here."

"I turned out just fine, I'll have you know. But I don't know who you are talking about. The only pickles Mother ever put up were Claussen's. She got them from Kroger and put them up on the middle shelf in the refrigerator door. Wonder bread contributed to these hips, and Mary Kate did beautifully on Enfamil, thank you very much."

I then worried she might actually faint. The parenthesis around her mouth turned chalky and her eyes began to swim. I extended my hand and helped her up as she described family recipes and experiences I had never known. Was she delu-sional? Was she having a breakdown? I led her over to the kitchen table.

"It's okay," I said, patting her hand. "I'd love to learn how to make fruitcake cookies. You can teach me how."

She looked into my face, studying my newly arrived crow's feet as if she had never seen me before.

"Corn bread, you certainly know how to make corn bread."

"Jiffy muffin mix," I whispered, feeling inadequate.

"Pound cake. Tell me you know how to make pound cake."

"Duncan Hines."

"Spaghetti sauce?" Her eyes started to tear.

"Prego Traditional. It's good, honest."

"Oh, Lordy. I'll have to start from scratch." Her head lolled against the back of her chair, rolling back and forth like a pendulum of regret. Then she sat up straight as a wooden spoon and grabbed my shoulders so I could not escape. "You will learn the traditions of our heritage if I have to hold remedial classes from a nursing home."

Realizing I was dealing with a sister possessed and that it would not be advantageous to put up a fuss, I nodded demurely and resumed my position at the counter with the other nuts. Sissie dug out the eight pounds of multicolored candied fruit that she'd stored since ought-one, refluffed herself, and took on her culinary duty with gusto. She instructed me on the proper way to chop our six cups of pecans. I was doing it wrong, of course.

"How many cookies are we making here?" I asked.

"Enough to feed the troops at Shiloh and every living friend and relative our family has claimed since I was born, except for Uncle Fred on Daddy's side, of course. Bill Ennis takes a dozen to his momma's grave instead of flowers each year. People are depending on us, so start chopping."

"And people really eat these things?"

I ducked as her hand whizzed past my head.

Then she explained how to ensure that our cookies had just the right amount of liquor to make them tasty but not so much that anyone would get soused.

"Liquor?" I said, perking up. With a shot or two of a decent libation I might survive this night without committing murder or hara-kiri.

"Apricot brandy," she replied with a dignified nod.

Not my favorite, but at that point I would've taken anything I could get. At first she refused the offer of a sip, but before long we were both chugging the stuff. Soon, we erupted into giggles and almost wet our pants.

When we recovered, I said, "I wish Mother had taught me these things. Maybe I would like fruitcake cookies if I had been introduced to them early on."

"Oh, you will like fruitcake cookies before this night is through," she reassured me. "If only I had Mother's recipe box, I could teach you everything you ever wanted to know about our culinary heritage. I wonder whatever happened to it?"

"You mean that old, green tin box?" I asked.

"That's the one."

Our eyes met. She knew what I was about to say, and it was everything she could do to keep from exploding into squeals before I got the words out.

"It's in my kitchen, in the cabinet over my stove."

The next thing she saw was my backside. Since I lived just down the street, I was back in record time, panting and holding the green box with all the reverence of the Holy Grail. I let her do the honors of lifting the lid. We gazed at the crumpled papers and note cards nestled within it as if we were looking into the womb of the Holy of Holies. Sissie fingered the edges of our mother's treasures and paused reverently before grasping one piece between her finger and thumb. She gave a tug.

Mary Horst's (that's our mother) Fresh Coconut Cake

We both *aah'ed* and tears welled up. I removed the next jewel.

Aunt Bill's Fresh Apple Cake

We took turns ushering each recipe out of its tomb with all the fanfare we could muster without falling apart, blinking convulsively to clear the watershed flowing from our eyes.

Aunt Willard's Angel Biscuits
Company Peas
Francis Stovall's to-Die-for Cheese Cake
Paula Ennis' Cranberry Orange Salad
Eggs a la King (no one claimed it)
Granny's Homemade Peach Ice Cream

For some recipes, Sissie would recite a memory to go with it. As we took turns reading each title aloud in a kind of litany to our lineage, we could taste and smell each delicacy—and we could feel our mother right there with us, sitting across the kitchen table, smiling at the sisters she'd raised so differently, yet so closely.

By the time we had emptied our green memory tin, it was four o'clock in the morning, we had sobered up, and twenty-four dozen fruitcake cookies had been baked, cooled, and tinned. Most important, we had revived a family tradition that will last for generations to come.

Now, the week before Thanksgiving every year, we bake fruitcake cookies with my daughter—just like Sissie did in her youth. We always clear a place at the kitchen table for Mother to sit and listen in.

I didn't miss out on anything growing up, thanks to a sister who keeps our mother's legacy alive and well—and who loves me enough to teach me how to make cookies I despise.

—*Julia Horst Schuster*

My Funny Mother

My mother speaks what I call cliché speak. Whatever the trial or tribulation, the difficulty or the heartbreak, my mother can always be counted on to come up with the perfect cliché to heal the wounds and soothe the heart.

I love my mother's clichés. Indeed, I call her at those moments when I am most in need of one of her comforting and oddly wise one-liners. She never lets me down.

"He doesn't want to be married anymore, Mom. He just doesn't want to be married," I sobbed over the phone.

"If he can't take the heat, he should get out of the kitchen."

"I don't know if I can ever fall in love again. How can I ever trust another man?"

"Pat, when you strike out, you just have to get up and bat again."

"He says he needs to 'find himself.'"

"Tell him to look under his hair."

And I felt better.

In a less-enlightened time, I worked as the only female in a department of males.

"They rig up the reels so that I get shocked when I touch them."

"They sound like real big, brave men to me."

"They tell the boss if I'm late or make a mistake."

"They want you to be 'job-scared.'"

"Gary locked me in a high-voltage cage, Ma. He thought it was funny," I complained.

"Tell him he'll think it's funny when it's on *60 Minutes*."

Just like that, she'd sent me back to the work world, madder than hell and wondering how to contact Morley Safer.

My mother can be a godsend when it comes to my own parenting challenges.

"She drives me crazy, Mom. She lies about being sick. She steals from me. She tells her grandmother that I spend her social security money." I relay the latest antics of my teenage daughter.

"Maybe you should write a book and call it *Daughter Dearest*."

"She told five different lies to five different people. We compared notes."

"You can fool some of the people some of the time. . . ."

"Now, I don't know when she is really sick or just faking."

"There *is* something going around."

Somehow, in just a few phrases, my mother convinced me that my daughter *is* a problem, that I am *not* crazy, and that she might *really* be sick. And she'd given me the confidence, clarity, and calmness to deal with it.

My mother used to be a beautiful woman. Even now, in her seventies, she is handsome. She was once hired to "swoon" for Frank Sinatra during an appearance at Baltimore's Hippodrome Theater. Though she has never had a "career" of any sort, she has been employed as a waitress and a barmaid and was once hired to model an iron lung.

Mom has given birth to seven children: three by one man, three by another, and one whom she gave up for adoption. We are all reasonably intelligent and not unattractive—except the adopted sister, who is extremely skinny and a crazy Elvis fan. We've all given her smart, attractive grandchildren.

When we argue, as mothers and children naturally do, she brings it to an immediate halt with the statement: "Don't ever forget. I'm the one who laid down and had you."

We all readily accept her eccentricities. She refuses to drive at night, ever. She never changes the route she drives, no matter how many expressways and byways they build. If the route changes—say, if a lane is added to one of "her" roads—she simply stops going to whatever place that route had taken her.

She does, I admit, do some strange things. The unkind would call them silly. The kind would call them unique . . . like the time she was following me to an unfamiliar destination.

"Just stay behind me, Mom. I know right where we're going."

"Let's get behind the wheel, McNeal."

We did fine . . . until we got to the tollbooth.

It was a normal tollbooth, the kind with several drive-through areas in which to pay the tolls. During non–rush hours, several lanes are usually open and waiting for customers. Such was the case the day my mother was driving behind me to New Jersey . . . and ended up in Pennsylvania.

The problem began at the tollbooths.

Because I had only a five-dollar bill for a one-dollar toll, I decided not to enter the "exact change only" booth, and within a split second, immediately realized the folly of my decision. I kept my eyes glued to my rear-view mirror and willed my mother to pull in behind me. Please, God, don't let my mother have exact change, I thought, knowing that, if she did, she would believe it mandatory to go through the exact-change lane. And if she entered a different booth from mine, she might pull out ahead of me, and, well . . . my mother gets confused sometimes.

My mother had exact change.

I watched in dismay as she pulled into the exact-change lane, tossed in her coins, and—while the collector counted back my change from the five I'd given him—took off. By the time I exited the tollbooth, she was out of sight and headed in the wrong direction. I had to search every exit and make countless U-turns, and it took more than an hour, but I found her.

I'm not sure why, but my mother goes into high hysteria whenever she cannot reach me immediately on the telephone. Her phone messages could be transcribed and submitted as comedy sketches.

"Pat, this is Mom. Listen, I really need to talk to you. Call me. Mom."

"Pat, please call me. Every time I call, I get this answering machine. Mom."

"Pat, this is Mom. Look, I don't know why you don't call me. I really need to talk with you. Mom."

"It seems like all I ever talk to is this answering machine. If I ever die, I told Ernie not to call you, to just drive down and tell you your mother is dead. Call me. Mom."

"Pat, look, I've got something really important to tell you. Listen, it's really, really important. Call me." Followed by the consecutive message: "Pat, I forgot to tell you who I was in the last message. This is Mom."

And so I call.

"Hi, Pat," she says. "Listen, I have a confession to make. I don't have anything important to tell you. But I knew it would make you call."

What can I do but laugh and settle in for a chat with Mom?

In my middle years, I decided to pursue a writing career. My mother doesn't read, at least to my knowledge, and I don't recall ever being encouraged to read as a child. In fact, she would often admonish me for reading too much. My mother has yet to read a word I've written, though she has often been the wellspring of many of my fictional characters. Yet, she wholeheartedly supports my passion for the written word. Though she doesn't understand anything about writing or the publishing world, she dutifully told all of her friends that her daughter had written a book.

She'd rather hear, than read, the tales of murder and romance that I weave. So, I spend hours on the phone, telling her my stories. She laughs and cries and gasps in surprise, just as though she were reading them. She listens raptly as I talk about plots and protagonists and bylines.

When one of my short stories was finally published, I thought, "Now, my mother will read something I've written."

"It's in *Birds and Blooms*, Ma. You can buy it in a magazine store."

"A magazine store? Oh, yeah. I think we have one in Columbia."

"I can order one for you."

"No, that's all right. I'll have Michael pick it up for me. No, wait, he's on vacation. I'll go myself. *Birds and* what?"

I knew it was hopeless. Finding a store that carried small specialty magazines and remembering the title of the one my story had been published in were beyond my mother's ken. I ordered her a copy from the publisher.

When I made it into a large publication that I thought even my mother was familiar with, I was sure my mother would at last read my work.

"*Reader's Digest*, Ma. You know, *Reader's Digest*. You don't have to go to a special magazine store. You can buy it at the supermarket."

"I think Ernie used to subscribe to that."

On the other end of the phone line, I rolled my eyes to heaven. She hadn't heard of even *Reader's Digest*?

I realized then that my mother would never actually read anything I'd ever write and that I would have to be content with telling her my stories. Still, this news was too good to keep to myself.

"*Reader's Digest* is distributed worldwide. It's an excellent opportunity. Of course, my piece is only two sentences, but . . . I don't care what it takes, Ma, I'm going to write for a living, even if the only book I ever publish is a payroll manual. I'm going to succeed at this."

"I have no doubt that you will."

I stopped still. The phone line crackled.

"You really believe that?" I asked. After all, most of my "success" talk was just a pep talk to myself. Other folks in my circle usually acknowledged such comments with a nod, if at all. Now, here was my mother, who'd never read a thing I'd written, much less anything else, saying with firm confidence that she had no doubt I would succeed as a writer.

"I wouldn't say it if I didn't believe it."

And I knew it was true. If she disagreed, she might say nothing. But my mother never said anything disingenuous, that she did not wholly believe.

My mother believes in me. Whether I succeed or fail, I will forever have that knowledge. I won't let her down.

—Patricia Fish

 Girly Girl

My daughter is crying. It is the final day of kindergarten—Teddy Bear Picnic Day—and fifty-two children are talking and shrieking, engaged in frantic activity. I know there are fifty-two children, because I just spent a half hour frantically stuffing hundreds of green, white, red, yellow, and orange gummy bears into fifty-two plastic bags. Now I'm helping eight five-year-olds of wildly varying ability sort their bags by color and graph the results. So few gummies, so little time, as they say. This is not great fun, but at least I'm not stuck at the Teddy Bear Sandwich Center. That mother has to carve teeny-tiny bears out of white bread and slather them with peanut butter.

My daughter is supposed to be at the Teddy Bear Coloring Center. Instead, she is tugging on my skirt, tears sliding down her tiny freckled nose. She is the only child crying, as usual. I try to swallow my impatience.

"What's wrong?" I ask.

"Cameron won't let me use the red crayon!" She sniffs. Cameron is short and funny, with a face and personality not unlike Dennis the Menace.

"Did you ask him nicely if you could borrow it?" I ask.

"Yes, and he wouldn't give it to me!"

I can see she's not going to let me off easily, so I walk her back to her table to investigate. Sure enough, Cameron is madly scribbling away with a red crayon, and as soon as he sees me, he begins puffing up his chest, mightily defending himself. He loudly explains that he's not yet done and that "she" tried to grab the crayon away from him. She screams right back that she "did not!" The other children at the table look on, perplexed, their stubby crayons poised in midair. My head is spinning.

"Use another color," I tell her. "Cameron will give you the red one when he's done, won't you, Cameron?"

Cameron is noncommittal. Then Davis, slight, cute Davis with a face the shape of a full moon, looks at my daughter and giggles. That's it. There's no hope for recovery now. She puts her head down on the table and sobs, big heaving sobs.

Instead of feeling empathy for her and feeling angry with the blond in short pants who has driven her to tears, I feel irritated with her. Why is she so darned helpless and thin-skinned? I think harshly. So sensitive? A child who makes flower stews, plays with Polly Pockets, and keeps roly-polies from harm. Sometimes I wish she would just deck someone. Why can't she be tougher, like me?

I was the last of four children. I was also the only girl. These two facts, I believe, shaped my destiny more than anything else. People often assume that because I was the only girl and the youngest, the baby girl as it were, I was hopelessly spoiled and protected. This always makes me laugh, it being so patently absurd as to make me wonder whether they've spent any time around boys at all. Pummeled and ridiculed, yes. Spoiled, no.

Being a girl in our male-dominated household meant having the status of a slave. My brothers were the aggregate boss, a position they constantly reminded me of. "Seniority rules!" my middle brother, Bill, the particularly mean one, would proclaim, shoving me out of whatever chair I was sitting in and planting himself in it with an evil grin.

Females were, in a word, worthless—giddy, foolish, obsessed with wimpy pursuits like books, cooking, and dolls. They were especially dense when it came to appreciating the cosmic value of sports. No matter that this was in the bad old days before Title Nine, when about the most strenuous activity girls were encouraged to engage in was paddle tennis or, at best, traditional female sports like gymnastics. I was accused of being adopted several times, because, among other obvious birth defects, I could not throw a football like my jock brothers.

Still, the worst crime in our middle-class, WASP family was to be sensitive. You could be lazy, you could be a jerk, you could even date a minority, but if you showed a quivering lip, a tear, or any sign of weakness, you were fair game. For a time my brothers could drive me to tears just by looking at me. They could make me cry even harder by calling me the s word. "Mona iiii-ss sensitive!" they'd chime. Then I'd oblige them, of course, by behaving exactly as they'd intended. I'd flee to my room in tears and fling myself on the bed, my face burning with a terrible emotion I now recognize as shame.

I figured out early on that if I was going to fit in with my family, feel a sense of belonging and power, I had one option.

Though I was never going to be a boy, I could act like one. So I did.

I built forts. I skateboarded. I wore shorts under my skirts and competed on the field ruthlessly. I grew tough. As it turned out, I was not half bad at being a boy. I was stocky and coordinated like my brothers, so athletics came naturally to me. In the sixth grade, when I took first place in the girls' pentathlon competition for the entire school, I was happy that I had won, of course. But the main reason I was happy was because I'd proven myself to my brothers, shown that I was not just a girl in a training bra and pleated pastel skirts, that I was something superior.

The result of all this sex-role imitating is that I felt better, stronger, and more competent, and less vulnerable to my brothers' taunts and insults. They could even criticize my muscular calves and I wouldn't crack and break down like some sleep-deprived torture victim. I might scream that they were jerks, but that was acceptable—that was anger. My sensitive side still lurked underneath, but by then it was more of a low-key hum than a deafening roar. My emotions were under control.

Having grown up with boys, when it came time for me to have a child, I wanted desperately to have a girl—someone like me on the surface, but perhaps different under the skin. I never gave much thought as to what kind of girl she might be. Shy, outgoing, difficult, artistic, funny, smart: I honestly thought it didn't matter. I would treasure her no matter who she was, I was certain, and give her the emotional support and validation I'd never had. It was hopelessly banal, but I saw having a daughter as a chance to redeem the past. I now see that I was fooling myself: Not only did I care about my daughter's emotional make-up—I cared deeply about it.

When my daughter was born, I felt like the little girl on Christmas morning who tears open the pretty paper to at last find the present she's always wanted. I felt blessed, thrilled, grateful beyond words. I loved her madly, instantly.

"You finally got the girl you wanted," my childhood friend Theresa said knowingly.

It didn't take long for me to see the person my daughter was: wise, inquisitive, nurturing, and feminine. A girly girl who loved jewelry, dresses, Barbies, and all things pink. A child who would break her cookie in two, then hold out the bigger piece to you in her small hand.

Perhaps the quality that struck me most was how self-reliant and independent she was. By the time she was crawling and pulling herself up on the bookshelves in the family room, we could leave her with some blocks, a few squeaky toys, and board books, and she'd play by herself for hours. By the time she was two, she could speak only a handful of words, but would pick out her clothes and try to wiggle them on. And not stripes mixed with prints or clashing colors, mind you, but outfits that actually matched! After producing an earlier male child who showed no interest in personal hygiene, much less fashion, this was a revelation.

But I also observed something else about my daughter. She was as delicate as a baby bird. She not only cried, she cried easily and often. If you spoke with the slightest edge in your voice, she cried. If she fell down or got a scratch, she cried. If she woke up in the middle of the night and found herself alone, which she invariably did, since we declined to invite our kids to sleep in our bed, she cried until you picked her up, and even then she was often inconsolable. I spent the early morning hours of my fortieth birthday driving her around on the Glendale and Ventura freeways because she was sobbing, keeping everyone awake. Thank God she had a brother who adored her and was sweet with her, or she might not have lived to see preschool.

Needless to say, all this crying was a bit wearying. At first I assumed it bothered me simply because of the noise or the need to so often bandage her fragile spirit. But gradually I realized my irritation was due to something deeper and more upsetting: a reluctance to accept that she was like me, the little girl who once got so easily hurt. When I realized that, my eyes filled with tears.

Almost six, she is most prone now to being wounded by her peers. A few weeks ago, she attended her first slumber party. When I arrived to pick her up, she was playing a board game with three other girls and broke down in frustration when her friend Lucia unwittingly went ahead of her. "It was my turn! It was my turn!" she wailed, hitting her knees with her fists. "Not again!" muttered one little girl—in an all-too-familiar tone—as she glanced at my daughter.

The truth is, I can't bear to see my daughter going through childhood as I did, suffering from too gentle and loving a heart. The world has precious little space for people like her, and I worry I will not be able to be the patient, wise mother she needs.

"Kate loves to be responsible and helpful," wrote my daughter's insightful kindergarten teacher in her report card. "I've enjoyed watching her grow and mature. Keep encouraging her to keep her head up high."

But my daughter has no choice about who she is. And thankfully, neither do I. One afternoon a few months back, we were over at her grandparents' house. My quiet father-in-law, who is seventy-eight, was sitting on the couch watching an NBA playoff game between the Bulls and the Jazz. He has diabetes, and my husband made a remark that his father wasn't feeling particularly well that day. The next minute my daughter got up from her chair and snuggled up next to him, placing her hand protectively on his knee. "Who do you want to win, Papa?" she asked. I have rarely seen a grown man look happier.

I know I still have a long way to go. But she has softened me, too; broken through my hard outer shell. Over time, we've evolved a bedtime ritual that goes something like this: After a bath and a story, we talk for a few moments, and then she takes my face in her hands. "I always wanted to have a mother like you," she says, her large blue eyes gazing into mine. Then it's my turn.

"I always wanted to have a daughter like you," I say.

—Mona Gable

"Girly Girl" was first published in Salon.com (Mothers Who Think), January 21, 1999.

I'll Give You a Dime

My cousin Lita and I were born in 1944, only three and a half months apart, the daughters of two close sisters. While Lita's father served in the Army, she and her mother moved in with us for a while. Our mothers often threw us together in the same crib, and we grew up feeling more like twin sisters than cousins. From infancy, Lita was my closest friend and a mirror to my soul. Although they moved out when her father returned from the war, Lita and her family stayed in the same city as ours, and our mothers visited each other often. So, we spent a great deal of time together. We confided in each other, divulged our dreams, and shared many of the same interests.

When we were old enough, we would spend the night at each other's house almost every weekend, well into our junior high school days. We might have continued the arrangement, but something even better happened. My parents moved into a house that was connected to Lita's by a short pathway through a patch of woods. At last we could see each other every day. We wore the trail down raw, crossing back and forth between our houses. We also walked to school and home together five days a week.

Our friendship wasn't always simple and carefree. Like siblings, we had spats once in a while. I can barely recall the reasons for any of our tiffs, because the outcome never changed; we always found ourselves drawn together again. The invisible thread that bound us might have frayed from time to time, but it never broke. I think we began to respect and understand that bond when we were both about seven years old—when we had one skirmish neither of us ever forgot. It put our relationship in perspective and securely tied us together for life.

Here is what happened: On one of her many visits, Lita brought over a comic book to read. We were both avid readers of anything, and comic books represented a special treat. At the time, the flimsy books cost a whopping ten cents. We could have gotten two ice cream cones—one for each of us—for that amount of money.

When Lita finished reading the comic book, she said I could read it, too, and handed it to me. I sat cross-legged on the floor of my bedroom and soon grew immersed in the stories. She tried to talk to me several times, but lost in a fantasy world, I ignored her. Archie comics were my favorite, after all. I never cared for the silly talking duck stuff, but teens doing things I longed to do one day fascinated me. Instantly, the book wove its magic on me. I laughed at the goofy parts, sighed at the slightly romantic parts, and dreamed of the day I might be a teen myself. Betty and Veronica even had a relationship much like my friendship with Lita. I slid into the world of the stories and forgot all about reality.

Lita hung around a short time, but finally, bored out of her wits, she left to do something else. I hardly noticed her absence.

At the end of the comic book, I found a Veronica paper doll, complete with several bright changes of clothing, garments I would have loved to own. The doll had a figure I would have loved to own, too. Without another thought, I reached for my scissors and merrily cut along the dotted lines, eager to see how Veronica looked in each of her spiffy outfits.

Lita stepped back into the room and cried out, "What are you doing?"

I stopped mid-snip and snapped back to reality. The book wasn't mine, and I had totally forgotten. Humiliated, I tried to explain my inexcusable lapse.

She threw up her hands and stormed from the room, refusing to speak to me.

I felt crushed and embarrassed. How could I have forgotten that the book was hers, not mine? Alone in my room, angry with myself and frustrated that I could not appease my best friend, I cried. Several times I left my room to find her, but she sat at the bottom of the stairs, brooding, and shunned me. She wouldn't even acknowledge my apologies.

Her mother arrived to take her home, and I knew I had only a few more minutes to make peace before they left. While my mother and hers sat and talked, I desperately dug into a drawer and found my piggy bank. I squinted through its pink, knobby glass at the few coins inside, to make sure I had what I needed, then I dashed downstairs and past Lita, who sat in preparation to leave. I hurried into the kitchen, opened a drawer, pulled out a butter knife, slipped the flat edge into the piggy bank slot, and jiggled and manipulated the meager contents until I finally withdrew the right amount of money. I ran from the kitchen and hurried back to the steps, only to find Lita still fuming, still sitting on a bottom stair, still waiting to go home.

I held out my shiny coin. "You can buy another comic book. Please don't be angry at me."

She would not look at me, so I stepped around to her other side and held out the peace offering again. "I'm sorry," I said. "I'll give you a dime."

Lita glanced at the ten-cent piece in my hand and looked up at my face, which was hot from embarrassment and wet with tears. She sighed, and her expression softened. "That's okay," she said. "I know you didn't mean it."

In that instant, our friendship deepened, as we both realized our friendship was much more valuable than a measly comic book. We hugged and ran off to play together again for the few minutes we had left before Aunt Anita took Lita home.

Life went on—about fifty more years of it. We went through high school and part of college together. As young adults, we both moved to Orlando, Florida, for a while, but I moved back home and then to Baltimore, Maryland.

Lita and I have lived in separate cities now for about thirty-six years, yet we remain close friends to this day. Like sisters, we still have similar interests, and we still squabble from time to time. We always make up, though, sometimes with a phone call that begins, "I'll give you a dime . . ."

—*Bobbie Christmas*

Moving Grandma West

Seen from the air, Aberdeen, South Dakota, is flat in all directions. In February the land is white-gray, like the inside of an old freezer. Train tracks crisscross the city. Small wood frame and brick houses line the streets. Dark tree branches claw the sky. As we make our final descent, I look to my stepmother, Carla, and make a series of silent prayers: *Let our tiny plane set down safely. Let this trip go easily. Let my father be okay. Let me not cry too much.*

We have come to Aberdeen to move my grandmother to New Mexico. She is my father's mother, and unlike my dad, she has never left the place of her birth. We thought she never would. After the death of my grandfather, we invited her several times to move to Albuquerque; the answer was always no. This stubbornness is not born from a lack of love. It's just that, in her world, there is no room for change. My grandmother does not dance. She does not dance because she never has. That is the way it is.

The thing that got Grandma Rose to change her mind is that my father, at the age of fifty-eight, has been diagnosed with Alzheimer's disease. She is moving to New Mexico to look after her only child.

When we enter Grandma's apartment, she hugs me quickly. "Are you hungry?" she asks. "Are you warm enough?"

A man in a baseball cap and denim jacket pushes himself out of a rocker and stretches out a hand. He is my dad's cousin, Bill.

"So, you're the daughter," he says.

"Uh, yeah."

"You gonna put yer dad in a home?" His eyes grow beady. "You know, I got the same thing. I just ain't been diagnosed yet. 'Course, your dad's always been crazy up here." He taps his head with a thick finger. "So, you gonna put him in a home?"

I want to have a strong, adult answer. I want to ask about his feelings of inadequacy. I want to bring up the frustration of being trapped in a small town, of watching his cousin live a life of creativity and adventure. I want to be smart and insightful, but, instead, I spew, "What kind of sicko question is that?"

I whirl into the kitchen, lean over the sink, and run water over my trembling hands.

From the living room, I hear Bill laugh, say he should be going. I stay in the kitchen until I hear the front door close. Carla comes to my side.

"I guess I wasn't really ready for that question," I admit.

Carla squeezes my shoulder. "Your dad says he was always a jackass."

We go to dinner at a place called The Flame, which has been around since my dad was a rebellious teen. Grandma orders a chicken sandwich; Carla and I order steaks, baked potatoes, and red wine.

"You know," Carla says, "I never eat red meat, but it seems sort of . . . appropriate."

"Yep," I agree, raising my glass. "To meat."

"I never had but one boyfriend," Grandma says.

Carla and I look at each other in surprise. We are not used to Grandma's sudden and random bursts of information.

"That was Grandpa, right?" I ask.

"I made him wait four years before we married."

"Why?" Carla and I say together.

"He wanted to save some money, to get us a place and some furniture."

When I was ten, I spent my birthday money from Grandma on a book of poetry by Shel Silverstein. I included some carefully copied poems in my thank-you note. She wrote back that she didn't read much poetry but Grandpa had written some poems for her when they were courting. I wonder how many poems he wrote, what they were about, and where they are now. Are they packed for the trip to Albuquerque, or have they been lost in all the years in between?

Back outside, Grandma refuses to let me take her arm, though the sidewalk has grown icier.

"I am not feeble," she says. "I am independent. Don't you two forget that."

Grandma has decided that Carla and I will take her bed. When we protest, she explains that the sofa folds out. I do not know if she sleeps. I do know she doesn't change out of the sweatshirt emblazoned with an appliquéd heart and plastic letters that read, "I love you, Auntie Rose."

Carla and I climb into Grandma's bed, both of us trying to leave the other as much space as possible. I have been dreading this moment a little.

"How's Dad?" I ask.

Carla can't even get through a sentence before I start to cry. She cries, too. We talk of money and of care, and I realize that the enormous love I have for my father is more than evenly matched by Carla's love for her husband.

Dishwater pale, the morning comes not a minute too soon. We start with a diner breakfast of doughy muffins, lots of coffee, and a visit with Ruth, Grandma's sister-in-law. Ruth's husband was killed in a car wreck when he was thirty-three. She did not remarry, and simply worked and saved, raising the children with the help of the family.

A widow herself for almost twenty years, Grandma pats Ruth's arm and says, "We're the type of girls who don't marry twice. We'd take the old ones back, but we don't go find more."

After breakfast, the bank is our first stop. Grandma carries all her important papers in a yellow canvas bag bearing a picture of a smiling frog. She remarks a number of times during the day, "It's my money. You don't get none of it. You got your own." We nod, smile, and say, "Yes. Yes."

Next, we head to the mortuary to wrap up the details of Grandma's final resting place. The plot has been paid off for years, death being, to my grandparents, the only real reason to splurge. Once the paperwork is in order, we drive to the cemetery and soon realize that flat brass grave markers are no help when covered by six inches of snow. Where is Grandpa? We scrape off the snow with our feet and find Brown, Drake, and Peterson, but no Ward.

"Are you sure?" we ask.

"I should know where my own husband is," Gram says.

And so we continue until, eventually, all the snow in the area is turned over and Grandpa is still lost. Carla and I seek help in the small, brick cemetery office, where on a wall covered with sheets of graph paper, penciled names in a smudged hand make up a map. We peer at the map and see that, there, across from where we've been looking, is "Ward, Everett."

We head back out to Gram and within a matter of moments we have found Grandpa. We pose for a photo next to the brass plaque. As soon as the shutter snaps, Grandma moves toward the car without a backward glance. I wonder if she is thinking of those four years before they married. Of the poems he wrote her. Of the furniture they moved into their first apartment. Or is she thinking she'd like a sandwich and a cup of milk? That it's colder this winter than the last? I don't know, and I realize I will never know. I come from a closemouthed clan. For not the first time, I wonder at my need to tell stories.

Dad's diagnosis came three weeks ago. Although it does not yet seem real, we are so much more aware that he is at home alone. On the phone that night, Dad tells me he is reading a book about the brain. He tells me to watch out for his cousin Bill.

"I love you," I say.

"I'm mighty fond of you, too," he says, chuckling.

The exchange is one we've shared thousands of times, but now it takes on new weight. How long will he continue to remember this joke? What will I say when he forgets?

My father is fifty-eight years old. Who will walk me down the aisle, and who will be a grandfather to my children? Dad's illness, like any catastrophe, is something we never expected. I look across the room at my stepmother and my grandmother. The troops are gathering. In Aberdeen, South Dakota, three generations of women are taking their first steps toward acceptance.

"What'll you charge me to wash my hair?" Grandma says.

"It's on the house," I reply.

She disappears into the kitchen. She reappears in a white brassiere and hands me a towel and a bottle of shampoo. Grandma leans over the sink, and I let the tap water flatten the wiry result of a permanent wave she gets every six months from "a girl across town." This is the first time I have seen the skin of her back, the soft dimples in her shoulders, the downy hollow at the base of her neck. This is a place I like to be kissed. Were my grandfather's lips ever pressed to this spot? Did his arms slide around her waist to pull her against him? Because my father exists I know this must have happened once. I want to think that it happened more than once. I want to think that there is something wild and restless in my grandmother. I want, most of all, to see some trace of my passionate father in this still and silent woman.

On our last day in Aberdeen the movers arrive. After only a few trips, the apartment is empty. Looking dazed, Grandma lowers herself onto the floor and hands me a chocolate bar.

"You know, your Dad's real sick."

I feel attacked by even the slightest reference to my dad's illness. I lean back, trying to contain myself. Grandma pats my hand.

"Eat," she says.

That night is spent with my father's cousin Dick and his wife, Ann. Dick is a cheerful man with graying hair and buckteeth. His limp is the result of the car accident that killed his father.

"Hey," Dick says, "You want to see me make fire from flint and steel?"

In the living room, we watch as Dick places straw and a piece of carbon cloth in the fireplace. He takes a bit of flint from a leather pouch and strikes it against a piece of steel. Sparks fly, Dick blows, his cheeks puffing with effort. The straw catches, then peters out. Dick blows harder, scattering ashes over the carpet.

Ann says, "The minute I get this room clean, Dick's back in here with the flint and steel."

"Here we go," Dick shouts. And there, on the edge of the fireplace, a tiny flame licks at the straw and begins to brighten.

The next morning, Dick and Ann accompany us to the airport. Grandma's lip begins to quiver. She hugs Dick and Ann so tightly that I know she has realized she will never see them again. She hugs them so tightly that for the umpteenth time I wonder if this is right. As we board the plane, Grandma reaches for our hands like a child.

Aberdeen grows small below. Grandma sits with her face pressed to the window and her hand clasped tightly in Carla's. She is crying soundlessly, the tears catching in her glasses and making dark spots on her turquoise coat. Carla tucks a tissue into Grandma's hand and rubs her shaking shoulders.

I realize that we will not return to Aberdeen until we lay Grandma to rest and find her name, written in fresh pencil, on the graph paper map at the cemetery. Grandma does not dance because she never has. She has never traveled; she does not know how to drive. Yet here she is, pulling up stakes so late in the game. Change has brought change. Right now, we can only guess at the transformation my father will undergo. So we must cling to what we know. We know we love him. That love will somehow lead us through one day and then the next. Dad's illness will bring us all to new territory.

Grandma may never learn to dance, but she has the capacity to change. If she can do it, we can, too. We gain altitude, and I send up a little bubble of hope and imagine it catching the sun over the flat, icy land below.

—*Tanya Ward Goodman*

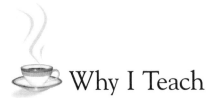 # Why I Teach

I know my students. Masses of awkward seventh graders swarm the halls of my rural middle school each day, hauling backpacks over one shoulder, talking and shuffling along the tile hallway floor from class to class. I watch them like a general from my post (my classroom door) and smile at the fact that I can call each one by name.

I know their secrets, their stories. Dora slouches and is shy, and I know it is because she spends all her time at home trying not to get noticed, so she won't feel the brunt of her stepfather's angry hand. Jay can pitch like a tenth grader, and all the girls swoon when he and his blond hair strut by, but I know he doesn't really even like baseball that much (he plays because his dad wants him to) and he is too scared to ask out the girl he likes. The kids think Keith is just the class clown, but I know of his dreams to become an astronaut (and I've recommended him for space camp). I know my students because I am their writing teacher. They trust me with their stories and so I am given the privilege of having a secret bond with each and every one of them.

I teach my students about the power of words, and I try to let them find release and expression through writing. We learn to trust each other in writing class because we learn how hard it is to write openly and honestly, and we learn that sharing your words takes courage. I see courage every day in my classroom, and I am always amazed at the words that come from my students' hearts.

One such example of courage took place during author's chair, a sharing session at the end of our writer's workshop in which students volunteer to share what they have written. We had a new student to the school, Al. Al was small and, with his dimpled cheeks and baby face, he looked younger than his classmates.

In fact, when Al was first introduced to the class two weeks earlier, one student said, "You're not in the seventh grade. You're a baby."

To that, Al quickly responded, "I'm Al Billslington, and I *am* in the seventh grade."

Despite his obvious courage, Al had been with us for only a short while and was still trying to fit in, so I was a little surprised when he volunteered to read during author's chair. I had one of those teacher moments, when I smiled and nodded for him to read, while inside I said a silent prayer that the other students would not tease the new kid after he read. The room fell silent, and Al began to read.

"If I had one wish, it would be to meet my dad. . . ." He started out loud and clear and held the attention of my usually restless seventh graders as he read on for what seemed like fifteen minutes. He told of how he had never known his father, who had left the family when Al was a baby. He shared the intimate details of his struggles to be the only man in the house at such a young age, of having to mow the lawn and fix broken pipes. He revealed to us the thoughts that raced through his mind constantly about where his father might be and why he might have left.

My eyes scanned the room for snickering faces of seventh-grade kids who I knew were prone to jump at a weakness and try to crack a joke, but there were no snickers. There were no rolling eyes or gestures insinuating boredom or pending attacks. All of my seventh-grade students were listening, really listening. Their eyes were on Al, and they were absorbing his words like sponges. My heart was full.

Al continued on, telling of nightmares at night, of never knowing a man so important to him, yet so unreal. I could hear his voice growing shaky as he read such passionate and honest words, and I saw a tear roll down one of his dimpled cheeks. I looked to the audience. There were tears on Jessica's face and on the faces of a few others seated quietly, intently listening.

They are letting him do this, I thought. *They are allowing him to share something he perhaps has never shared before, and they aren't judging him or teasing him.* I felt a lump in my own throat.

Al finished, struggling now to read his last sentence. "If I had one wish, it would be to meet my dad, so I wouldn't . . ." His tears were rolling now, and so were ours, ". . . so I wouldn't have to close my eyes in bed every night just wondering what he looks like."

Without any cue from me, the class stood up and applauded. Al smiled from ear to ear as they all rushed him with hugs. I was floored.

This is why I teach. I teach because I am allowed to learn the stories behind the faces. I teach because I can watch kids grow and laugh and learn and love. I teach because of students like Al.

—*Whitney L. Grady*

Leaning into the Harness

Her name doesn't follow "I love you" in a greeting card very often. When it does, it's an occasion. But if you look closely, her signature is written in the stoop of her tired shoulders, in the deep creases worn into her brown face by silent smiles and unspoken worries. Her signature isn't often written for her children; her signature is her children.

She is mother to eight, all grown. Some live near her, others are at a distance. Yet geography has less to do with closeness than one might think, and intimacy isn't dictated by a span of miles.

She has always been practical, always gotten things done. Over the years, she has spent more time flattening tortillas than tying bows into her daughters' hair. But there was a double portion of love pressed into those tortillas.

Through divorce, death, alcoholic husbands, and too much hardship, she set one foot in front of the other and met the basic needs of her children. They were fed, clothed, housed, and loved. But there were no frills.

She is a woman who has lived her life as a workhorse, and when there was an added need to be met, she leaned into the harness just a little bit harder. At the age of seventy-two, that part of her nature hasn't changed. Not one bit.

Indeed, she looks for the needs that must be met, and she does what she must do to meet them. She goes to work at the Riverside Wal-Mart as a greeter and works her shift in pain. She has lupus, arthritis, hearing loss, and glaucoma, in addition to the expected aches and pains of any woman her age. She is recovering from a bleeding ulcer, and when she was too weak to return to work standing, she returned in a wheelchair.

Why? Because there was a need. And as has so often been the case, it wasn't her need, but someone else's.

Her youngest son and his family needed help making ends meet, and she just doesn't have it in her to give any less than her best. She wastes no time on laying blame for the lack of income and instead invests herself in filling the gap.

But the price is her time, and there never has been enough to go around.

For each child's tear that she wiped away, another slipped down a cheek beyond her reach. For each sorrow she helps her children and grandchildren endure, there is another that she knows nothing of. And no price can be put on those unconsoled tears and unrelieved sorrows.

But she is human, she is finite, and she is doing the best she can.

As her life continues to unfold, she invests each day. She resolutely sets her face toward the goal of helping those who struggle, those with obvious needs.

Some of her grown children feel shortchanged and often rightly so. People with successful personal lives and careers don't need their mother less. Yet, it must be remembered that this woman's life is an elaborate weave of hardship and modest victories. And there are secrets in her fabric. There are reasons she is burdened by the needs of those who flounder.

Maybe she still wakes up at night and remembers what childhood was like after her own mother died. Her well-intentioned father took his children to live with his sister while he traveled on a railroad job. It took all his savings to buy them a decent bed to sleep in, and then he tearfully said good-bye.

Before he was out of the city limits, that bed was taken over by another relative, and the kids were introduced to the cold clay floor. They slept every night on the hard-packed earth with a dirty quilt to keep them warm—except when their father came to visit.

Her life has never been about accumulating possessions for herself. It has been, and still is, about making sure her children and grandchildren don't have to do without the basic comforts of life. Over the years, her routine of necessity has become her routine of happiness. Leaning into the harness is the equivalent of being needed; it is what she does best. Yes, tears are shed that she knows nothing about. And yes, she sheds private tears of her own.

Hers is the kindly brown face in a California Wal-Mart. She doesn't often sign greeting cards, but her signature appears like clockwork on the back of the small paycheck she shares. In her own way, she will always stand between her children and the harshness of a cold clay bed.

Hers is a practical, unassuming courage—and for one small family, it makes all the difference.

—*Christy A. Caballero*

Walking into the Wind

The wind howled, whipping the rain against the den windows. On that angry winter afternoon, darkness began chasing the last rays of daylight shortly after 3:00 P.M.

Eden, my four-year-old, had been watching *Sesame Street* with me when she suddenly left my side. She padded to the front hall and for the next several minutes struggled to pull on her boots. I waited for her to ask for my help, but she didn't. Mission accomplished, she yanked her red jacket off the hook.

"Are you going someplace?" I stifled a laugh. Surely, she would soon head for her playhouse in the basement. I would be invited to tea, served through the curtained window of her miniature kitchen.

"To Danielle's." Although tiny for her age, Eden spoke with the assuredness of my forty-year-old boss.

My jaw clamped shut. I refrained from motioning toward the windows or saying that the storm might suck her all the way to Oz. Her dressing for the weather demonstrated a degree of mature judgment I wasn't about to squelch.

She retrieved her Minnie Mouse umbrella. Her arms, too bulky in the coat, could barely come together to hold the handle. Her sweater must have bunched up at her elbows. I resisted the urge to straighten, watched in silence.

"I'll drive you," I finally said. In good weather, the five hundred yards to Danielle's was an easy walk with no streets to cross.

"I'm not a baby." She opened the door and peeked out.

I could have used the vocabulary of menace—dark, dangerous. Or I could have reminded her that her sister would return from dance class soon, and we would bake cookies.

"How about a kiss?" I said, instead.

She beamed at me, her right dimple deepening. Her wet lips left a warm circle on my cheek. Her arms, confined by the jacket, lay for a brief moment against my chest. Then she pushed open the screen door and stepped out.

I dashed to the phone. "Eden's on her way to you," I sputtered to Danielle's mother, and hung up. I threw on my coat, drew out an umbrella, and raced into the rain in my rubber-bottomed slippers.

I stayed fifteen feet behind my baby. She struggled with her umbrella against the wind, plodding on, never looking back. In the glow of the streetlight, rain pelted her umbrella and cascaded onto her foot-long back.

This was a rite of passage that I had no clue was coming. The baby who had learned to walk not long ago already belonged to herself, was already walking away from me into the dark, unafraid. In the storm of the night, my child was lost to me. In her stead appeared the woman who would one day travel the globe.

The rectangular light of an opened door indicated that Danielle's mother waited. Eden was ushered in, never knowing about the salty tears in my mouth.

Before spring, my nine-year-old daughter, Tomm, announced that she was ready for sleep-away camp. Her erstwhile passion for all stray animals—from caterpillars to rabbits—suddenly a childhood fad, she now wanted to attend a drama camp.

"Which of your friends is planning to go?" I asked.

She fingered my earlobe, checking my earrings. "No one."

This was the kid to whom I had relegated emptying the dishwasher when she was only two and a half. And she had never broken a plate. Why was I surprised at her confidence?

In the following weeks as we sat through camp presentations, I stifled my desire to pin my beautiful child to velvet, like a rare and precious butterfly.

"Mommy," she said one night when I tucked her in and settled down to tell her the bedtime stories that were ours alone. She brought her almond-shaped eyes as close as our noses allowed. "When I grow up, I want to be like you, not a PTA mom."

My laughter had the nervous lilt of the guilty career mother. "What's a PTA mom?"

"You have a life."

You are my life, I wanted to say. You and your sister are the center of my universe. But you test me. To pass, I must let you be whoever you want to be rather than the carriers of my hang-ups and fears.

But I didn't say it.

The pink backpack dwarfed her when I put her on the bus to the camp of her choice. Coltish legs poked above her sneakers, and her eyes were dark and grave. Only the huge yellow flower in her hair offset the look of a lost Bambi.

"I don't know anyone," she whispered in my ear, as though the thought had just occurred to her. Her warm breath, with a whiff of her bubble-gum-flavored lip-gloss, made me want to take her back home.

"You'll have a friend by the time you get there," I told her. And she did.

When it was time for Tomm to go to college, she picked the largest institution that had accepted her, and several months later took the five-hour train ride for student orientation. I flew in a day later for a parallel parents' meeting. She and I were to meet at the counselor's office.

I sat through the parents' discussion about the anguish of separation, the mourning over being discarded. All around me, befuddled adults agreed that freedom was confusing to their children—and yes, dangerous. As astonishment rose on the horizon of my consciousness, I wondered whether I was missing a secret chromosome. The type of bonding these parents described seemed like a color that eluded the blind me. While I had felt so anchored in my relationship with my Tomm, my parenting must have been flawed all these years for neither of us to feel the angst of separation . . . I hadn't talked with her since she had left the day before. Perhaps she hadn't even arrived. Maybe I shouldn't have let her travel alone or should have at least insisted that she call. And what had made us assume, oh so cavalierly, that the coming months and years would just fall into place?

Suddenly, I wondered whether I should have been a PTA mom. Luckily, I still had a second chance with Eden.

I transferred Eden to a private high school that nourished her insatiable thirst for knowledge and where I could get more involved. But within a couple of years, she charged into adolescence and demanded to return to the public school, where the sandbox for her activities was bigger.

Five years later, on one of her college breaks, Eden took me out for sushi. She had decided to become a movie producer, she said, but only if she could make it big. Did I think it was impractical? It was a flesh-eating industry, she explained, and she'd have to relocate to California. But she had no connections. The easy alternative, she said, would be to make it safely in the New York corporate world. There had been offers for internships.

The dimple of the four-year-old still puckered her right cheek. My baby still walked into the wind, still struggled with her Minnie Mouse umbrella, pelted by rain, unafraid.

My mouth felt cold. My hands around the ceramic tea mug were hot. This was my opportunity—my last—to keep my youngest close and safe.

"You'll make it," I whispered, realizing that my job had always been to get out of the way.

—*Talia Carner*

Home Is Where the Hearth Is

There is an old Gaelic expression that states, "May the roof above you and the hearth before you always be your own." Reflecting upon the history of war-torn, famished Ireland, it is not difficult to understand why a safe haven, a home, has been so highly regarded by the Irish.

Such were my thoughts as I surveyed the brownstone on West 18th Street, bordering New York City's Greenwich Village. The day was cold, gray, and dreary as I stood outside the wrought iron gate surrounding the home. At the turn of the century, this modest building meant the world to Maggie O'Connor, an immigrant from County Clare. One of my biggest regrets was that I'd never had the opportunity to meet dear Maggie, who was my great-grandmother.

Bursting with optimism, eighteen-year-old Maggie landed at Ellis Island in 1892 with little more than five dollars in her pocket and the clothes on her back. But she wasted no time lamenting what little she had and secured a position that afternoon as a cook's helper in a wealthy Park Avenue household.

A year later she married a fellow Irisher, a handsome longshoreman from Donegal. The two set up housekeeping on the third floor of the brownstone that now stood before me. Seven years and five babies later, he was killed, tragically, crushed between the dock and some itinerant cargo.

How often I have wondered what thoughts must have gone through her mind at that time. Did she consider returning to Ireland? Putting her children up for adoption? Turning to her mainstay, the Catholic Church? I like to imagine her squaring her narrow shoulders, jutting her chin forward, and swallowing her fears. Women in my family have always been a pillar of strength, and I like to attribute that trait to Maggie.

My grandmother remembered little about her father. What was very clear to her, however, was that shortly after his death, the family moved "downstairs." In hindsight, it seems that without her husband's income, Maggie could no longer afford the upstairs apartment, and she lost no time in relocating her young family to the basement quarters. Once situated, she convinced the owner of the brownstone to accept a bartered arrangement. Every morning, she would fill each open heating grate of the twelve units above with coal and then prepare breakfast and later prepare dinner for all of the boarders. In exchange, she and her children could live in the basement quarters rent-free.

The owner must have agreed, as my grandmother recalls Maggie herding the five children into that "downstairs" apartment. But my grandmother's memories were not depressing. Rather than "dark and damp," as one might expect, my grandmother described their home as being "light and bright." And she said that every day brought a new adventure.

But if Maggie had painted a rosy picture for her children, in reality her life was one of continuous work and little leisure.

Every morning she carried buckets of coal to the twelve families living upstairs. Then, while keeping an eye on her own brood, she would prepare breakfast for the boarders, serving them in the large dining area. Her own children would then eat in the kitchen, and my grandmother recalled that leftovers had never tasted so delicious.

Several hours each afternoon, Maggie worked as a laundress, and the children accompanied her to various homes along "the Avenue" (Seventh). During the late afternoon, they returned to the boarding house to prepare dinner. As time was a commodity not to be squandered, she filled the evening hours by taking in "piecework," sewing by the fire.

If times seemed hard, she never complained. There was food on their table and a roof over their heads. In Ireland, she had had neither, for famine and poverty were everywhere.

So many times in my life I have thought about Maggie, my great-grandmother, and how hard she worked. It was through her back-backing labor that my grandmother was able to learn a trade, that my mother was able to attend college, and that I was able to obtain a graduate degree. Because of her sacrifices, I have inherited a life of more ease and luxury.

Over the years when enjoying a relaxing weekend, I have often wished I could have spent part of it with Maggie. Perhaps we could have enjoyed tea and scones at a five-star hotel, indulged in a manicure and massage at an exclusive spa, or taken in a movie or a play at an upscale theater. But somehow, I knew she would not have enjoyed these experiences; she would have been nervous, frightened, and perhaps even suspicious of such pampering and leisure activity. I can almost imagine her politely declining my invitations and escaping to the safety of her basement apartment, her familiar mending nestled in her lap.

So deep were my thoughts as I stared at the brownstone, that I did not notice that the drizzle had become a downpour. As I struggled with my umbrella, the present owner opened the door. He seemed to be of a gentle nature, and smiled shyly and asked if he could assist me.

"Oh, I'm sorry," I stammered. "I was just admiring your home. Someone I knew used to live here a very long time ago."

He brightened visibly and asked if I would like to take a look inside. He seemed to be quite proud of the brownstone.

"I'd love to," I responded, climbing the porch steps.

As I walked through the large foyer, dining room, and parlor, I could appreciate his pride. The home was magnificent and had been restored to its Victorian splendor. But my interest was not on the main floor.

"Would I be able to see the basement?" I asked.

The owner smiled. "The basement? Now, that's an unusual request. How did you know that is my favorite part of the house?"

The stairs were located behind the kitchen, and as I descended, I thought of dear Maggie hauling endless buckets of coal up those very same steps.

Reaching the bottom, I gasped. Despite the gray afternoon and the rain beating against the high basement windows, the entire area seemed to be bathed in light. With overstuffed chairs and ottomans surrounding an open hearth, the room felt like a homey refuge. But there was more. An inexplicable benevolent force seemed to permeate the room—as if it were almost a holy place, a place that housed only love.

On the mantel was a Greek statue, and I inquired about it.

"It's Hestia, the goddess of home and hearth," the owner answered. "She watches over this house. While I love what she represents, I am not fond of the name 'Hestia.' It seems a bit too formal, a bit cold, doesn't it?"

"Have you ever considered calling her Maggie?" I asked him. And suddenly, rays of sunlight streamed through the basement windows.

—*Barbara Davey*

Tender Is the Night

My teenage son had a crying spell last night. Not an unusual thing for girls, friends with daughters tell me. An argument or missed phone call triggers an outburst, and they recount a day's worth of faux pas and petty humiliations that make life at this moment unlivable. They heave their misery like poisoned food, loudly, dramatically, desperate to purge until there is not one tear left. And then, dawn breaks over a new sky, and there is hope again. It's like that, their mothers say, several times a week at worst.

I have only sons. They are sensitive, for boys, and can be emotional. But when adolescence descended on them, it came with a blackout curtain. And the worries and wonders they used to share at bedtime became private matters.

Boys are easier, I hear, as teenagers. Less histrionic. More independent. Steadier. That's true, I think, from my one-sided parenting experience. But it's deceptive, this face of self-containment. From all appearances, life is good. My son gets passing grades. He has a delightful girlfriend whose presence softens him. He actually enjoys school for once. He mountain bikes with buddies on the weekend and comes home mud splattered and endorphin charged.

But there's a bravado to him now. He carries it like a polished shield. I see him pumping it up in the car ride to school. The leather jacket. The spiked cherry-red hair. The earrings. The slouch. The tight jaw. All accoutrements to the image he hones. His voice is deeper when he grunts goodbye.

I imagine high school as a mass of projected self-images, sparring and jostling in the halls, desperately shielding the ghost children behind them. Newly sprouted fears and insecurities are snatched like plunder if exposed. It's a matter of survival, regardless of gender, to get through a day ego intact. We all did it, growing up. With luck, by senior year you've found a niche. An interest, a passion—or, if nothing else, a clique—to foster confidence and growth. You come out the other end with a stronger sense of self.

My son is just a freshman, struggling with the hardest part. Trying to figure out who it is he wants to be seen as, before he can get to the part about who he really is. And I don't get to help. At least not in ways I normally consider helpful. Questions are considered intrusions, embraces are assaults, family time is a bore. I've learned to give him a wide berth and take the openings when I see them. I feel gratitude for the smallest things: a smile flashed my way at the funny part in a video, an unexpected hug while I make dinner, an unprompted thank-you. Mostly, I simply have to take at face value the side he shows to me, because the rest is inaccessible.

But last night he called out from his bed, where he lay crying, unable to stop. He held out his arms and clung tight like he hasn't for years. An earring had started it. A garnet stud swirled down the bathroom drain. It triggered an avalanche in him that stymied us both.

"Is there something else?" I asked. "Something that's been bothering you? What's going on?"

"I just need to cry," he wailed. "I need to get it all out. It's not fair how I never get to cry anymore. All day at school, I walk around holding it in."

I thought he liked school. "Is it that bad? Is someone hurting you?" I envisioned a bully by the lockers twisting his arm, gangs of ruffians surrounding him at the bus stop after school. What undisclosed maliciousness had been tormenting him?

"No, it's not any *thing*. It's just the way it is. You have to be tough all the time. If you start to feel something that isn't cool, you have to hide it."

I remembered how upset he'd been when his class watched a movie that showed wild animals being killed and someone in the room had cheered when the elephant was brought down. How furious he'd been when a classmate once suggested that all retarded people should be euthanized.

He let out a long, thin wail and rolled his head from side to side. "It feels like a balloon getting blown up inside of me. All these feelings. I can't ever let them out. Not with my friends. And at school, you're dead meat if you cry. Even if you're really hurt bad."

It's true. High school is a cruel Darwinian society, and the weakest are smeared. I remember seeing a boy taunted to tears in my own high school, and it was like watching someone being handed a death sentence. Everyone knew. There was no coming back from this. I didn't know what to tell my son, except, "You're right. You have to hold it in. But when you're home and safe, let it out, and we'll be here with you."

I remembered him coming home the previous weekend, his leg bloody from biking. A friend was with him, and he brandished that sheared shin like a trophy, bragging about how deep it cut and how little it hurt. Only after his friend left would he let me bandage it. He swung his leg up on the kitchen table, still full of swagger and talk. And I thought how far he had grown from the little boy who wanted kisses and a *Jurassic Park* Band-Aid for every little scratch and bruise. *Growing up*, I'd thought. *Tougher than me now*.

But last night I was grateful for the chance to hold him again. To pat down his stiff red hair and wipe his tears. To feel the bird-thin bones beneath new muscle and realize, *My God, he's still such a kid*.

You forget, when they peer smugly down at you from gangly new legs. They bang their way around the kitchen making meals you never knew they could cook. They can get themselves all around town without asking for a ride. They don't come to you for advice, and snap at you if you offer it. It's easy, then, to think you've reached the downhill part, that most of the lessons you've taught already, and this is your time to coast. You leave him alone when he doesn't want to talk and believe him when he says he's okay. You remember things you forgot to do, like learn Italian and write a book. And you think that maybe the time has come at last for you to focus on yourself and your child-weary partnership.

But really, this is the trickiest part of all. They want you there, right next to them, when they need you—knowing all the right things to do and say. And then . . . *poof!* The distance barrier inflates like an airbag, and you find yourself dumped on your ass, wondering what it was you said or did.

I'm left navigating a million double-messages, trying to distinguish real boundaries from false fronts, poking the ground for hidden passages. I stumble against my own needs and insecurities, never sure how my advances will be received. But I'm the mom, and it's up to me to read the signals, take the chances, and absorb the blows if my timing was off or the angle was wrong.

No doubt he will come home from school today more gruff and disinterested than ever (just to make sure I don't get any ideas about last night). But I'm reminded now that behind that fifteen-year-old façade, my child still lingers, and no matter how deftly he dodges connection, he still counts on me to know when to come in there after him. And as much as I hate that he has things to cry about, I love that he still cries.

—*Jennifer Meyer*

Christmas Is Delicious!

We were so excited and happy about taking our first trip to Radio City Music Hall with our son, Michael. The famous Christmas Spectacular was back in New York City, and it would be a wonderful experience for us all. My husband had never seen the show as a child, so it would be a first for the two men in my life. The weather was cold and crisp, and the city shone with holiday decorations and twinkling lights. Dressed in colorful red and green sweaters, we set off on our big adventure.

Our son's midtown Manhattan nursery school had planned a field trip for fifty of us, with our two- and three-year-olds in tow. We had purchased a block of tickets for the performance. Although I'd grown up in the city, I hadn't seen the Christmas show since I was ten years old. I looked forward to seeing the beautiful Art Deco building again, this time through the eyes of Michael, who had just turned three.

As we made our way to the theater, childhood memories flooded back to me. As the eldest of three daughters, my father chose me to accompany him on a yearly father-daughter "date" to Radio City. I could still remember parts of the Christmas show and my delight in going to an expensive seafood restaurant after the show with my dad. I hoped that Michael would remember this day and look back on it fondly as he grew up.

Michael was excited just to stand in line to get into the five o'clock show. He rarely saw the city by evening and was mesmerized by the traffic, the bright Christmas lights, and the crowd of children and adults. He kept up a steady stream of excited chatter throughout our wait.

"Where's Santa?" he asked.

"Are all these people Santa's helpers?"

Michael charmed everyone in line and proudly introduced us to the people standing in front and in back of us. In the contagious party-like atmosphere, we waited outside in the cold without complaint.

We made the requisite stop for snacks and souvenirs before going to our seats in the second mezzanine, having spent nearly the down payment on a house for five-dollar candy, five-dollar sodas, ten-dollar programs, and wildly expensive holiday novelties. Michael chose a stuffed Rudolph the Red-Nosed Reindeer as his special companion to hold during the show. The main lobby fairly vibrated with excitement, as children and parents rushed around making purchases before finding their places.

Our group spanned almost six rows of seats, and we were a noisy, overstimulated bunch of theatergoers. As the lights went down, handsome men and beautiful women skated onstage on a revolving set. We *oohed* and *aahed*. The colors! The costumes! The beauty of the holiday season and the telling of the Christmas story unfolded beneath us on the stage. All the while, Michael's classmates busily slid down from their seats to visit friends and to point out items of interest to all. I seemed to spend as much time relocating toddlers as I did watching the show.

Michael's eyes shone with joy and excitement. Before this, he had visited only a department store Santa, which had both thrilled and terrified him at the same time. Now, as the dancers came onstage, he grew more and more excited and pointed out everything that he saw to us. He commented on the characters and asked if he could go downstairs and touch the snowmen. I explained to him that this show did not include audience participation, as *Sesame Street Live* did. Still, he kept up his steady stream of happy toddler chatter, oblivious to the muted *Shssshs* lovingly directed toward him. Thank goodness we were in a child-friendly atmosphere, where his excited exclamations blended in with those of other children.

As the Nativity scene rolled onstage, Michael's eyes widened to the size of saucers. He asked us to tell him who the characters were, and I explained that they were Mary, Joseph, and the baby Jesus, along with the Wise Men and his favorite live animals: horses, cows, goats, and sheep. The love between parents and child were evident to Michael, and I kept my explanation simple, using words and descriptive phrases he could understand.

As soon as the words "baby Jesus" had left my mouth, Michael unexpectedly jumped up in his seat and shouted, "I love baby cheeses! And Swiss cheeses! And Bonbel and American cheeses, too!"

(At the time, we carried string cheese along with us wherever we went. Some children had security blankets; Michael had his cheese.)

Immediately after he shouted the words, nearby rows of parents broke into hysterical laughter. The superb acoustics of the hall amplified Michael's comments, and his exuberant voice traveled all the way down to the stage, as if he had spoken into a microphone. You could say that he stopped the show, for we noticed that Mary's and Joseph's shoulders were also shaking with silent laughter.

When I explained to Michael that it was "Jesus," not "cheeses," he was a bit disappointed. However, he quickly recovered, and said that he "loved baby Jesus and baby cheeses, too." Word of Michael's outburst had gone from tier to tier, all the way downstage. The show was stopped for almost five minutes, to allow everyone to recover and go on with the festivities. It took us much longer to regain our composure and settle down to enjoy the rest of the performance. Once I had clarified Michael's mistake, he sat happily, chewing on his beloved cheese, offering some to baby Jesus. "He looks hungry, too."

How simple, and yet rich, are the wonders and joys of childhood. In trying to create a Christmas memory for Michael, I'd forgotten that sometimes the best memories are unscripted and unplanned. And little could I have known that my three-year-old would inadvertently create a joyous moment for me and a whole theater of people. What a delicious, unforgettable way to commemorate this holiday season!

—*Robin E. Woods*

 Pass It On

When I was about fourteen years old, my parents took me aside and hesitatingly told me I'd probably never go to college. As much as they wanted to provide tuition for my sister and me, it was out of the question due to my mother's heavy medical expenses. I looked at my mom's sad face and resolved never to bring up the subject again. Still, I had hope, and I carried it with me always, like a good-luck charm.

My father was a high school teacher and took extra jobs ushering at local ball games to pay for a few extras. Though Mom wasn't able to contribute to the family's income, she was a wizard at creating something special from little or nothing. She would take a few scraps of cloth here, adapt a pattern there, and sew up one-of-a-kind skirts and dresses for my sister and me. When we'd walk down the street in stylish outfits made just for us, it was hard to feel sorry for ourselves. Mom was so talented with various crafts that we never felt poor.

Still, when an older neighbor, Sharon, went off to college, a huge lump constricted my throat. I thought she was the luckiest person I knew. Seeing my strained expression, she suggested I look into scholarships, but when I did, I found out they usually paid for only a limited portion of tuition and expenses. My savings totaled $100, not even enough for one semester's books.

Soon, I was a junior in high school and busied myself babysitting for three different families. At a dollar an hour, the babysitting did little for my small bank account. College expenses seemed to increase each year by as much as I was able to put away. The fact that my father taught at my high school and helped students plan their college careers seemed especially cruel, but my mother's medical expenses were constant and my parents had vowed never to borrow money to meet them.

During my senior year whenever anyone asked about my college plans, I would break out in a sweat and mumble something about going to work instead. The empty words mirrored my feelings on the subject, but graduation seemed a long time away.

Near the end of the school year, my counselor called me to her office to ask about my post–high school plans. I fidgeted for a long time, then finally admitted there was little money for college and that getting a job seemed the only course of action. Then she asked me what type of job seemed likely. I stammered and stuttered as the realization hit me—hard—that I'd actually have to job-hunt in a few short weeks. When I lamented that I could barely type and had no experience, she said the only things I could do in an office were file and answer phones. She showed me the day's job listings; every single one of them required education or experience, or both—even for file clerks and receptionists!

She asked me what would I do if I had the resources to pursue anything I wanted. Without hesitation, Cornell University in New York popped out of my mouth. That's where my neighbor Sharon went, and her descriptions made the place seem idyllic, even if it was thousands of miles away on the other side of the country from my home state of California. In fact, every time Sharon came home, I could hardly wait to hear about her college life. In retrospect, I was probably a pest, but she never turned me down.

My counselor said that Cornell was far more than I could afford. Even with all my babysitting money, I had saved only about $500. She suggested a compromise: attend a local junior college at night and work part time as a waitress during the day. That was a far cry from Cornell! I immediately put the preposterous idea out of my mind. I wanted the whole college experience of living in dorms, walking around a huge campus loaded with history, and attending classes in classic buildings taught by astute professors. I left having resolved nothing, with no clear plan for work or college.

I stopped by Sharon's house that night and spoke with her mother, Mrs. Echeverra, really just wanting to hear some news about goings-on at Cornell. I told about the counselor's suggestion and moaned about my state of affairs. Mrs. Echeverra scolded me gently, saying I was better than someone who whined and complained, especially when my mom had done so much for me, often when she was ill. She was disappointed in me and told me so.

Mrs. Echeverra was someone we all admired. She was lovely and gracious, and, as I fully realized, she had looked out for my sister and me the many days my mom was sick.

She taught me how to make chili, vegetable soup, and from-scratch spaghetti sauce, things my mom couldn't do. She'd also loaned me books and through her example had shown me how to make a warm, welcoming home. I felt terrible that she'd witnessed me wallowing in self-pity. I realized I'd done that a lot lately.

The following week, I visited Mrs. Echeverra to apologize and to tell her I'd found a waitressing job and registered for classes at the local junior college. Mrs. Echeverra said that if I completed my work there, I could probably get a partial scholarship to transfer to a state college. The rest of my expenses could be paid by loans and working more in the summer. Then she mentioned a special scholarship and said she'd see to the details when the time came.

Over the next two years I learned how hard waitresses work. My feet burned, and I was often bone tired. No matter how badly I felt, I had to smile and be friendly, even when customers snapped at me. To get through my coursework faster, I attended school full-time during the day, rather than at night as the counselor had suggested, and worked out a system of waitressing during the odd hours between classes. It was tough, but I wasn't alone. Many other students at the junior college also worked; some of the other girls were also raising children.

After graduating from junior college, I applied to the local state college and arranged for loans. With Mrs. Echeverra's help, I also obtained the scholarship she'd told me about, which provided just enough to make up the difference between what I had and what I needed. It wasn't Cornell, but the teachers were enthusiastic. Sharon put the frosting on my cake when she mentioned that some of her classes were huge and it was hard to speak with a professor. Not at my school! The University of California at Bakersfield had relatively small class sizes, and we worked directly with the professors, never a teaching assistant. Deciding I could easily forgo dorms, I instead shared a small apartment with a roommate. The campuses' many squat temporary buildings and palm trees weren't as picturesque as the ancient oaks and ivy-covered architectural masterpieces I'd envisioned at Cornell. Instead of rolling hills of manicured grass and shrubbery, there was a lot of dirt. The state college was, after all, built in the middle of oil fields, but the place fit the city's history of oil exploration and farming, and it seemed right.

Due to my work schedule, it took three years to do two year's work, but in time I finished college, framed my degree, and went off into the world, settling in the Midwest. Several years later while visiting my family in Bakersfield, I went into the financial aid office at the college. I was making my last loan payment and wanted to do it in person. I handed the clerk my check, and she brought up my records on the computer. When she realized this was my last loan payment, she congratulated me. I mentioned the scholarship and said what a help it had been, but she looked puzzled and said there was no record of a scholarship.

There must be some mistake, I insisted and explained about the scholarship for teacher's children. She shook her head and said no such scholarship existed. I pressed her for details, but she was unable to provide any further information.

Mystified, I called the school the next day and spoke to another clerk. She, too, said I hadn't received a scholarship.

After some prodding, she finally revealed that someone had made payments to the school every semester I was there. She said the person asked to remain anonymous and that was all she could reveal. But I knew.

Mrs. Echeverra had moved, and no one seemed to know where she'd gone. I had to find her. My family asked around, and we finally tracked her down in a nursing home. She was one of the livelier residents and remembered me on sight. We talked about our families and what we had done since we'd last seen each other. She quizzed me on my cooking skills, and I said that whenever I made vegetable soup or chili, I always thought of her.

Finally, I told her what I knew and that there was no way I could ever thank her enough.

She beamed and assured me there was: "When you find someone deserving, pass along a little kindness. That's the best way to honor someone you love."

—Kathleen McNamara

My Jar of Self-Esteem

Karen and I met when our first children were both eight months old. She was a new member of the church in which my husband was a pastor. We soon discovered that we had a number of things in common: a particular favorite shade of blue, a passion for obscure hymns, similarly designed wedding bands, and a mutual faith. Both creative, I expressed myself best through music and Karen through art.

As a pastor's wife, I'm usually friendly with the people who attend the churches that my husband serves, but I usually don't form deep friendships with them. Another pastor's wife had even advised me not to pursue close friendships with parishioners. However, when I met Karen, I knew immediately that she saw me beyond my role in the church and that I could trust her.

Our instant bond strengthened as our lives continued to run parallel with one another's. Although completely unplanned, Karen's three children were born within two weeks of mine. Our friendship grew with our families, forged on barfy pregnancies, colicky babies, and early childhood illnesses. Our husbands both worked long hours, and so our daily phone calls became our mutual lifeline, a connection to reality filled with laughter and reassurances to one another that we would live through whatever challenges life presented us.

Just before the birth of our third child, my husband was transferred to another city. It was difficult to say good-bye to Karen, but we knew our friendship would continue somehow. Neither of us could afford daily long-distance phone calls, so at Karen's suggestion, we did "one-ringers." Every afternoon when the kids were down for their naps, I would make myself a cup of tea, call Karen, let it ring once, and hang up. Karen would have tea ready at her end, dial my number, let it ring once, and hang up. That way, even though we couldn't talk, we could still enjoy our tea together.

About that time, my middle child decided that she was never going to sleep again . . . ever. I had a four-year-old who wanted to play all day, a nineteen-month-old who wanted to scream all night, and a baby who wanted to eat constantly. I dreamt about sleep the way starving people dream about food. Sleep deprivation eroded how I viewed the world and myself. I couldn't think clearly. I couldn't have reasoned myself out of a damp paper bag. The left side of my face twitched for two years.

Karen couldn't offer me sleep or a helping hand with my children, but she helped adjust my perspective and lift my spirits with two thoughtful gifts. The first came in the mail: a pretty flowered mug filled with my favorite tea. On the wrapper of each tea bag, she had written a different verse that I was to find in my Bible and read while we had our tea times together. My dear friend couldn't be there to talk with me across the table, but those verses of hope and encouragement spoke for her and meant even more to me than they'd meant before.

A few months later, when Karen's husband was in town on business, he brought me another package, a special gift he said Karen had been working on for a long time. It was a beautifully decorated ceramic quart container with a label in Karen's handwriting that read, "Sig's Jar of Self-Esteem. Use as necessary," with a prescription to apply whenever I doubted myself or felt lonely. The jar was packed with slips of fancy pale blue paper, rolled into capsule-sized scrolls, each containing a message just for me. There were dozens of them.

> *God smiled at me when He sent me a special gift named Sig.*
> *I treasure your friendship.*
> *I'd love to live within 100 feet of your kitchen.*
> *You are raising kids that will be well-equipped for life.*
> *You have the gift of hospitality.*
> *I appreciate your consistency.*
> *You are the person I would most like to be stranded in a mall with, provided it had a daycare and a German coffee shop.*
> *I really believe you could do anything you wanted.*
> *You challenge me to be the best me. Thanks.*

In beautiful calligraphy, each little blue "pill" reminded me that I was special, that I had gifts to offer, and that I was loved. I laughed and cried as I read the notes. The first night, I almost overdosed on them. The jar found its way to the kitchen, where I could reach for it just before my face started to twitch.

Fifteen years later, my jar of self-esteem still has a special place in my heart and in my kitchen. I don't use it as often as I used to; apparently the magical potion of friendship helped to rebuild my self-esteem. The twitching returns only when I don't get enough rest, which is quickly rectified by a dip into my jar of self-esteem.

I now work full time, so we no longer do the one-ringers, but we can now afford the occasional phone call. She and her family visited our home recently, and over steaming cups of tea we discussed, among many other things, the future. We called our teenaged children into the room and asked them to please promise us that, when Karen and I can no longer make decisions for ourselves, they will place us in the same nursing home. They agreed. It dawned on us afterward that we hadn't planned for our husbands, who are also friends, to join us. We decided that they could come, too.

—*Sigrid Stark*

 Incidental Kin

Whenever he bleeds now, it is my blood he sheds. On mornings when I am especially rushed, I often mishandle the razor while shaving my legs in the shower. While the water rinses the wound, I imagine that he might be shaving his face, untold miles away. Perhaps he, too, has inadvertently nicked himself; the blood coloring the tissue he uses to stanch the flow is the same blood that streams down my shower drain. Even the most expert pathologist could not detect a difference, because no difference exists.

He bleeds my blood because of simple chance, the exquisitely random circumstance of gene variety and selection. He needed a bone marrow transplant, and I, a stranger to him, proved a perfect match.

I am curious about him, but rules made to ensure privacy and for the protection of both parties prevent me from knowing anything other than his gender (male) and his age group (young adult). The odds that he would find a suitable blood match were one in 20,000. I ask myself: What are the odds that I might find him revolting? What if we differ in political views or moral philosophies? What plans does he have for the rest of his life? What, I wonder, has he cherished, vowed, hoped, forgiven?

Because he could be anyone, he becomes, instead, the nameless, faceless everyone.

One month before the scheduled donation date, I went to the transplant center to give additional blood and urine samples to confirm my physical well-being. As I returned to my car, two little girls, perhaps three and four years old, exited the elevators of the parking garage, followed by a man of indeterminate age. Although taller than I, he appeared to weigh much less, and he carried his wasted frame carefully. He slowly made his way to his truck and with obvious effort, boosted both girls, slight as flowers, into it.

I sat in my car, watching him, wondering if he could be the one who would receive my marrow. I knew the odds were against it: On any given day, 3,000 potential recipients wait for a donor.

Soon afterward, I learned that my recipient had commenced chemotherapy to destroy his own marrow and make room for mine and to suppress his immune system so it would be optimally receptive to the new cells. Once this process has begun, there is no going back. Either the patient receives new marrow, or he dies.

The marrow aspiration took place on a cool fall morning two weeks past my thirtieth birthday. The hospital staff was courteous and efficient. I was given an epidural and put to sleep. The surgery lasted forty minutes; later, I learned that the doctors worried whether in the quickness of the procedure they had removed more liquid than cells. Postsurgical tests run on the marrow, however, showed a high cell count.

I woke up after the surgery a bit woozy, the second of two autologous blood units dripping into my vein. For me, the intravenous fluids represented little: hastened recovery, renewed energy. But in a place not far from where I lay, another intravenous tube transferred my marrow into the recipient's bloodstream, from which the cells would instinctively find their way into his bones. For him, these roughly two pints of spongy, red material represented nothing less than his future.

I've always considered myself to be an optimist, yet I could not fathom the tremendous amount of hope contained in those bags. No, not hope—something beyond hope. The substance in those bags was pure prayer: earnest, liquefied prayer.

The anesthesia left me nauseous for about twenty-four hours, but I experienced no major complications. I was back to work in three days and resumed light exercise in two weeks. I impatiently awaited news of the recipient.

Once in a while someone asks me why I donated bone marrow to a person I knew nothing about. I usually reply that it's he who has done the amazing, by risking his life in order to save it and by having such faith in a complete stranger. It's an easy, stock answer, and one that seems to satisfy most. But even I know it doesn't begin to explain the reason why.

A few years ago, my father's eldest brother fell ill with cirrhosis of the liver. He immediately quit drinking, but the damage had been done. By the time he started throwing up blood, all the late-arriving assistance we could summon was just that: too late.

When I went to visit him in the facility where he was being cared for, I was shocked to find him shrunken almost beyond recognition. He gave no indication that he even knew I was there. He seemed thirsty, and I gave him some water, but his teeth chattered as if he was chilled by a coldness that ran inside-out, far beyond the reach of any earthly relief.

My uncle was dying and with him would go my father's last remaining sibling from a family of five children. Feeling both inept and irrelevant, I kept my visit short. Upon hearing of his death a few days later, I immediately regretted what I had been given the opportunity to do, but had not. I wished that I had climbed onto his bed, placed his head in my lap, and stroked his forehead until his teeth stopped chattering and he fell asleep.

This is what I wished, and I wish it now as I wished it then, without hope, in the truly forsaken manner that I will continue to wish it for the rest of my life. It is this fervent, hopeless wish, and the cold undercurrent of shame that still flows strong and black beneath it, that serve to remind me that I am not noble. On the contrary: I owe, I am in debt.

Three weeks after my aspiration, I receive word that the recipient is doing well and the marrow is engrafting onto his bones. The impossible has happened: Someone whom I've never met shares my personal—yet no longer individual—genetic typing and is closer to me, in some respects, than a blood relative. I think of the person whose veins now carry my blood and of the 3,000 others who today need a donor. Some of them will not last the day, having run out of time. May a kind hand stay and soothe them to sleep.

—*Brenda Fritsvold*

The Last, Best Gift

It was my twelfth Christmas and school had finally let out for the holidays. The kids on the bus were bouncing and laughing, showing off trinkets from class parties. When we got off at our stop, though, all joy drove away with our schoolmates, leaving us in a cloud of smelly exhaust on the long, empty road. We turned toward home to walk in single-file silence: five skinny, blond-haired, blue-eyed, look-alike kids.

Bits of wood flicked as Roddy, the oldest, whittled away at a little wooden warplane. Len, the youngest, stretched his stride to match Roddy's footprints. I watched Len's sodden shoelaces, flapping and frayed. Our sisters, Lis and Ellie, lagged behind as we slogged through the slush to face our first Christmas without Dad.

It was 1946. My friend, Quinn's, dad had died in the war, and the ladies' society had brought special things for his family's Christmas. But not our dad, and not for our family.

In a way, though, it was the end of the war that killed him. He lost his job as custodian when the Baxter Army Hospital closed. After that, between his carpentry and our little go-broke farm, Mom said he just worked too hard and worried too much. We'd all stood there after the ambulance drove away, watching the snow whip across the porch light, feeling as bleak and hollow as that endless January night.

Then our own little war began.

Survival.

Come spring, Mom sold the farm and we moved to five acres and an old one-room schoolhouse. We slept in an army tent, worked on neighboring farms, and spent every spare hour adding a kitchen and two bedrooms to the building.

Now the lights of our little house beckoned in the early dusk of Washington winter.

As we threw open the door and stomped the slush from our feet, Mom called, "There's a surprise when your chores are done."

Coming back from milking I saw it, propped behind the house—the most enormous Christmas tree ever.

We didn't question how it got there. Roddy and I wrestled it through the door. Its sharp fragrance penetrated our lungs as we nailed boards on and stood it up. Mom quietly fingered its deep green needles, which glistened from the melt of light fallen snow. Our eyes feasted on it. Its spike scraped the ceiling, and the branches almost blocked the doors to the bedrooms. Best of all, it crowded out the gloom that had followed us home.

Len ran in circles, whooping with delight.

Ellie begged, "Can we decorate tonight?"

Mom nodded. "If you can find the ornaments."

Ellie grabbed her coat from the school hooks by the door and dashed out with the flashlight, Len close behind.

"Try the big shed," Mom called. "And tie those shoes, Len."

The old farmhouse had been double the size of this little place, and we hadn't gotten rid of a thing. The two sheds and the old tent were pretty jam-packed, and the house, with its abundance of cubbyholes, was crammed. Everything was there, somewhere, but we could never find what we wanted when we needed it. Except for Dad's old carpentry tools, which I'd carefully oiled and hung in the smaller shed. I had a few tools of my own, one of which I'd found on the road last summer—a beautiful screwdriver with an oversized handle of inlaid wood. Dad would have liked it.

His tools were just about all he'd left to us. Those, and three end-rolls of paper he'd brought home way back when he was custodian at Sunset McKey Salesbook Company. Dad was supposed to toss them into the furnace to heat the building, but he just couldn't see burning a thing before its best use was realized.

They stood propped in the corner of the living room, two rolls of tissue paper and one heavier, good enough to draw on. I think that, until that moment, we'd been saving them, as if holding on to a piece of Dad himself.

Lis dragged out the heavy one. "Let's make a banner, Rich."

We cut a piece from the roll and smoothed it across the floor. As Lis poked through the stubs, she asked Mom, "Did you finish your Christmas sweater?"

"Mm-hmm." Mom smiled as she rocked and nodded.

Somebody had given her the yarn, and she'd been knitting every night for a month. We kids tried not to bicker and helped each other with homework, so as not to interrupt her. With Mom's new job on top of everything else, that Christmas sweater was the first thing she'd done just for herself since Dad had died.

Roddy joined the little kids in hunting for the decorations, and then we unpacked our memories—the tin carousel that turned in the heat of its candles, the old glass ornaments from Norway, the wooden crèche Dad had carved for us kids to paint, faded paper Santas from each child's kindergarten, and miles of crinkled tinsel and tangled lights.

It was the next day, Christmas Eve, before the last piece of tinsel went on. We fed more wood to the shiny porcelain Heat-a-lator, and the room took on a glow all its own.

"Let's eat supper by the tree," Lis suggested.

"Like a picnic!" Ellie chimed in.

And we did. Hot dogs, macaroni, and green beans. With hard-boiled eggs from our own chickens, milk from our own cow, and ginger cookies we had all helped drizzle sugar frosting on.

It took forever for me to fall asleep. Roddy, next to me, didn't move a muscle after pulling up the quilts, but I could tell by his breathing that he was awake, too. Len rearranged the covers several times, but none of us spoke. Away from the warmth of the big room, the cold emptiness of Dad's absence enveloped us. He should have been tucking us in and closing the door with his traditional Christmas admonition, "You stay out of Santa's way, now. And no peeking!"

Nobody had even mentioned hanging stockings. We all knew Mom could afford only one small present for each of us. We all knew. But we weren't prepared for just how small that pile of presents would appear under that great huge tree when we crept out of our bedrooms in the morning.

The puddle under Mom's boots told us she'd already done our chores.

Ellie, Lis, Len, and I all scrunched on the couch and sat straight as pokers with our hands folded. The bentwood rocker creaked as Mom lowered herself into it. She pulled the hem of Dad's old blue corduroy robe around her ankles. I thought I saw tears in her eyes, but I wasn't sure.

"I'll stoke the fire again," Roddy said.

I think he was more intent on prolonging the gift opening than warming the room.

We all waited, trying not to stare at the base of the tree. I wished we kids hadn't drawn names.

Len's feet began to bounce in impatience. "Let Rich open my present first," he said, as Roddy took his place in the olive green overstuffed chair. Dad's chair.

Everybody said Len looked the most like Dad, but Roddy turned to Len with Dad's eyes and Dad's tone. "Hold your horses, sonny."

Dad had always started at the bottom of the pile so the first gift would be a surprise. But this pile was a single layer, so Roddy did the next best thing. He stirred them around with his hand to choose the first at random.

"Let's see here . . ." He turned the tag to read it.

For each gift, he stirred and drew, and slowly read the tag. But no matter how he tried to make it last, those presents were opened in no time at all, and we sat, each with two gifts in our hands. I held a paper ornament Len had made at school and a little pickup truck, real metal, with a red cab and a green box.

Lis got up first. She placed her gifts on her spot—"Don't anybody sit on these"—and knelt to look under the couch.

Her bathrobe sleeve jammed way up as she stretched her arm underneath.

I couldn't tell what she pulled out, even though she was mere feet from me.

Ellie, who had a better view, got a funny look on her face. Then she, too, scooted off the cushion and left her presents behind to dig through the pile of mittens by the hooks. Then Lis hauled one of Dad's old tissue paper rolls into the girls' room.

Suddenly—it must have been magic, because I don't know how we knew—we were all looking for things, under furniture, behind boxes, and in cubbyholes, secreting what we found into the pockets and folds of our robes.

The second giant roll of tissue paper went to our bedroom, and scissors and tape were passed back and forth as we hid what we were wrapping from the others. With new gifts piled under the tree, we took our places again, not quite so poker-straight this time, and Roddy handed them around.

I unwrapped my long-lost penny whistle. Ellie hugged her missing baby doll. Mom had a matched pair of gloves again. We kept it up all morning.

We got dressed and searched the tent and shed, finding things, wrapping them, ripping them open again. We threw the paper every which way, bounced lost balls, tried on missing hats, played jacks. We got sillier and sillier.

We even sneaked into each other's drawers and wrapped things that hadn't been lost at all. Somewhere in there, Mom put cranberries on to boil and a chicken in the oven.

The aroma rose, filling the house. So did the mountain of crumpled tissue paper. We had to wade through it to get to the kitchen when she called us to eat, while the last set of gifts waited under the tree.

After dinner, I'd never felt so full. Not just of food, but of fun, of pure joy—and anticipation. I could hardly wait for the others to open what I had for them.

This last pile had more gifts than all the others. Roddy drew the nearest first and handed it to me. It was small but heavy. The scrawl read, "To Rich from Roddy."

My heart quickened, but I opened it slowly.

"Your best knife," I whispered. I was afraid I might cry.

The most magnificent magic had just begun, for this time we had each sought gifts for the others from among our own treasures. My heart about burst watching Roddy open my screwdriver with the inlaid handle. Lis and Ellie ended up with each other's favorite dolls. I don't remember it all, but Len got two from everybody, because we each gave him our shoelaces.

As we sat amidst our bounty, eating Baby Jesus' birthday cake, Lis asked, "Why aren't you wearing your new sweater, Mom, your new Christmas sweater?"

Mom's eyes sparkled as she raised her eyebrows and said, "Maybe we're all wearing it. Maybe the whole room is wearing it." She rocked back and forth in the old bentwood rocker, her face glowing in the light of the splendid tree.

Roddy's jaw dropped; you could hear him suck in his breath.

"What?" said Lis.

"She traded it," Roddy said quietly, "for the tree."

All eyes turned to Mom.

"I couldn't have done it without all of you," Mom said. "Don't you remember being extra good so that I could finish on time?"

This time she didn't stop the tears in her eyes as we gathered around, hugging her all at once. And Dad was right there with us. In Len's face and Roddy's eyes, in the old blue robe, in the traditions and ornaments . . . and in that grand mound of tissue paper that had wrapped our Christmas and taught us the best use of things.

We hugged Mom until her chair almost rocked right over. Then we jumped and played in the paper like a pile of leaves. Finally, handfuls at a time, we wadded it up tight and tossed it into the shiny porcelain heater, watching the flames and feeling the warmth, one wad at a time, until they were gone.

It was my father's last, best gift.

—*Kathryn O. Umbarger, as told by Richard J. Olsen*

Love Lessons

I tiptoed to the kitchen and placed my ear against the door. Inside, I heard a deep voice and then laughter.

My mother had a male visitor! Who was it? The only other male visitors to our home had been family—grandpas, uncles, and cousins. My curiosity finally got the best of me, and I peaked around the corner and stared in awe. Sitting at our kitchen table was a dapper gentleman wearing an Army uniform adorned with rows of medals pinned across the chest. His dark wavy hair brushed back from his smooth forehead above two flashing brown eyes. It was his dazzling smile and beautiful white teeth that really sent me spinning. He was the most handsome man I'd ever seen. And the minute I saw him, a gap-toothed smile spread across my face.

My mother was a young widow then with three small children. My sister was ten, my brother four. I was six, and I missed having a daddy. Our father had been killed in a car accident. After a while, I realized he wasn't coming back from heaven, but in my childlike faith, I figured that since God had taken away my father, He could send me another one. So, I prayed and prayed for a new daddy, never doubting that God would hear my prayers and send one to me. Peering into the kitchen at the dashing soldier with the dancing eyes and brilliant smile, I knew he was the one.

"Thank you, Lord! Hallelujah!" I said, imitating Sister Riley. Then I marched right into that kitchen.

"Hi! I'm Patty. What's your name?"

"George," he said, flashing his pearly whites at me.

"Are you a hero?"

"No." There was that smile again.

"Then why do you have all those medals?"

"I've just come back from a war, and they gave me these for good conduct."

Looking toward Mom, who was making coffee, I asked, "Don't you think my mother is pretty?"

"Patty!" Mom scolded, her face turning crimson as she glanced at George. "Go outside and check on Benny."

George leaned forward and whispered to me, "Yes, I do. I'll see you later, Patty. I think we're going to be good friends."

George started calling on Mom more often. I don't think they went on many dates, and when he came to the house to see her, Mom had to share him with me. I would wait anxiously for my new friend to arrive and then rush to him with so many questions and things to say. He always seemed happy to see me and never grew tired or impatient with my endless questions. He played games with my brother, sister, and me, and when it came time for us to go to bed, I would refuse to go until George read me a story. Most of the time, he'd nod off in his chair after I'd pretended to be asleep.

In spite of me, Mom and George decided to get married.

I was so hurt when they didn't take me along on their honeymoon. I couldn't understand how George could leave such a good friend as me behind. But I was thrilled the day they returned, knowing my favorite friend would now be living with us.

After the wedding, we all moved to a farm. I loved animals, and it was a dream-come-true for me. For George, who'd never been married before, coming out of World War II and into a ready-made family took some adjusting. One evening was especially bad. Benny was throwing a temper tantrum on the kitchen floor. Annie was complaining loudly and clearly that it was not her place to take care of that spoiled brat. While showing off trying to help Mom, I had spilled a whole crock of buttermilk. Our dog, Freddie, in his hurry to lap up the milk, skidded across the floor and bumped into me, making me drop and break the crock, which had been in Mom's family for ages. George stood there with a dazed look on his face and muttered, "I must have been in shell shock to marry a woman with three kids."

Mom fled to their bedroom in tears, and George walked out the back door.

I hurried out to the porch. "I'm sorry. I'll be more careful next time. Please don't leave!"

He picked me up, and gently wiping my tears, he said, "We're the best of friends, right?" I nodded. "Well, friends never desert the people they love. Don't you worry, I'll always be here." Then he went in to console Mom.

It didn't take long before we three children started calling George "Pop." He approved of the name.

"You kids had a wonderful daddy, and I would never try to take his place. I'll make my own place."

And he did.

Pop made a point of taking us to visit with our dad's parents often. "I'm sure it eases their pain to see you children," he would tell us. Bringing comfort to my grandparents also made me feel better and needed. They, in turn, grew to love George as much as we did.

Pop didn't send us to church—he took us. I insisted on sitting by Pop and sharing a songbook. I loved to sing, even though I couldn't carry a tune, and I'd belt out the hymns at the top of my lungs. Pop said he didn't mind, but then, he couldn't carry a tune either. Sometimes, if the preacher was extra long-winded, I would fall asleep with my head on Pop's arm. Mom would scold that, just because I went to sleep didn't mean Pop could, too, to which he'd reply that he was just keeping his friend company.

Pop also taught us the meaning of work. He encouraged us to do a good job regardless of what the task was, and living on a farm, there were plenty of tasks to do. Pop never made us work—he worked with us, and made it a fun and educational experience.

Once I climbed up on top of the chicken house, thrilled at my daring and how far I could see. I ran across the roof, which made the chickens squawk. When I climbed down, there was Benny.

"I'm going to tell Pop! You're going to get in trouble!"

"You're a brat!" I yelled.

When Pop came home from town, Benny was waiting, and sure enough, he ratted on me.

"It's not nice to tattletale," Pop scolded Benny, much to my surprise. "Friends never tattle on each other."

"She's not my friend! She's my sister!" Benny yelled.

"Well, you're no friend of mine either!" I yelled back.

"If you can't be a friend with your brother or sister, how do you expect to be friends with anyone else? I want you two to treat each other as though you're best friends." He made us shake on it.

It wasn't easy to keep that promise. But to this day I count my sister and brother as two of my best friends.

On one trip to town with Mom and Pop, I asked for a pair of fancy boots. They had sold some livestock, and I knew they had some money.

"I'm sorry, Patty, but this money isn't mine to use as I please. Your mother and I have some debts to pay. When you owe someone money, the money in your pocket isn't yours. It belongs to the people you owe money to."

To this day, I make sure to pay all my debts before I spend money foolishly.

Pop always told us that friends don't tell each other's secrets or discuss one another's problems with other folks. We knew that we could tell Pop anything and that he would hold it in his confidence. We did, and he did. Pop was easy to talk with, and our talks always helped, because he was a patient, careful listener. I've tried to be a good listener in turn.

Pop was upset on my wedding day. He worried that my fiancé and I weren't good enough friends. "Love is good, but you need friendship in a marriage," he said. He was right. The marriage didn't last. When I married the second time, I was certain that my husband and I not only loved each other, but that we were also best friends.

Over the years, Pop has always been there for me, through many ups and downs. Whenever I've tried to thank him, he just smiles that marvelous smile and says, "That's what friends are for."

Pop is in his eighties now. I still go to him with my problems, including when we lost my beloved mother ten years ago. He's as good a listener and teacher as ever. His lessons in friendship are being passed along to my children. Recently, when he was honored at a veterans' hall of fame in our hometown, I found out that he was quite the war hero after all. He'd been through the invasion of Normandy, the Battle of the Bulge, and all over Europe.

Another gentleman at the awards ceremony asked if George was my father.

"Yes, sir," I said. "He is my Pop and my best friend."

—Pat Curtis

A Little Child
Shall Lead Them

I had just opened my classroom door to the balmy spring afternoon when a woman entered and surveyed the bustling crowd of kindergarten children, my aide, and several volunteer mothers.

"Who's the teacher?" she asked.

I glanced around the room. Debbie was tying her classmate Leonard's shoelaces. "Now, watch so you can do it, too," she directed in her high-pitched voice.

"The teacher?" I said, smiling. "Oh, today it seems to be Debbie."

In the years I was surrounded by children in their first year of public school, they often amazed me with their innocent wisdom and unself-conscious interaction. I learned much from these "teachers"—five years old and three feet tall.

Of all my students, Jason, Bethanne, and Tahn stand out most in my memory. Tahn, a refugee from Vietnam, joined my class one February. Like many children in that mostly Asian neighborhood, he started his school experience with little knowledge of English.

On the first day I handed out boxes of large Crayola crayons. Tahn splayed his out on his work space and tested each color on his sheet of newsprint. Then, with a grin of confidence, he picked up a crayon and drew a tree trunk. Within five minutes, he had drawn a tree, a strip of sky, and a smiling boy with black spiky hair.

When I looked down to admire his work, he picked up two blue crayons and gave me a quizzical look. He pointed to the purple crayon in another child's hand, then back to his box. No purple. I explained that we were sometimes sloppy about the crayons and they ended up in the wrong boxes. I spoke English at my normal speed and in my usual tone of voice, knowing that my words would make no sense to him.

Yet, he understood. He got up with a blue crayon and walked around the room inspecting boxes. When he found one without blue, he dropped it in, then extracted an extra red and searched for a box without red. He repeated this process with amazing efficiency. By the time others had finished their pictures, each box contained the correct eight colors. In a few minutes, Tahn had completed a task that usually took an aide a half hour.

Tahn breezed through all his activities quickly, then looked around the room to find something that needed organizing, cleaning up, or rearranging. With art projects, he finished first, always. He would go to a child who was having difficulty applying papier-mâché, getting two pieces of clay to stick together, or cutting along lines on a piece of paper. At first, I wondered if he would take the experience away from the other child, but I soon found that he acted like a coach, showing the other child how to do the task.

That spring, I collected plastic berry baskets and taught the class how to weave rug yarn through the holes. As usual, Tahn finished first and then helped others. Meanwhile, I picked up almost-finished baskets and tucked in the last bits of yarn. I continued this process while my aide took the children to recess. A little head emerged near my hands. Tahn watched while I repaired a particularly pathetic basket.

"Tahn, you didn't go outside with everybody else."

I did not know whether he actually understood my words or just the essence of their meaning, but he answered, "I watch."

I overturned the basket and maneuvered the last bit of yarn into place. I plopped it in front of Tahn. "There!"

He rewarded me a wide, impish grin and said, "Veddy gooot, Teacha!"

The year Bethanne showed up, I had been blessed with a small class. It enabled me to give individual time to each child, and no one needed it more than Bethanne.

Not that I could teach her much of a cognitive nature. She had no language skills—neither English nor her native Philippine Ilicano dialect. A seven-year-old weighing 130 pounds, she communicated with grunts, couldn't hold a pencil or a crayon, and pawed through books with little control of her hands. Her parents had been afraid to bring her to school.

But she could hug. She would throw her arms around me and look into my face, beaming. She embraced her much-smaller classmates, too, but always with gentleness.

We often sat on the floor in a circle, which was hard for Bethanne, but she managed to plop down, turn around, and with her hands on the floor, hoist herself back up again. When she was seated, children scrambled to sit next to her, leaning up against her comforting bulk while she sat passively, a faint smile on her face.

The other children tried to teach her to talk. I remember Jamilla sitting with her, an open book on Bethanne's lap. "This is a sheep, Bethanne. Say 'sheep.'" Bethanne only smiled.

Once, while taking the class to the gym, we passed a group of older children. "Hey, look, there goes that big, fat kindergarten girl," someone yelled, and his classmates laughed.

The kindergartners did not. When we got back to the classroom, Douglas said, "Those big kids made fun of Bethanne." Others nodded solemnly.

The school counselor and nurse arranged testing by a medical team, and we were told what Bethanne's parents had been afraid to find out. Bethanne's mental capacity was so limited and her physical size so unmanageable that she probably would not live into adulthood. She would never be able to care for herself beyond the most basic functions.

I realized that I did not have the skills to give her what she needed—except for the loving environment that she experienced with the children in our wonderful little group. But she needed more. She was placed in a special education class at another school, and I hoped it was for the best. Several weeks later at a meeting, I met the aide from her new class.

"Are you the person who sent us that obese girl who wants to hug everybody all the time?" he asked me.

"You mean Bethanne?" I said. "That's how she communicates. She needs to love, and hugging is the only way she can express it."

"Well, let me tell you what that loving lump did." His sarcasm was acid. "She escaped the classroom a week or so ago, went into the parking lot, and snapped the antennas off all the faculty cars."

I tried to imagine her rage. *At her new class? At me, for abandoning her?* I felt sick.

I swallowed, forcing myself to control my anguish and anger. "What do you plan to do about her?" I asked.

He told me that the school was working on a placement at the experimental school on the University of Washington campus. A few weeks later, Bethanne was transferred to one of the best places for mentally disabled children in the country.

Another year, when I greeted my kindergartners at the classroom door after Christmas break, I noticed that many children were wearing new jackets, hats, mittens, and backpacks, obviously Christmas bounty. During our opening circle, we admired each other's newly acquired possessions: clothes, a pair of shoelaces, socks, a barrette, a haircut. I showed them my new watch. One pair of items stood out among the new treasures: Jason's sparkling silver sneakers. We observed the look of joy on Jason's brown face.

"Hightops," he told us proudly. "And purdy soles." He lifted one foot with his hand and pivoted his leg for all to see the pattern of colored lines and circles on the bottoms of the new shoes.

For recess, the children took out balls, jump ropes, and chalk. I watched them fan out in their habitual directions, each group finding its own area on the playground. Jason and the usual cluster of runners lined up at the edge of the schoolyard: taut, expectant, eager.

"Ready, set, go!" they yelled.

I watched them take off. Five boys and two girls sprinted away from the starting line, Gary in the lead. Gary, who always took off on the word "set," usually arrived first at the edge of the concrete and tumbled, panting, onto the grass before the others joined him, laughing, piled into a disorganized heap. Winning was important to Gary because his older brothers played hockey and he understood competition. The rest of the small runners, Jason included, were content just to feel the power of their bodies sprinting through space. I never intervened. Soon enough, in a year or two, they would learn about being the first, the best, the strongest, and playing by the rules.

But this was a special day for Jason. I watched him take off on "go," and his obvious excitement propelled him faster than usual. His new shoes gleamed like hubcaps in the sunlight, a blur of speed. He left the others far behind, caught up with Gary, and reached the grassy finish line well ahead of the veteran winner.

"Oh, man," I heard Gary complain. "It's those shoes, Jason. No fair!"

Jason ran up to me, chest heaving. I looked down at his excited face.

"You were great, Jason!" I said. "How did that feel?"

"It's my sneakers," he gasped. "They're really fast. I can go like the wind now! My Grandpa told me I'm gonna be an Olympic star, just like Jesse Owen!"

In the following days and weeks, I watched Jason live up to his belief about the shoes. He not only ran the races, he ran everywhere, and I enjoyed seeing his skill, speed, and agility improve daily.

That spring, a new student joined our class. From the moment he entered, the other children were agog with excitement. Tanned by the Hawaiian sun of his former home, fully a head taller than most of his new classmates, Samuel exuded confidence and maturity far beyond his years. At recess, each group vied for his participation, but he chose to join the runners.

"Ready, set, go," the sprinters yelled.

Gary left at "set," Jason at "go." Samuel hesitated, but only briefly, before catching on. He sped away and overtook the two in the lead. The new boy was beauty, grace, and speed in motion. His muscled, sun-browned body and gleaming honey-blond hair reminded me of the Greek messenger god, Mercury. I watched as he ran far past the indefinite finish line and to the end of the playground.

Poor Jason, I thought, dismayed. He had slowed down and then actually stopped to watch Samuel. His mouth hung open, but only for a few seconds. As Samuel walked back toward the others, who now lay sprawled on the grass, I watched in amazement as Jason approached him and, extending his hand, pumped Samuel's hand vigorously.

Jason trotted back to me, his eyes shining with excitement. "Did you see that new boy, Samuel?" he asked.

"Yes, I did," I replied. "He's pretty good, isn't he?"

"He runs so fast," Jason panted. "He runs just like the wind! He's gonna be an Olympic star someday!"

I hunkered down and hugged Jason, my eyes welling up with tears, and I thought, *Someday, Jason, when I grow up, I want to be just like you.*

"Maybe so," I told him. "But I know you'll be a star, for sure. You have enthusiasm and a generous heart."

"Yeah." Jason grinned. "And silver sneakers."

For nine years, I nurtured my kindergarten students, rewarded cooperation and creative expression, and planted the academic skills needed to launch them into the first grade. But often the teaching flowed both ways. Many times, I felt more like student than teacher, learning from such role models as Tahn, the organizer and friendly coach, affectionate Bethanne's compassionate classmates, and Jason of the generous heart.

—Annemarieke Tazelaar

A Long Way from Anywhere

The seven-year-old girl sat quietly on the concrete steps of the old, gray apartment complex, waiting for her mommy and daddy to come down with the last few items that would fit into their dilapidated, old Ford. She wrapped her torn and stained blue blanket around her chubby shoulders and cuddled her handmade clown doll to her chest. Taking a deep breath, she blew out a resigned sigh and watched her warm breath turn to crystal as it touched the early-morning air.

Here we go again, she thought. *Another trip to who knows where.*

Her bright blue eyes grew dark as her parents hurried down the stairs with only a few items between them.

"Where is Mr. Fuzzy Teddy?" she asked.

Without a word, Mommy gently ushered the little girl into the backseat of the car. The child sat with her arms crossed. She knew another toy was being left behind because there "wasn't room" for it. She had heard the line so many times she wondered why she still asked. The last time they'd moved, her favorite doll had been left behind. The time before that, it was her Appaloosa rocking horse. The time before that, her four-foot-long, green stuffed snake with the rainbow-colored spots.

Each time something was left behind, if felt like a piece of her heart had been sliced off with a big sharp carving knife. Since she was an only child and had no friends, her toys were her companions. To lose them was heart wrenching, but she suffered in silence. If she said anything, Daddy would just feel bad and go even more quiet than normal. His cold shoulder was harder to take than the breaking of her heart.

As they drove away, a salty tear rolled down her plump, pink cheek as she watched the red and green lights flash by her window. It was Christmas Eve, and they were on the road again. She really thought that this year they were going to have a "real" Christmas. Mommy and she had put up a tiny, scrawny tree they'd found out in the field. She had helped decorate it with popcorn and paper stars. They had even placed a teeny straw baby Jesus on one of the branches.

Now, they were driving away from the promise of Christmas. She wasn't sure where they were going, only that they were heading in the direction of California. They always headed to California when the money was running out. Daddy had a sister there who always let him "borrow" money and let them stay with her a few days until Daddy could "get back on his feet."

As the blustery day wore on, the little girl played in the backseat with her blanket, handmade clown doll, and a bright green plastic jump rope with missing handles. Sitting on the edge of the Ford's tattered bench seat, she'd drop the rope down a rust hole in the floor right beneath her feet. With a little help from her fingers, she had made the hole big enough so that she could watch the rope dance and jerk as its end hit the road flashing by. It kept her quiet for hours.

As day rolled into stormy night, her stomach tied into a tighter and tighter knot. Christmas would be there in no time, and they had no tree, no fireplace, and no place to stay so Santa could find her. Yet, she remained silent. Words were of no help when Daddy was involved.

As night fell, they pulled into a small, well-used truck stop diner for dinner. They ordered two of the "specials," which, in honor of the holiday, consisted of sliced turkey, dressing, and mashed potatoes and gravy. Everything tasted so good to her. She even got to share a piece of pumpkin pie with Mommy and Daddy. Maybe Christmas Eve on the road wasn't so bad after all. At least they were together.

It was late by the time they'd finished dinner, washed up in the bathroom, and hit the road again. The tired child lay down on the backseat, curled up under her thin blue blanket, and imagined the Christmas they would have next year. She pictured a big home with enough rooms so that everyone had their own special place. She saw a big Christmas tree sparkling with hundreds of green, yellow, red, and blue lights. Silver tinsel hung from every branch. Popcorn and paper chains encircled its limbs. Under the tree sat dozens of brightly colored packages, many with her name on them. In her mind she opened the biggest package and out popped a three-foot panda bear. She fell asleep with a smile on her face and a tear on her cheek.

Morning seemed to come early, and they were still driving. When she woke up, she felt the chill of the icy outside air as it poured in from the hole in the floor and the leaky windows. She wrapped the blanket closer around her shoulders, sat up, and crossed her legs under her to keep her feet warm. After yawning and wiping the sleep from her eyes, she turned to look out the window.

There by her side lay a little, bald baby doll wrapped in a pink blanket, a brand-new Mickey Mouse coloring book, and a fresh box of eight Crayola crayons. She picked up the toys without a word and just stared at them for a while.

"Mommy," she finally said in a whisper.

"Yes," her mom whispered back.

"Where did these toys come from?"

"Santa brought them," she said.

"But how?"

"Santa always finds good little girls and boys, even when they're a long way from anywhere."

The little girl sat back in the seat and played quietly for hours with her new toys.

That little girl was me, and I found out many years later that my mom and dad had stopped at a convenience store and used their last two dollars to purchase those toys. What should have been the worst Christmas of my life turned out to be the best Christmas, because my parents gave me more than toys. They gave me a belief in miracles.

—Candace Carteen

A Midwest Miracle

Quentin Merkel is not a man easily moved to tears, but twenty years ago, he found himself crying late at night.

Two years earlier, his wife, Sharon, had been diagnosed with a debilitating disease that was robbing her of the ability to do even the simplest household tasks. Her prognosis was grim. She had amyotrophic lateral sclerosis, ALS, a degenerative, fatal disease that wastes away the muscles and eventually paralyzes its victims.

Exhaustion had set in for Quentin. He was working full time as a high school teacher and coach, then coming home to cook, clean, and care for the Merkels' five young children and his increasingly ill wife. His day would start before dawn, getting every kid up and dressed and out the door before 7:00 A.M. It would end at midnight, after a full day's work, followed by dinner, dishes, homework, baths, laundry, and caring for his beloved Sharon. Every night, he'd fall into bed and cry and pray. He prayed for strength to keep going, fearing that he could not. He prayed for help, night after night, but none came, and he began to wonder whether his prayers would ever be heard.

One morning at school, fellow teacher and friend Leo Schultheis approached Merkel and asked, "How is your wife? Do you need help?"

"No," said Quentin. "We're fine."

Later that night at home, a deeply fatigued Quentin began his prayer again. That's when he got his answer. It went something like this: "Who the heck do you think you were talking to this morning? Here you are, asking for help from above, and help is being offered by someone standing right next to you."

When Quentin returned to school the next day, he told Leo the truth: Things were bad and getting worse. In response, Schultheis and his wife, Marilyn, began Project Merkel, the genesis of an amazing effort that continues today. It began as a group of volunteer adults and teenagers who cooked dinner, did laundry, bathed children, and helped with homework and housework. The sicker Sharon Merkel got, the more tasks they took over.

That Sharon Merkel is still alive and at home today surprises people who are aware of the cruel reality of her disease. Many know it by another name, Lou Gehrig's disease, coined for the 1930s-era New York Yankees baseball player who died from it at age thirty-eight. With ALS, the nerve cells that control the body's motor functions degenerate, and paralysis eventually sets in. Many of its victims die from pneumonia, unable to cough off congestion in the lungs.

Sharon was diagnosed with the disease in 1981, when her youngest child was a year old. It began with muscle weakness. Within a few years, she was in a wheelchair. Twice over the next four years, she fought off what she and her family feared would be fatal pneumonia. After the second bout, which put her in the hospital for four months, her family had an excru-ciating decision to make. Medical advisers were pushing them to put Sharon in a nursing home. They told Quentin that he wouldn't be able to take care of his wife at home, that if he put her in a nursing home, he could get on with his life. Quentin recoiled from their suggestion. Sharon *was* his life! He'd vowed to love, cherish, and take care of her in sickness and in health, till death parted them, and he was not about to back out on that sacred promise.

It was not an easy promise to keep. Raising five children on a teacher's salary was a stretch to begin with. Sharon required around-the-clock care, and the equipment she needed was costly, beyond what insurance would cover. Requests for help from the government were turned down; Quentin made too much money for his wife to qualify for Medicaid or other government assistance. She couldn't get help from the Social Security Administration, either. The purpose of the benefits, they were told, was to replace the earnings lost when a worker becomes disabled. The irony was appalling. Sharon hadn't been "working" before the disease struck; she'd only been raising five children.

Once again, friends stepped in. They assured Quentin that they'd find the money to keep Sharon at home. A small group of people set up a fund, dubbed it the Friends of Quentin and Sharon Merkel Committee, and began asking for contribu-tions. Every year since, they've raised the money needed to pay for her care. The cost now exceeds $70,000 a year.

Sharon is now almost completely paralyzed. She is totally bedfast and dependent twenty-four hours a day on a ventilator and other medical equipment, which require continual monitoring. Three trained caretakers take turns by her side night and day.

But her mind is sharp and fully engaged. She communicates by blinking out messages using an alphabet chart that two of her sons rigged up for her. Family and friends say she is still the heart of her household, still directing the daily traffic of family life from a bed in the living room, still the mom of the house. Not long ago, her youngest son, Shawn, came home later than expected, only to find his mother waiting up for him; she gave him a royal chewing out. Against the medical odds, she's survived to see all five children graduate from high school, two of them graduate from college, and one get married. Her life, though difficult, has been fuller and longer than the experts and strangers would ever have thought possible. Of course, they don't know Sharon Merkel's tenacious spirit and friends.

For more than two decades, scores of people have contributed staggering amounts of time and money to keep Sharon Merkel alive and in her home, and to keep her family afloat and together. Over the years, people have often asked Quentin Merkel whether his family has ever prayed for a miracle. A soft glow seems to light his face as he answers quietly, "We did, and we got it. The circle of friends who've answered our prayer for help, that is our miracle."

—Maureen O. Hayden

 Dear Mom

After thirty years, I am finally beginning to appreciate the mother you have been to me. Although Jana is only ten months old, I feel I have learned more about you in the short time since her birth than in all my years of growing up and breaking away.

As I go about my new life of caring for Jana, I constantly wonder, how on earth did you do it? You, who raised not one, not two, but six children. I'm still feeling shock waves from the change and upheaval one child has made in my life, and I know that what I have experienced so far is only a glimpse, the barest hint, of all you went through raising us.

"You learn to sacrifice when you have children," was one of your stock phrases when I was growing up. To you, sacrifice was a necessary virtue, an accepted part of parenthood. But I didn't go for that. I considered sacrifice not only unnecessary, but unfashionable and downright unappealing as well.

Well, Mom, what can I say? I'm learning.

Lately, I've begun to look on motherhood as an initiation into "real life." I don't think I realized until Jana's birth that the life I'd led previously—relatively free, easy, and affluent—is not the life led by most people—past or present. By becoming a mother, I seem to have acquired automatic membership into a universal club made up of uncertainties and vulnerabilities, limitations and difficulties, and sometimes, unsolvable problems. Of course, the club has its benefits, too.

When Jana wakes from her afternoon nap and, so happy to see me, gives me her radiant full-face smile, I smile back and feel on my own face the smile you used to give me when I woke up in the morning. Or, when Jana does something particularly cute, I'll glance up at Gary, and in the look we exchange I see the one I remember crossing between you and Dad at opposite ends of the dinner table. It was a look full of feelings I never knew until now.

When I hold Jana close to me and look down to see my hand tight across her chest, or when I tuck a blanket around her while she sleeps and touch the skin of her cheek, I see your hands (those hardworking hands with their smooth oval nails, steady and capable and caring) doing the same things. Then I feel as if some of the love and security you gave to me through those hands is now in mine, as I pass that love on to Jana.

The other day Jana fell asleep against my arm. I must have spent fifteen or twenty minutes staring at her, marveling at the wheat color of her hair, the suppleness of her skin, her perfect tiny red mouth, moving now and then in sleep. What a rush I felt, of love and wonder, of care and luck, and more. I suddenly remembered something I saw on your face last summer, when I was home on a visit shortly after Jana's birth.

We were sitting on the glider swing in the backyard. It was a lovely morning, cool there in the shade, and the air was full of fragrance from your rose garden. I was holding Jana, who seemed to enjoy the gentle movement of the swing.

But I wasn't enjoying anything just then. I'd had a rough night. Jana was six weeks old and had been up every few hours. I, fretful and nervous as only a new mother can be, had been having trouble falling back to sleep between her feedings. I was cranky and tired, and not feeling cheerful about this motherhood business at all.

Sitting on the glider, we talked—or rather, I talked, letting loose my load of anxiety and frustrations on you. And out of the blue, you reached over to touch my hair.

"It's so pretty," you said, an odd expression on your face. "The way the sun is hitting it just now . . . I never noticed you had so many red highlights before."

A little embarrassed, preoccupied with other thoughts and problems, I shrugged off your comment. I don't know what I said, something short and dismissive, no doubt, as I waved away the compliment. But your words affected me. It had been a long time since someone had seen something truly beautiful in me, and I was pleased.

It has taken me this long to realize that the look you gave me that day is the same look I give her almost daily. And it makes me wonder: Is it possible that you still see the miracle in me that I see in Jana? Does the magic continue even when your children are grown and gone and parents themselves? Will I look at Jana in thirty years and still feel the same rush of love for her that I do now?

It almost hurts to think of that kind of love. It's too vulnerable, too fragile. I know well the barriers that spring up between parents and their children over the years, the frictions, the misunderstandings, the daily conflicts and struggles, the inevitable pulling away and final break for independence. It hurts to think that someday Jana will grow up and wave away my tentative words of love as I did yours.

What happens to that first, strong rush of love? Is it lost somewhere along the way, buried beneath the routine practicalities of caring for a growing child? Or is it there all along, unvoiced and unexpressed, until, perhaps, a new child is born and a mother reaches out to touch her daughter's hair?

That, it seems to me, is the real miracle: the way a mother's love is rediscovered, repeated, passed on again and again—as it has been handed down in our lives from you to me, from me to Jana, and from Jana, perhaps, to her own children. It is a gift in itself.

I guess what I've been meaning to say all along is, thanks, Mom.

—Christine Goold

Monday Morning

"We can play in the RAIN! It will be so FUN! I love the RAIN!"

I wake up to the sound of William singing to himself. There is no real tune except that the last word of each line is slightly higher in pitch and volume. I roll over to squint one eye at the alarm clock: 6:35. I close my eyes, hoping that somehow it's not 6:35, it's not Monday morning, and I don't have to be out the door with William in about an hour.

"And the RAIN! It came DOWN! It's so WET! Go away RAIN!"

The singing persists. I lie in bed and think about what is to come: We are about to begin the daily tug-of-war, William pulling me toward the world of pretend and me pulling him toward the reality of picking out clothes, eating breakfast, and getting to school and work. I'm already frustrated because I know how to win this game and he doesn't even know he's playing.

I drag myself out of bed and stumble up the stairs to William's room. He is lying on his Winnie the Pooh sheets, legs spread-eagled, wearing his Toy Story jammies, which I just then realize are on the edge of too small. When he sees me, he sits up, smiling. His hair is doing its usual crazy morning dance with swirls and eddies all over the crown. I almost never have time to tame this nest and won't today. Instead I kid with his day-care workers that he is doing his Ethan Hawke grunge imitation.

William starts talking as if the night that has just passed was merely a pause in our ongoing conversation.

"Backhoes get dirty."

"Yes, they do, William."

"The wheels get dirty when they drive."

"Okay, sweetie." I am using my patient voice. "Let's leave the backhoes for a minute. I need you to pick out clothes, because we have to get moving this morning. You have to go to school, and Mommy needs to go to work. Your green pants and your stripy turtleneck are clean. Do you want to wear those?"

"But why do the wheels get dirty, Mommy?"

"William." There is now an edge to my voice. "We can talk about the backhoe later. Right now, we need to concentrate on picking clothes. Do you want to wear the stripy shirt?"

"But, Mommy, why do the wheels get dirty?" His voice goes up in pitch.

"William, if you don't answer my question, I will just pick out your clothes for you!"

"But don't pick out my clothes!" He's raised his voice to meet mine. He slowly drags himself over to his dresser, laboriously opens a drawer, and pulls out a short-sleeved shirt. It's December.

"You can wear that if you pick out a sweatshirt," I say, knowing this will cause an argument later. He agrees.

When we get downstairs, it's 6:52, and I'm roughly on schedule. I head to the kitchen and put on the water for tea.

"Mommy, will you play with me?" William is holding a dump truck in one hand and offering me a small Tonka grader.

"Buggy, we really don't have time right now. I would like to, but we're very late."

We're not actually late yet, but this sentence is a reflex in the mornings. "Now, what do you want for breakfast? You can have cereal, a bagel, or eggs and toast." I want to bite my tongue as I say "eggs and toast." It's his favorite, but he will want to help.

Sure enough, he cries, "Eggs and toast!"

After I break three eggs into the bowl, William stands ready with the eggbeater. I resign myself to his "help," but regret this as I watch the countertop get splattered with a sticky, yellow slick. "Watch what you're doing, William. Please keep the eggs in the bowl!"

My sharp tone of voice makes him look up at me. "I'm sorry, William, but we're late!"

At last, William is seated. He's piled all of his eggs on top of his jellied toast and is driving this concoction around his plate, making the sound of a fire engine.

By 7:37, I've showered and dressed while William watches *Sesame Street*. Ideally, we'd be backing out of the garage in three minutes, but that looks doubtful. We've got more dressing to do. When I bring William his boots, he greets me with, "Mommy! Look what I can do!" He is sitting astride one of the arms of the easy chair as if riding a horse. I keep myself from saying, "We're late!" and manage a half-hearted, "Great!" as I start pushing the hiking boots onto his floppy feet.

"These are my construction boots, right, Mommy?" He says "construction" with determination and seriousness, elongating the middle syllable, eyes squinting with effort. It's not that he's struggling with the word; it's just that construction is serious business for William. Then we have to confront the sweatshirt.

"William, you need to put on your sweatshirt."

"But, I'm not cold," he insists. It's now 7:42.

"William, you may not be cold now, but it will be cold in the car. Put your sweatshirt on. Now."

"But . . . I've got a good idea!" He changes tactics. "I could put it on once I'm in the car!"

"Not while you're buckled in your car seat. Put it on here!" My voice is getting frantic.

"But Heather and Rachel say—" This is his final strategy: appeal to the wisdom of his teachers.

"William!" I explode. "We are not going to do this today. We are not. I am going to put on your sweatshirt for you. We are really late, and you must wear your sweatshirt. If this makes you cry, I'm sorry."

It does. And I am.

As William climbs into the backseat, his eyelashes are still wet, but the tears have subsided to a slight shiver when he inhales. I maneuver into the driver's seat. The dashboard clock says 7:47 as I back out of the garage and turn on the radio to catch the news. I half listen to an interview with a military expert about the technology of the Gulf War.

As I stop for the red light at the entrance to our neighborhood, William is pushing one of his trucks around his lap, making quiet engine noises. The interviewer asks the expert about "smart bombs."

". . . and they can go down a chimney and into someone's living room. . . ." the voice explains.

"Mommy! Mommy!" William is breathless. I glance in the rearview mirror. His eyes are wide and shining, his lips slightly parted. In a reverent tone, he breathes, "They're talking about Santa Claus!"

As the light turns green and we merge into the Monday-morning traffic, William asks, "Mommy, why are you crying?"

"I'm okay, Buggy," I say as I look in my rear-view mirror at my child's shining face. It suddenly doesn't matter that we are late again, that our countertops are constantly sticky with egg, that William will never leave the house with all of his hair going in the right direction. William's innocent confidence that it is only Santa Claus who comes down chimneys forces me to see the world through his eyes. The tension, the hurry, the irritation of the morning fades in the face of my son's innocent beauty. William is four years old, and he believes in Santa Claus.

—*Ellen Jensen Abbott*

Daughter of the Bride

My mom announced her engagement on my answering
machine. It was one of those rare middle-of-the-night
phone calls delivering good news, and I missed it. Submerged
in a flu-induced New Year's Eve hibernation, my husband and
I had turned off the phone ringers that evening and called it
a year.

I played the message the next morning, expecting to hear
loud greetings from a missed party. Instead, I heard my mom's
happily tearful voice announcing the perfect introduction to
a new millennium: She was getting married after more than
a dozen years of single parenthood, self-taught independence,
and dating misadventures.

I immediately phoned home, hating the hundreds of miles
between us. This kind of news is best relished in a kitchen
counter conversation—a lengthy, looping, mother-daughter
discussion held while perched atop the kitchen counters, pref-
erably with ice cream.

When my mom answered the phone, I let out a celebratory
shriek and burst into tears. It is an inherited response. Wordless
joy, overflowing pride, abundant surprise are all tear-worthy in

our emotional shorthand. As my mom described the evening's events that had led to Paul's proposal, memories clicked like so many slides across a silent screen, a progression of shifting relationships that defined personal evolutions.

I remembered my mom curling into bed with me the night that she and my dad announced their separation, anchoring me in love even as she spiraled into unknowable grief.

I remembered telling my mom about my own engagement as we waded in the balmy curve of currents off the Florida Keys, hugging and laughing under an October sun.

I remembered driving my mom to her surprise fiftieth birthday party and watching her walk into a room of women who were family by choice, friends through school, weddings, baby-sitting club, Lake Michigan summers, and unexpected transitions.

I remembered watching my mom speak at her mother's funeral, now a motherless daughter after years of tackling the daily, open-hearted tasks of parenting a parent.

I remembered my mom preparing for her first date with Paul, wary of yet another endless dinner with a stranger who might drone on about himself through dessert and then calculate her share of the bill to the penny.

Instead, the dinner had opened a relationship that encompasses past lives, laughter, loss, grown children, compromise, and hope. I listened long-distance to my mom's giddiness and incredulity at meeting such a gentle, thoughtful man—especially now, a beginning after so many endings.

As months went by, I felt like a junior high school confidante, an eager accomplice in the unfurling he-said/she-said girl talk that somehow makes a relationship feel more real. I even fell a little in love myself. How could I not adore the man who so clearly complements my mother?

And now my mom is getting married. This time, she is a bride without the veil, trousseau, or parents to give her away. While she is quite capable of giving herself away, I somehow feel responsible for my mom's heart. For better or for worse, I am a maternal daughter, always taking care, watching out, keeping the peace.

As an unmatronly matron of honor who has a thirty-year history with the bride, I feel I am giving part of the woman I know to Paul. This woman who loves chocolate éclairs, golden retrievers, and late afternoons at the beach with a good book. This woman who is the first to ask what she can do for you, roots for Indiana University basketball, and is always grammatically correct. This woman who sleeps too little, gives too much, and has a gift for hearing what is unsaid.

I think a certain amount of grace is inherent in any transition. For so many years, my mom has been that grace for me, propelling me forward with unconditional love. Now, it is my turn. Next month, when my mom says, "I do," I want her to know that I do, too.

—*Molly Hulett*

Marching Orders

"Let me go!" my teenage son, Lamont, yells at me.

I clench my jaw, determined to hold back tears.

"Let me go!" he yells even louder.

Today is the last muggy day of freshman orientation on the tree-studded campus of Morehouse, a historically black, all-male college in Atlanta, Georgia. Lamont finally is shouting the words he has choked back all week.

I am new to this "college goodbye" business, and it shows. My heart is pounding, and my muscles are tense. I take deep breaths to calm myself. I never thought that letting go of my "baby"—in this case, a six-foot-one, mustached, and self-assured history major—could hurt so much. It feels like childbirth without the epidural.

Of course, I am proud Morehouse accepted Lamont. This campus of manicured lawns and preantebellum brick buildings is known worldwide as the finest institution of higher learning for African American men. My son will walk the same cobbled pathways and take exams in the same classrooms as did civil rights leader Martin Luther King, Jr., former

U.S. Ambassador Andrew Young, and film writer/director/producer Spike Lee.

What an adventure for him. And what terror for me, this imminent last goodbye. I am a single mother to an only child, a former overextended workaholic now on an indefinite stress leave from work. I will fly back to California tonight, but my entire life will remain in Georgia.

I remember when I first discovered that Lamont and I were kindred spirits. Barely out of training pants, Lamont and the four-year-old girl from next door were best friends. One day, I washed dishes as they played in the living room.

"We're gonna play house," Lamont announced.

I wiped the soap from my hands and crept to the doorway. Far be it for me to interrupt innocent child's play, but I stood ready to halt any inappropriate prekindergarten tryst.

"I'm the daddy," he told her. Before I could speak, Lamont explained domestic responsibilities to his "wife."

"Your job is to be quiet," he said. "I have some very important studying to do, and I can't be disturbed."

I muffled a giggle. At the time, I was enrolled in an MBA program, and so I understood the reference. I pledged to spend more time with my son, then puffed out my chest and strutted back into the kitchen. The kid was a regular chip off the old block. I have always been the bespectacled brainy kid who routinely requested extra homework. Though not as nerdish as me, Lamont also takes his education seriously.

Today, I sit here in the Morehouse auditorium because of his academic hard work and determination. Several thousand other parents occupy seats around me in the upper rows during the orientation's closing ceremony. Though I cannot see him, I know Lamont is up front, shoulder to shoulder with more than 900 other African American young men, the incoming class of 2007. They fill the first twenty rows of seats, a squadron of teenagers—some looking awkward, some looking confidant—in white shirts, Windsor-knotted ties, and dark suits.

The vice president of academic affairs, a tall, regal woman in an ivory pantsuit, is on the stage. The timbre of her clear, deep voice matches the solemnity of the occasion. The ceremony reminds me of a black Baptist church service, complete with a local minister's singsong opening prayer and Bible reading followed by soulful Christian hymns sung by a Morehouse choir swaying to the beat.

The associate dean welcomes us and summarizes the past week of orientation workshops and seminars. She turns her attention to our sons.

"Class of two thousand seven, please stand."

The young men stand amid muffled squeaks of leather auditorium seats.

"Turn to face your parents and guardians," she continues.

They turn from facing the stage to facing all of us in the upper rows.

"Gentlemen, today you stand before those who have nurtured and cared for you through the few milestones of your young lives. These individuals supported you with love and understanding—even when you felt undeserving of such unconditional devotion." The associate dean's booming voice rises and falls in the syncopated rhythm of a country preacher. "They taught you right from wrong, and instilled in you the dedication, faith, and intellect that led you to gain admission to this magnificent institution, Morehouse College. Their job is done."

I feel the pinprick of tears. Several women near me sniffle.

"I now request that you tell your parents and guardians that you are ready to move on to the new opportunities and challenges ahead. Gentlemen, address your parents, repeating after me," she commands, her voice rising:

"I . . . ," she booms.

"I . . . ," the loud, deep voices of Morehouse's class of 2007 respond.

"Now, say your name," she commands.

A roar of garbled voices rises from the group as each young man shouts his full name.

"Understand and appreciate the sacrifices you made for me . . . ," she thunders.

"Understand and appreciate the sacrifices you made for me . . . ," they echo.

"And I will make you proud . . ."

"And I will make you proud . . ."

"But for me to be all that you hope and pray for . . ."

"But for me to be all that you hope and pray for . . ."

"You must please . . ."

"You must please . . ."

"Let me go!" she shouts.

"Let me go!" Lamont yells at me from somewhere in the vast auditorium of other young men yelling at their parents.

My son is giving me permission to do what I was so afraid to do until this moment—say goodbye.

"Let me go!" the administrator repeats, this time louder.

"Let me go!" Lamont and his classmates yell louder.

She pauses and gazes into the upper reaches of the auditorium where family members sit.

"Mom, Dad, and guardians, it is your turn to stand."

We do, many in the audience wiping away tears.

"I want you to think back to when your young man was just a little boy. Remember when he got that first bicycle without training wheels and you taught him how to ride?" she asks.

Nervous laughter ripples through the auditorium, as many others and I nod our heads.

"You remember, you ran alongside of him, your hands next to his on the handlebars while he peddled as fast as he could. After you had gone a fair distance, remember what he said to you, Mom and Dad?"

She pauses.

"He said, 'Let me go!'"

Another pause.

"He said, 'Let me go!' And you didn't want to. You were so afraid he would fall and hurt himself. But you forced yourself to let him go, anyway. He wobbled a little at first, but then he gathered balance and speed, and soon he was riding on his own."

I smile and nod my head, as do many of the caretakers around me.

"Well, now it is time to let him go again," she says in a booming voice. "Now, repeat after me. "Son . . .""

"Son . . . ," we parents and guardians repeat.

"I am so proud of you . . ."

"I am so proud of you . . ."

"And I am officially . . ."

"And I am officially . . ."

"Letting you go," she yells.

"Letting you go," the other parents and I yell.

"I am letting you go!" she yells louder.

"I am letting you go," we repeat louder.

My tears fall slowly at first, and then I am sobbing and fumbling in my purse for a tissue. I find one and blow my nose, noticing that most of the women and some of the men around me are crying, too. But the tears are ones of pride and acceptance. It feels so good to finally release the sadness that has weighed me down all week. My tears flow down my cheeks and into my huge grin.

Later that evening, Lamont and I are at the curb outside of his dormitory. My cab to the airport idles nearby. We have exhausted the "leaving home" details that I feel compelled to squeeze into our last moments together. No, he won't forget to call regularly, even if it has to be collect. Yes, he has enough quarters for the laundry. No, he doesn't think he will need a heavier coat. I hug him tightly for about a minute, a good thirty seconds longer than he would have allowed any other time.

"Bye, Lamont," I say as he closes the door of the cab for me. "I love you."

"I love you, too, Mom," he says as I roll down the window. "Goodbye."

As the cab drives off, we wave to each other. Both our faces break into wide, stupid smiles—his because of the wonderful adventures that lie ahead and mine because I finally recognize that this parting is, in fact, a good one.

—*Jeanette Valentine*

 Pink Organdy

Esther stood at her closet, trying to decide between the navy suit and the gray wool skirt and cardigan. Esther disliked making choices, but she particularly disliked choosing clothing. Sometimes the effort even gave her a headache.

It wasn't that she had little to wear or that her closet didn't contain a wide variety of fine garments. She just never felt the confidence to choose the right outfit for the occasion.

Today, they would attend a band concert in the park, an outdoor event where the audience sat leisurely on the grass and sipped lemonade through straws. Most likely, the young people would wear jeans and the middle-aged would wear slacks and sweaters. Esther didn't want to be too dressed down for her age or too dressed up for sitting on a blanket in the park.

She was tempted to call her husband into the bedroom and ask his advice, as she had been throughout their marriage but never had. Once again, she fought the urge. Getting a grip on herself, she pulled out the gray skirt and cardigan, looked at each piece, sighed, laid them on her bed beside the pearls he'd given her for her birthday, and started to change.

Suddenly, a distant memory entered her mind—one that had broken her teenaged heart all those years ago.

He was three years older than she, a popular high school senior; she was a lowly sophomore. They shared no classes together and their paths never crossed, but she had seen him often from afar. And to her, he was the most magnificent boy she had ever laid eyes on. Tall and slender, he had brown hair with a wave that fell over his forehead and shoulders perfect for leaning on. He wore white canvas shoes, which gave him a devil-may-care appearance that she somehow knew in her heart was not really like him at all.

Through sly detective work, she found out his classes and his homeroom. She also learned that his first name was Alan. But she never approached him, never so much as said hello. Then, at the end of the school year, she heard something from other girls at school that made her heart thump in her chest: He had a summer job bagging groceries at the store where her mother worked as a cashier.

Her mother usually did the grocery shopping at the store before she came home from work, so there was no reason for Esther to go there. But realizing that Alan would probably leave for college at the end of summer inspired Esther to do something she would never have done otherwise. She stopped by the store one Saturday for a pack of gum. Her mother couldn't help but notice Esther's gaping mouth as she stood at the cash register looking out the window to the parking lot. Alan, the muscles in his arms and back straining against his white T-shirt, that devilish strand of hair gleaming in the sun, seemed to float across the parking lot in those white shoes as he helped an elderly woman load her car with shopping bags.

"Esther, are you all right?" her mother asked, grasping her arm, no doubt fearing that her daughter was about to faint. Esther wondered the same thing.

She was so taken with seeing the boy she'd adored from the other end of school hallways and across school lawns that she couldn't speak. Her hands shook, and she felt queasy with fear and embarrassment. She couldn't let him see her. Without a word to her mother, she ran from the store and all the way home, slammed the door behind her, flopped down on the couch, and cried.

"Esther," her mother said when she got home from work and found her daughter in her room, deep in the pages of a novel. "Why don't you ever go out? All you do is sit in this room and read. Other girls belong to clubs and go out on dates and shopping together. All you do is read."

Esther sulked behind her book. Her mother always tried to get her to join in, but Esther was usually content with her books and record player. Besides, she got out enough to suit herself. She attended high school football games, didn't she? She visited the library every Saturday, didn't she? What more did her mother want?

"I want you to be happy, Esther. I want you to meet a nice boy," her mother said.

Esther put down her book. "I don't want to meet a nice boy, Mama."

"Well, you will meet him. He saw you at the store today and told me he wants to ask you out, to a dance at the university," her mother said.

Esther jumped up. "Mama! I don't want to go to a dance! And I don't have anything to wear!"

"You have a closet full of clothes, Esther."

"But—"

"Yes, I know, you have nothing suitable for a dance. I'll give you the money to go downtown and choose something lovely. You'll have a wonderful time at the dance."

What choice do I have? Esther thought. She'd always done what her mother asked. Well, she'd go, but she wouldn't dance. She would say she didn't know how. She would say she'd hurt her foot.

"Who is the boy?" she asked, dejected.

Her mother smiled. "You'll like him, Esther. He's very nice. He's the new bag boy at the store."

Esther's heart fell to her toes. It couldn't be! She couldn't do it! She wouldn't be able to speak! She'd spend the entire evening shaking!

Esther had no idea what to wear to a dance, especially at the university. She milled around the store, leafed through all the dresses, and finally chose a knee-length, pink organdy dress with a high collar and elbow-length sleeves. Then she realized she had no shoes to wear with it. It was the fad then to buy cloth-topped shoes and have them dyed to match the outfit. Esther went home with pink shoes.

The dance was a disaster. Esther sat in a corner, trying to be pleasant but totally forlorn. The university girls, with upswept hair, long pencil-slim black skirts, and scoop-necked or off-the-shoulder blouses, seemed so much older and more sophisticated than she felt. No one wore pink shoes. Everyone danced except Esther and, she was certain out of sheer kindness, Alan.

While Esther was panicking inside and willing herself to fade into the nearest wall, Alan seemed to enjoy himself. He talked with her, smiled at her, circled the rim of the dance floor to fetch her soft drinks and snacks, and talked with passersby. But with each look at the dance floor and all those lovely university girls, Esther felt more out of place, more ashamed that she had ruined Alan's evening and his chance to dance with the prettiest of them.

At home that night, she buried her face in her pillow and sobbed. She would never, ever show herself to Alan again. She had made such a fool of herself, wearing pink organdy and pink shoes like a six-year-old in a Sunday school play, sitting in a corner, unable to dance, like the wallflower she was.

Alan called her the next week to ask her out again. No way. Never. She was completely humiliated, and she was certain she had humiliated him as well.

Esther felt a hand on her shoulder.

"Almost ready?"

She turned toward him, straightening her sweater over her skirt. Gray skirt. Gray sweater. Gray hair.

"You look lovely," he said.

"Thank you, but I'm all gray."

"But when you smile at me," he said, stroking her hair, "Your cheeks turn a radiant pink, and your eyes are like a starlit evening sky."

"Do you think I'll pass, then?"

"More than pass, my beautiful Esther."

He took her into his arms, and she felt completely loved and protected in his warm embrace.

"But you know, Esther," he said, "as beautiful as you are now, you'll never look lovelier than you did the night I fell in love with you, in your pink organdy and pink shoes."

She snuggled against Alan's chest and knew she had made the right choice about much more than pink organdy.

—b.j. lawry

 Time Out

I flung aside the covers and bolted upright, wide-eyed. "Wake up!" I shook Mike's shoulder gently, then harder. "We overslept!"

I raced to the girls' room, frantic and smelling of morning breath, pulled the two older ones out of the bunk bed and led them to the bathroom with their eyes closed. Trusting that they could walk through the morning routine in their sleep, I pulled open drawers and laid out their clothes, while the baby slept on in her crib. Then I sped down the hall, pulling open the bathroom door in transit. "Your clothes are on the bed! Dress fast; we're really late!"

"Can we have pancakes today, Mommy?"

"No! Daddy will butter some toast for you to take out the door. Hurry!"

I threw on a pair of yellow slacks and a matching T-shirt. Dress at the school where I taught was casual. Permanent press, great! No time for ironing. No time for a shower, either. I ran a brush through my hair and while I dashed on a little makeup, I listened to the girls in the next room.

"I hate these overalls."

"Me, too. I wish Mom didn't know how to sew."

"Me, too. I wanna wear a pretty dress."

"I wanna wear my orange T-shirt with the sparkles, and my jeans with the silver studs."

"Can you reach my pink dress?"

"Sure. Will you pull out my T-shirt? It's under your bed."

Ordinarily I would have intervened and ensured they wore appropriate and clean clothing, but under the circumstances I decided to prioritize and let it go. Five minutes later we convened at the front door. Mike handed out lunch boxes and toast to go, and we were off and running!

Sasha looked up at me as we left our building. "You look pretty, Mommy. I like yellow."

"Let's walk a little faster," I replied. What a sight we were— the harried, wild-eyed mom with a book bag slung over one shoulder, herding two tousled little girls who had forgotten to brush their hair, but were dressed to kill, one in sequins and studs and the other in ruffles. We navigated a long city block with commendable speed, darting around slower pedestrians and speaking as little as possible except for an occasional "hurry up." Amazingly, we were only a few minutes behind schedule. If we kept up a brisk pace, I thought, I'd be able to drop them at their elementary school in ten minutes and sprint to my own school in time to clock in at 8:30—with a little luck.

It didn't happen. As we approached the first intersection, the light changed and we had to stop. Now, if you've ever been in New York, you know that nobody actually waits for the pedestrian walk signal before crossing. Savvy pedestrians watch the opposite traffic signal and step off the curb when it turns yellow, look both ways, and start walking when it turns red. The pedestrian walk sign comes on when you're about halfway across. I stepped off the curb, looked left and right, and jumped back as a bus beat the light. Though I'd given myself plenty of room and was in no danger of losing my life or incurring bodily harm, I hadn't seen the mud puddle.

"Oh, no!" So much for the split-second timing that had gotten us out the door almost on time. I stared down at my slacks, splattered with dark mud spots from waist to cuffs, doing lightning calculations of how many minutes it would take to dash back home and change, weighing that against the pros and cons of just going to work as I was.

Suddenly, Sasha's head disappeared from my peripheral vision. I whirled around to see her sitting on the sidewalk, opening her lunch box, and I blew up. "You know we're running late, and you saw what just happened, and all you can think of is you want a *snack*! What's the matter with you?"

Her bottom lip quivered. Great, I thought. On top of everything else, she was going to start crying right here on the street.

Big brown eyes looked up at me and brimmed over. "I was just getting you a napkin so you could clean your pants."

My frustrations melted along with my heart as I knelt down to hug her. Suni put a comforting hand on my shoulder. Droves of commuters skirted around us, a little island in the rush-hour hustle, and when the light turned red again, we were still in a huddle.

"Mom . . . I have an idea." Suni usually did. Her ideas matched her favorite clothes—neon with lots of glitter. "Let's not go to school. Let's all call up and say we have a cold.

Actually, I think I do, a little." She coughed. "And Sheila can stay home from the baby-sitter's . . . and Daddy can make us all pancakes."

"Blueberry!" That was Sasha's idea of heaven on earth.

"And then we could spread a blanket on the floor and play Chutes and Ladders." Suni was on a roll, and she knew it.

My priorities took a new turn, for the better, I think. What would I actually lose if I took a day off? And how much more would I gain? We threw our half-eaten cold toast in a trashcan and ran laughing hand-in-hand back to our building, conspirators in a grand plot. The blueberry pancakes were the best we'd ever had, and we played Chutes and Ladders until everybody won at least once.

The mud spots came out in the wash. Most bad things do; life is like that. I'm happy to say that, after being mentored by a sweet little girl sitting on the sidewalk getting a napkin out of her lunch box, my priorities remained firm: Punctuality is important, but not as important as your family.

One of my girls called me the other day. Married just one year, she and her husband had called in sick and spent the day together. They didn't play Chutes and Ladders, but from the sound of her voice, I gathered that whatever they'd done, they'd both won! She's going to be a good mother.

—*Nancy Massand*

A Pair of Nothings

I held my breath as I watched my brother's finger trace through the newspaper listing of teachers assigned to third graders. I squeezed my eyes shut tight. *Please, please, don't let it be Miss Ball.*

"Miss Ball."

My brother's words hit me like a punch to the stomach. Wasn't it bad enough that third graders had to learn their multiplication tables before they could pass to fourth grade? No one wanted to be in Miss Ball's class to do it. She was scary.

According to my father, Miss Ball's badly scarred face was the result of smallpox in her youth. Knowing the cause didn't diminish the effect. Tall and slender, with eyes as black and shiny as onyx and lean fingers that could snap like a rifle shot, she was the most intimidating figure on the entire second floor.

That September I dragged my newly shod feet into class, completely demoralized by my class assignment. With such a stern demeanor, Miss Ball would have even less of a sense of humor than the teachers I'd experienced previously. No tolerance for a creative imagination in her class. I prepared myself to hate every minute of the next nine months.

Reading was the first class. A breeze for me. My older brother Doug had taught me to read when I was four. Geography was a snap, too. Same with history. When we came back to the classroom after lunch recess, there it was on the blackboard: the first row of the dreaded multiplication table. The "zero times." The school chili gurgled in my stomach. By the end of the day, we would be repeating the numbers in that mindless prisoner-of-war style I had learned to resent from my first day of first grade. I planted my face on my fists.

Zero times zero made sense. I could even accept one times zero. But I had to question why two times zero was still zero. I was just a farm kid, but I knew when you had two of anything you had *something*. My hand shot up, wagging.

"Doesn't that two mean anything?"

Miss Ball stared at me, her black eyes unreadable. My classmates stared at me. I held my breath until my vision blurred. Maybe it really was possible to slither to the floor and sink into one of the cracks between those worn hardwood slats.

Then Miss Ball did something beyond my realm of experience. She smiled. A gentle smile. Not that evil smile teachers get when they sense a smart aleck in the class. I'd expected reproach. What I got was goose bumps. This was definitely new territory for me. Now everyone was staring at the woman at the front of the room and not at me. I could breathe again.

She turned to the blackboard and drew a large rectangle, which she divided into halves. "This," she said, pointing to the blank interior of the left block, "is a nothing. A zero." Next she gestured to include both portions of the divided rectangle. "And these are two nothings. Class, what do you get when you have one nothing and one nothing?"

"Nooothiiing, Miiiss Baaall."

I stared at that divided rectangle long after Miss Ball and my classmates had moved on to discuss other zeroes. A blank domino. A pair of nothings. I wanted to hug myself with delight. At last, a teacher who could illustrate a point, who could make me visualize rather than merely saying, "Just because." Even back then, before analysis of learning behavior became popular, she was perceptive about some students learning better through visual aids and reinforcement rather than auditory instruction.

In later lessons, when her personal stock of colored chalk appeared, I discovered Miss Ball could draw flowering trees with nests hiding in them, clouds with exotic birds flying around the sky, and rays of sunshine and rippling water with lily pads that looked real. She could write poems, too. Short poems with exciting new words that expanded my vocabulary and my horizons.

Miss Ball was a kindred soul. A creative soul. A beautiful soul.

Later in the year a box appeared on the activity table. It was full of 3-by-8-inch cards. On each card was a word. On the back of the card was the definition of that word. Nothing in my education to that point had ever struck such a spark of excitement. Words were some of my most favorite things in the world. I found words fascinating, not so much the sounds they made when you spoke them as their appearance, their meanings, how they could be employed in a sentence to alter meanings. These were all new words, big ones, 250 of them. This was not the vocabulary you learned on the farm. Not a single domestic animal resided in their midst. The box represented the lexicon of journalists, scholars, and philosophers.

Like a new kid in class, the words became my friends. I copied them, played with them, and introduced them into my conversation. And, like any other eight-year-old, I'm sure I mistreated them on occasion. I hardly noticed that none of my classmates shared my enthusiasm. The words were my companions on the baseball field and playground as well as in the library and the classroom.

Tears stung my eyes that final day with Miss Ball. I had more to learn from this wonderful teacher. She had so much more to teach. There were more boxes full of those musical, magical new words.

Fifty years have passed since I sat behind that old wooden desk with notches and initials carved by generations of students and darkened with decades of varnish, ink, and grime. Of all my teachers, I remember Miss Ball most, not for her flawed complexion and intimidating demeanor, but for her ability to spark the imagination of a dirt-poor, pigtailed country girl. Thanks to Matilda Ball, the desire to learn burns as brightly for me today as it did when she drew that simple white-chalk rectangle filled with a pair of nothings.

—*Kathleen Ewing*

A Plane Ticket, a Phone Call, and a Country Song

It all started with a plane ticket and a phone call.

"How'd you like a visitor the second week in July?" I asked my big sister, Deanne. I knew the answer. In fact, I had already booked my flight to Nashville.

"What? You're kidding! Dawn, that'd be great!" she exclaimed in her impossible-to-place accent.

We've been told we sound alike. I find that extremely odd, since I speak like the stereotypical Long Island girl, while her accent is a smattering of all the places she's lived—Southern California, New York, Tennessee, and a bit of God-knows-what-else thrown in.

I shared the details of my trip with Deanne. The owner of the publishing company where I worked as an assistant editor had just sold one of his magazines and was giving the entire company a week off and each of us a nice bonus to celebrate.

A few weeks later, Deanne picked me up at the Nashville airport. We headed straight for her rural home just outside of Paris, Tennessee. Over the next few days, I enjoyed my first genuine Southern "bar-bee-que," hung out at the local

Dairy Queen with my teenage niece and nephew, and got to know the waitress at the neighborhood greasy spoon. Mostly, Deanne and I did what most sisters do when they get together—shopped and gossiped.

Then we headed back to Nashville, just the two of us, for the rest of the vacation. By the last day of our trip, we'd seen the Country Music Hall of Fame, Earnest Tubbs Record Shop, and Studio B on Music Row. I'm not sure how two girls born and raised in the suburbs of New York grew up with an affinity for country music. Perhaps it had something to do with our dad singing George Jones and Kenny Rogers every morning while he shaved.

After a long day of touring country music landmarks, we sat in Nashville's Red Roof Inn downing TGI Friday's mudslides from little plastic cups. We poured them straight from the bottle, no blender, no ice, just sweet chocolatey rum. I gazed out the window at the burning Nashville sun, grateful both for the air conditioning and that our trip had been blessed with such good weather. Even with the constant humidity hanging in the air, we hadn't seen one drop of rain.

"We should go to the Grand Ole Opry," I suddenly blurted out.

Deanne smirked at me. Between our dinner at Ruth's Chris Steakhouse and five days of nonstop shopping, the trip had already broken both our banks and then some.

"Seriously," I said, jumping up from the bed and grabbing the stack of tourist brochures we'd picked up in the hotel lobby. "I want to go to the Opry."

"That'd be cool," Deanne said in a voice that warned me not to get my hopes up.

Tickets would probably be expensive, sold out, or both. But my quest had already begun. She shrugged as I dialed the phone.

"Do you have any tickets available for tonight?" I asked. I caught Deanne's eye and a wide grin spread across my face. "Thank you. We'll be there." I gave the girl my name and thanked her again.

"Well?"

"They have tickets, only twenty dollars. Our reservations are set. We pay at the door."

Deanne silently performed calculations in her head. "Let's do it," she said finally.

My hands trembled with excitement, and I couldn't keep still. I paced the room to burn off the nervous energy. "We're going to the Opry! We're going to the Opry!" I chanted, the thought dancing in my mind like the refrain of a song.

"Who's playing?" Deanne asked, catching my enthusiasm.

I opened the trifold brochure and hunted for the correct date. I skimmed through a few lesser-known names that sounded vaguely familiar, then got to the current stars. "Terri Clark. Steve Wariner—"

"Steve Wariner!" we squealed in unison.

"He'd better play 'Two Teardrops,'" I said.

"I hope he does 'Kansas City Lights.' Do you think he will?" Deanne asked. At my blank stare, she added, "Oh, that one was from before you were born."

"I've heard of it," I said indignantly, the little sister never wanting to be shown up or left out. A favorite tune sprung to my mind. "If he plays 'Holes in the Floor of Heaven,' I'm going to cry," I said.

"Yeah," Deanne said, matching my somber tone. "I love that song."

The song, a Top Forty hit on country radio stations at the time, traces the stages of a man's life as he loses first his grandmother, then his wife. The falling rain in the chorus symbolizes the tears cried by loved ones who have passed on.

I thought of our own family's beliefs. We've always told the younger children that Nana and Grandpa watch us from stars in the sky. Many nights, I would look up in the sky, find the two brightest stars, and know Mommy and Daddy were looking after me.

"Well, let's get ready," I said, opening my suitcase to get my sister's opinion on a choice of outfits.

Hours later, we stepped into the Opry and found our seats amidst the rows of red velvet chairs. I'd been in theaters both larger and more impressive but few exuding as much history and tradition.

"Daddy would have loved this city," I said. "This theater, the Hall of Fame, everything. I can't believe he never made it here."

There were too many cities that our dad, who died of a heart attack at fifty-two, had never seen. By the time I was twenty-three, I'd already been to Chicago, Nashville, San Diego, Orlando, San Antonio, and New York. Over the next five years, I added Anaheim; Albany; Cleveland; Washington, D.C.; Baltimore; Key West; and Sydney, Australia, to the list.

"Fifty-two was so young," I said to Deanne, a sudden realization.

Looking at my sister's face, I had another realization: She's nearly forty. And I'm reminded that she's got our mother's eyes.

In the picture of Deanne hanging on my living room wall, she is dressed in her U.S. Navy blues, young and smiling, holding a squirming three-year-old—me. That photo represents one of the few recollections I have of her as a child. I barely knew her growing up. She left for the Navy when I was three, came back as a stranger when I was six. For many years, she was a voice on the telephone with which I felt a vague, tenuous connection. But as time goes by, a sixteen-year age difference shrinks to a blip. Strangers grow into sisters, then into friends and finally confidantes. In Nashville, sitting together drinking diet Pepsi from collectible mugs and listening to music that crosses generations, we became contemporaries.

I felt my heart pounding in my chest as I looked down and saw him—the star, Steve Wariner—a tiny figure from that distance. Deanne and I sang along to each of his songs, dancing and clapping during the bluesy "Burning the Road-house Down."

Then we heard the telling first chords and the emotional first line: *One day shy of eighty years old, my grandma passed away. . . .*

My sister looked over at me. A lump grew in my throat. By the end of the first verse, the tears in my eyes had burst into two streams pouring down my face. Deanne grabbed my hand. Thankful for the contact, I gripped hers tighter. We sat there, two sisters, fully grown orphans, alone and together. Identical tears fell from identical blue eyes down identical round, rosy cheeks. We sat, wordlessly, motionless, holding hands, listening and feeling every note, every word.

When the song ended, we sniffled simultaneously, wiped our tears, and enjoyed the rest of the show, saying nothing more about the song. Bittersweet smiles said all that needed to be said. And yes, he did sing "Kansas City Lights." And yes, I knew the song.

After the concert, we sat on a bench in front of the Opry, resting our feet and enjoying the waning sun as the traffic dissipated. I shivered as I felt the slightest tickle of something wet on my bare arms.

"Did you feel that?" Deanne asked.

I had felt it, too, but had dismissed it as my imagination. I looked down at the pavement, speckled with freshly fallen drops. Aside from a few fluffy clouds over the Opry, the sky remained sunny and blue.

"Yes, I did," I said, smiling. "Mommy and Daddy must be watching."

—Dawn Allcot

 Sister Power

"Mom . . ."
"Can we . . ."
"Have . . ."
"Ice cream . . ."
"Please?"

There they stood, five little girls, hair moist from the heat, proud of their newly discovered power to deliver single sentences in five sequential parts. How could I resist five sisters cooperating? They got ice cream. It was the first time they'd used their united strength to get what they wanted, but it wouldn't be the last.

When my daughters were teenagers, boyfriends were careful to be nice to all the sisters, not only to the one they wanted to date. If the sisters decided they didn't like a boy, the guy didn't stand a chance. Phone calls were not forwarded and doors were not opened to the unwelcome.

One day I arrived home to find one of these poor suitors at our door, ringing the bell.

"I know they're in there," he said.

I opened the door, ushered him in, and sure enough, there they all were, drinking tea.

After he left I asked, "Why didn't you let him in? Where are your manners?"

"We don't like him."

"He's not good for her."

By the puzzled looks on their faces, they obviously thought I was the one who didn't get it.

One sister was so scared to bring her current boyfriend home that she met him away from the house for almost a year before he made it in.

College found the sisters in different schools but never farther apart than the telephone. When one needed consolation, she got it from four comforters; when one claimed a victory, the whole group celebrated. If one sister ran out of money and needed a place to stay between jobs or between schools, another opened her home until the crisis passed. They helped one another find jobs, and they lent and repaid loans to one another. Of course, they also fought and disagreed with each other, but they always stood united, ready to take on the next challenge, arm in arm.

Marriages and children did not ruin their collective front. The babies who came along year after year found not just Mom and Dad welcoming their arrival, but also four sets of doting aunts and uncles with arms wide open. During one sister's labor, the hospital staff referred to the waiting room full of sisters as the "aunt trap." When nurses would pass by, one of the soon-to-be new aunts would intercept them and ask how things were going in the delivery room.

Babies were born to the first three sisters. Everyone was waiting for the fourth sister to make an announcement. She attended many baby showers with a smile on her face and an ache in her heart.

People outside the immediate family would smile and say, "You're next!" Or they would scold and say, "Don't wait too long. You're thirty; you can't wait forever."

They didn't seem to consider, maybe she can't get pregnant.

She didn't talk about the miscarriage at six weeks. Imagining the pain of mothers who lose a full-term baby or endure multiple miscarriages, she counted her blessings and kept trying. But the wait got longer and harder for her. Her husband researched all their options, and they picked a fertility clinic in the city where they lived.

For five years they tried to conceive a child, and each year their odds grew slimmer and their options fewer. Near Christmas of the fifth year, her younger sister gave birth to a healthy baby girl. Amidst the family's shared joy in the newborn's arrival, everyone, especially the new mom, felt the childless couple's sorrow.

With no baby to spoil, the childless couple doted on the nieces and nephews. So unselfish were they with their love for the new baby, it was hard to watch them go home with empty arms.

My four girls in Canada worried and talked about the toll it was taking on their sister in Atlanta. Her clothes hung too loosely, her cheeks were sunken, and the circles under her eyes were too dark for makeup to cover.

"It is time to give up. Accept. Adopt," I said. "Whatever it takes, but stop hurting like this."

Soon after Christmas, I got a phone call from one of the sisters.

"She is going to try a clinic in Toronto. They will work with the clinic in Atlanta and try some new procedures the facility in Georgia doesn't have. We are going to help."

Even though the treatments would involve thousands of miles of air travel and two fertility clinics, the sisters were determined. They had to try.

A pattern was established. Home base was a town near Toronto where four of the sisters lived. One sister stayed home to babysit and to fix meals for the travelers' families. The other three drove to the clinic in Toronto. One sister went into the operating room to hold her sister's hand. Afterward, pale and shaken from actually witnessing the pain of harvesting eggs or the invasiveness of that day's procedure, she reported the progress to the two sisters in the waiting room, where one sister knitted a blanket for the baby they all were sure would come.

Sometimes, the father was needed at the clinic. The sisters met his plane and embraced him, tried to ease his embarrassment, and afterward took him back to the airport immediately. With the mounting costs, missing work was not an option.

The first egg was implanted, and everyone held their breath. Three weeks later when it became clear a baby was not on the way, the sisters rallied around the couple, extending their support to the next procedure . . . and the next, however many and however long it took. The days following each procedure seemed unbearable. Each time a fertilized egg was implanted, the calls went back and forth between five sisters for three weeks, no one daring to ask: What are the odds?

One time it was so close they felt certain her dreams were finally coming true. They were wrong. Another time, the doctors knew right away that the numbers were wrong and cancelled the day she arrived. Finally, after six months of treatments, the doctor told her, "It is not going to work. Your eggs are not viable."

The sisters mourned. They cried and prayed for another chance.

The whole family became so unnaturally quiet, it was scary. No one could relax. My computer hummed as I combed the Internet, researching adoption organizations. I knew the sisters, too, were searching for solutions.

Still, I had to sit down when I heard the voice of one of my daughters on the phone.

"Mom, there is one chance for her to have a baby: I'm going to donate an egg."

Now, two sisters would be caught up in the world of medicine and invasive procedures with no guarantee of success. Two families would have to cope with women on monthly doses of hormones that would rock their minds, upset their emotions, and distress their bodies. It took some time before I could support their decision. They didn't wait for me. The mighty force of five sisters was in full forward motion.

All sorts of good-luck routines became rituals: Leave for the city at an established time. Stop for chai tea at a certain place on the way. Keep exacting records of dates and times in a sacred, shared book. Light candles in a special room prepared for the travel-weary sister to recoup between procedures in the clinic so far away from her home.

The time between appointments was not easy. The donor sister took massive amounts of hormones; one month's medication filled a grocery sack. She wondered how her sister had been going through this and keeping her job as a substance abuse counselor. Some days, she cried all day. Others, she was lucky if she was able to sit and watch television. Coordinating a house full of kids with varying schedules was too much, so her sisters took turns caring for her children.

Four sisters learned how to give injections without fainting. They took turns driving. They cooked and cleaned for each other, so they could all keep their jobs. They worked together for six months, five families totally committed to helping each other get what one of them wanted.

At last, the tests were positive. The sudden inactivity was frightening. Every ringing phone was answered with fear. How could they stand it if it didn't work? Showers were planned; gifts were made with cold hands and worried hearts. Privately, I wondered whether the baby would be all right, whether, after all of this, the baby would be whole and healthy, whether she could carry it full term.

Finally, the twenty-eighth week, the date the doctor had said the baby would be reasonably safe, arrived. Everything looked fine. The sisters took a collective breath of relief.

Two drove and two flew to their sister's side when the doctor said it was time. He knew this was not a usual delivery when the father asked if all four sisters could be there. Generous nurses let the sisters give the water, wipe away the sweat, comfort, and encourage.

There they stood, four proud sisters surrounding the bed of one beloved sister, hair moist from the heat, eyes wet with tears.

"Mom . . ."

"We . . ."

"Have . . ."

"A . . ."

"Baby!"

—*P. Avice Carr*

 Caroline's Prince

My three-year-old daughter, Caroline, believes that people come in three categories: princesses, princes, and workhorses. Inevitably, I (her mother) fall into the workhorse category, while she presides over the princess line. Hers is not a Habsburg chin or an iron fist but a natural talent to rule and to show by example. Minutes after she was born, her father carried her around the delivery room, and to everybody's astonishment, she held her head up high and looked around the room with the attitude of Queen Victoria.

A platinum-blond princess, she wears tiaras at breakfast, high heels for lunch, and ball gowns for dinner. Her six-year-old brother, who has tired of all the hoopla, has but one term for her: *piece of work.* Her second alias is "Cato," after her Dutch great-grandmother Catherine and her Norwegian great-grandfather Cato. But I am beginning to think that, in Caroline's case, the name Cato is more closely related to the Roman statesman Cato, who was known for his wisdom and wit. Caroline's wisdom is the only one that counts, and anyone who dissents falls out of grace and can expect a kick in the rear, no matter that Her Royal Highness is wearing high heels.

The three workhorses (her father, her brother, and me) are hardly worthy of her. However, she, aware of her *noblesse oblige*, puts up with us as if we are a bunch of indentured but loyal and rapidly aging servants. Besides, in order for her throne to rise above her subjects, she needs losers like us to lean upon.

At three, she is conscious of the arts of affectation, grace, and elegance. Unfortunately, however, her finer sense of elocution leaves much to be desired. A booming voice may come with the territory, but when Workhorse #1 took her to the bathroom of the Chinese restaurant to pat her on her diapered regal bottom because she pitched her fork at a bald man's head in a fit of royal rage, Princess Caroline yelled so loud that the entire restaurant could hear her indignant, "How dare you hit me!"

Besides her voluminous voice, she is unabashedly uninhibited for an aristocrat. One hot afternoon she threw off all her clothes and sported her naked body in front of her mortified grandfather.

"Wanna see my kagina?" she proposed, as if she were consulting him on a flower arrangement.

Her grandfather had no desire to see any kaginas, and William, Workhorse #3, told his sister that even princesses have "vaginas," to which Her Majesty replied that she knew best, and then turned up her royal bottom in his direction and let out a princely pretend-fart.

By the way, Shrek is her favorite matinee idol. On her more imaginative days, she tells me that she will play Princess Fiona if I am prepared to turn green and play an ogre. But an ogre is not the Prince Charming she has been waiting for. Her prince turned up in the guise of her swim instructor this summer. Although Princess Caroline wondered why she should bother with swimming when she would one day have a royal yacht at her disposal in every harbor, when she laid eyes on Prince Kevin, she was sold on the idea of getting wet.

Kevin is, after all, a prince in every way: He is *dark* (tan like a Californian surfer) and *mysterious* (Caroline still can't "read" him; when he walks by, oblivious of Caroline's hungry looks, she tells me he is "sooooo funny!"). Furthermore, he is *young* (fourteen, maybe fifteen) and *handsome* (he beats Shrek in that department) as well as *polite* and *courteous* (even when Caroline opens her treasure trove of trivia to him, he patiently listens). Above all, since he is *strong* enough to drag all of Caroline's pudgy forty pounds through the pool, he'd be strong enough to slay her dragon, too. (Workhorse #3 would disagree here and tell me that Caroline *is* the dragon.)

All joking aside, after meeting Kevin, Caroline told me that Workhorse #2 (Daddy) would no longer do as a potential hubby. She may still consider dancing with Workhorse #2 at her wedding, but as a groom he is completely out of the picture.

Since I had never seen a three-year-old falling head over heels for a much older man, I decided to observe her tactics. It might come in handy if I were to become widowed young and needed to find myself a trophy husband with gray hair and prostate problems.

Her mating game went like this: First, there was coyness—her little (big) head would avoid any eye contact. She would look down at her toes or pretend to be counting the polka dots on what she calls her "ballerina" swimsuit (it has a little skirt in the back). I had never seen Princess Caroline so humble and civilized. But soon this kind of evasion and hiding behind the cellulite-legs of Workhorse #1 gave way to open flirtation.

This also meant that Kevin had advanced from distant prince status to outright hunk status. She bragged about Kevin's good looks and great talents as a swim instructor to Workhorse #3, who, deeply immersed in reading *Pippi Long-stocking,* could not have cared less.

It also meant that I no longer had to drag her into the water to where Kevin was sitting at the beginning of each lesson. Instead, she would bounce and skip toward him like a Playboy bunny on steroids. She'd show him how she could hop on one leg and how she could fold up her outer ear and stash it inside her ear canal. Then, unable to hear Kevin's compliments on her ear acrobatics, she'd say *"What?"* like a deaf grannie.

She relished the body contact she had with him in the pool: the way she draped her hands on his broad shoulders when practicing the breast stroke; the way his head would touch hers as she practiced the backstroke; the way she would blow bubbles with him and throw her voluptuous body at him during diving practice. She was in swim heaven, and all because of Kevin.

For years, every time we'd wash her goldilocks in the bathtub, she would scream bloody murder and tell us she was going to divorce us all. Needless to say, when Kevin asked her to put her face in the water, she went underwater with a smile on her face—heck, she'd stick her head down the toilet, if he asked.

Then came vanity. After all, with drenched hair, she was not assured of her royal good looks. In between head dunks, she would straighten up and comb back her wet hair with her fingers and pull it behind her ears, or ask Kevin whether she was having a good hair moment.

"Yes, your hair looks fine," I heard him utter several times with a boyish nonchalance in his maturing voice.

Once Kevin had seen her with wet hair, the degree of intimacy went up, and Caroline deemed it proper to move into her all-out casual mode—that is, incessantly listing all the characters in *Dragon Tales* and chatting so much about her favorite television shows that Kevin started throwing looks of desperation at me. Obviously, he wanted her to shut up and get on with the lesson. Meanwhile, she was hopping on one leg again and recounting an episode of *Powerpuff Girls*: "And 'member on the *Powerpuff Girls* when Professor Utonium . . ." The summer can be long and dreary when you do nothing but teach three-year-old girls to swim.

When Caroline ran out of her TV repertoire, she became daring and began stalking Kevin all over the pool terrain. The moment she'd spot him, her face would light up and she'd think up a little plan to sneak up on him and surprise him with the forever-fascinating trivia from a day in the life of Princess Caroline.

One afternoon as she watched his wet limbs come out of the water, her scenario planning kicked into full gear.

"What if," she told me, grabbing her pink bath towel, "I pull this towel over my head, walk up to him, throw off the towel, and tell him my dog's name is Smokey?"

"Excellent plan, my darling," I replied. "And such an important piece of information," I whispered to Workhorse #3, who was painstakingly and prudishly covering up his six-year-old nudity with his own towel.

Off she went, a pair of chubby legs underneath a pink towel. The towel with legs was seen all over the terrain, trailing Kevin. I think Kevin was embarrassed, for he kept walking away at the pivotal moment. So, she came back, perspiring with disappointment. As she reported back to me, her glance hovered past my shoulder, and a new plan popped into her little pageboy-styled noggin.

Showing off her one dimple, she said connivingly, "Oh wait . . . he is walking to the canteen. If I go sit on the little bench over there, he'll see me when he comes out."

It was sheer genius—had Kevin not already walked away, passing behind the little bench. But Caroline hadn't noticed his departure, so she sat down on the bench, folded her hands in her lap, and waited. She sat and patted her hair, making sure it was all pretty. She sat and licked her lips—toddler lipstick. She sat and looked at her nails, regretting that the pink nail polish was wearing off and uneven. And she waited and waited. People started noticing her, and someone finally asked, "Who are you waiting for, little girl?"

With the composure of a princess, she batted her eyelashes like Scarlett O'Hara and sighed with the passion of Miss Piggy: "Kevin."

The guy at the canteen overheard her, grabbed his mike, and called across the land: "Can Kevin come to the canteen?"

At that point I walked up to her, but as soon as she saw me approaching, she said "Shoo!" as if I was a bothersome and intrusive fly that needed to be chased out of the room. When I failed to get the hint, she yelled, "Get lost, Mom! Kevin is coming!"

For a moment I had a flashback to when I was sixteen, minding my own business on a beach in Portugal. A Portuguese Romeo with sideburns down to his jaw lay down next to me and told me that northern European women, with their blond hair and fair skin, were goddesses. My mother, witnessing all of this from her hotel-room balcony, had marched in a beeline to the beach and told me to pack up and leave.

And here I was—I had become my mother.

So, Caroline had her little rendezvous with Kevin, telling him that she had a Band-Aid on her knee, a dog named Smokey, and a mother who turned up at the most embarrassing moments.

She returned to me triumphant at having accomplished her mission—and seeming more thirteen than three. Later, I told Workhorse #2 (her dad) that we should consider hiding birth control pills in her cereal the moment she started having periods.

At bedtime, I tucked her in, brushed her soft cheek with mine, and inhaled her sweet innocence. She framed my face with her little hands, and gazing earnestly at me with clear blue eyes, she said, "I love you, Mommy." As always, it was the moment that made my day.

As I left the room and flipped off the light switch, I looked back at her little round-bellied shape on the bed and whispered, "Good night, sweet Caroline—I'm glad you've found your prince."

—*Inez Hollander Lake*

 Reverse Psychology

My firstborn, Scott, would have been a challenge for any mother. For a brand-new mom with little child-rearing know-how, he was, as they say, "a handful." With an intelligence and a sense of humor that exceeded his years, combined with an energy and a curiosity that topped the charts, Scott managed to find mischief where no mischief had gone before. So it was that, shortly after this whimsical little man came into my life, I found myself buried in how-to books on disciplining children, raising responsible kids, tough love, and other parenting advice. As time went on and Scott's antics continued and, if anything, became more creative, my realm of study expanded to include child psychology classes as well as listening to parenting tapes and radio programs.

Now, don't get me wrong; Scott was not a "bad" kid. He wasn't malicious, he didn't deliberately look for trouble, and he wasn't a nonstop challenge, 24/7. In those fleeting moments when he wasn't pulling pranks or being rambunctious, he could be a downright sweetheart. But he was very active and more than a little ornery, and he had an uncanny ability to outsmart other people. Not many children regard April Fool's Day with as much enthusiasm as they do Christmas.

Staying a step ahead of my wily male child was not only challenging, it was, at times, next to impossible—especially as our family grew to two, then three, then four children. That's when the books in my library started changing from how-tos to "how comes."

Just when I thought I'd reached the end of my parental resources, and rope, with Scott, I happened upon a radio talk show hosted by a well-known child psychologist, Dr. James Dobson. Impressed with his apparent expertise, I immediately went out and purchased a set of his audiotapes. Whenever the rare opportunity arose for me to listen and learn, I did so eagerly.

One weekend, my mom and dad invited Scott to their house for a sleepover. With my little mastermind out of my hair—er, the house—for a day or so, I finally had the opportunity to soak up a few of Dr. Dobson's tapes. One particular tape, which focused on handling a challenging child and gaining his or her respect, really piqued my interest.

In that session, Dr. Dobson used an experience from his own childhood to illustrate how his mother had applied "reverse psychology" to show him how she felt when she had to discipline him. Mesmerized, I listened as he explained the concept and described his youthful turnabout.

He had done something naughty and was standing before his mother, anticipating his punishment. She held in her hand a paddle. But before administering the blows, she had something to say to her young son—the proverbial "heart-to-heart talk" most kids dread but often dismiss. She told him that, to have a son who was constantly compelled to get into mischief, she must not be a good mother . . . and so, being a bad mother, *she* should be the one to receive punishment.

Now, she instructed solemnly, it was up to him to spank her.

He gasped in horror! Spank his mother? The person who had rocked him and nursed him as a babe, who read stories to him, fed him, mended his hurts, dried his tears, attended his sporting events, and rubbed his back until he fell asleep at night? How could he possibly spank his mom, who loved him so much, to atone for his mistake?

Tears rolled down his cheeks as she handed him the paddle. He didn't want to spank her. He didn't want to hurt her, ever. She was his mom, and he loved her. In that moment, he realized how his mother must have felt every time she had to spank him. And he vowed to try harder not to give her reason to punish him again.

Needless to say, he didn't spank her. And, of course, he didn't never again do anything wrong. No child is that perfect. But he learned a big lesson that day, which inspired him to improve his behavior and to think before he acted out, and which gave him a new respect for his mom.

Eureka! This was the answer I'd been looking for to teach my little Scott a new attitude toward his mommy. I almost couldn't wait until he misbehaved again, so I could administer this very valuable lesson.

Upon Scott's return home from Grandma and Grandpa's house, it didn't take long before he was tormenting his three sisters again and the opportunity arose for me to put my plan into action. If there was an Oscar for "actress playing a sorrowful mother," I would have received it. As a tear rolled down my cheek, I took Scott by one hand, and gripping the paddle in the other, led him into the "time out" room. I knelt before him and said my well-practiced lines.

"Scott," I began. "I must not be a very good mommy to you. No matter what I try to do to help you stop picking on your sisters, you just don't seem to listen. It hurts me inside to think you don't want to behave. It makes me feel like I'm a bad mommy."

For the first time in his little life, he stood before me quietly, truly listening to my words. It was hard for me not to chuckle under my breath, but I was going for broke here. I continued:

"My son, I hope you can forgive me for being a bad mommy. God wants me to be a good mommy to you, not a bad mommy. So, I feel I am the one who deserves a spanking today."

With that, another tear rolled down my cheek, and I stood up. I handed him the paddle. His eyes widened in what appeared to be horror. Slowly, I turned my back to him and then bent over.

My heart was pounding so hard I thought it would jump out of my chest. Moments passed in what seemed like hours, and I started reveling in the knowledge that Scott had learned a valuable lesson, and planned on boasting of my success to his daddy. With my back turned to my seven-year-old son, I envisioned his sad face, how he was going to beg my forgiveness and promise to change, how he—

Whack!

What was that stinging reality I'd just felt?

Whack!

No! As I turned to look at my son, it dawned on me that the look I'd construed as horror wasn't horror at all—it was euphoria! He wasn't begging for my forgiveness. He wasn't saddened by this course of events. He was basking in sheer delight!

Whack!

I began to run! He began to chase me!

Having never been allowed to hold the paddle in his hands before, he was now wielding it like a weapon and loving every second of it. Glancing behind me, all I could see was the blur of his Cheshire-cat smile and his spindly legs carrying him wildly closer.

Any hope I'd had of teaching my son a lesson flew straight out the door—with me right behind it and my son in hot pursuit. I don't remember how many neighborhood blocks he chased me before I finally turned, tackled him, and wrestled the paddle from his grip. What I do know is that it wasn't my son who learned a lesson that day.

Though I didn't win any acting or parenting awards for that performance, I did put reverse psychology back where it belonged—in the psychologist's office. And I did learn, in due time, that the real guide to raising a responsible, loving son comes from understanding, and accepting, and loving, and nurturing who he is, as an individual.

Today, my son and I are very close, and I am extremely proud of the man he has become. He and my daughters are my pride and joy—never mind the sometimes rocky road we traveled to get here. We often reminisce about their childhood escapades. Scott naturally lays claim to more than his fair share, and he inevitably retells the mommy-spanking debacle, always amidst gales of laughter. But perhaps I will get the last laugh, after all.

You see, Scott is now the proud father of a wily, strong-willed, beautiful two-year-old little girl. Perhaps for his birthday, I will give him my collection of Dr. Dobson tapes.

—*Cheryl Glowacki*

The Rising of the Sun

I was asleep when I felt him touch my arm and shake me. I tried to ignore him, but he was persistent . . . as usual. I rolled over and glared sleepily at him.

"What do you want?" I snapped.

His face was hidden in darkness, but I could sense his excitement. His whole body tensed with it.

He whispered hoarsely, "Wanna watch the sun come up?"

I did want to, very much. So I got dressed in my sleeping bag, while he heckled me, whispering: "Who wants to look at you, anyhow? I can't see you. Who'd look? What do you got worth lookin' at? Hell, I could iron a shirt on your chest."

And so he continued until I squirmed free of the sleeping bag. Taking my hand in his, he led me past the other sleeping bags and toward the tent flap. Climbing over our sisters was easy. Climbing over Mama was nothing short of life threatening. She was small but tough, and if she caught us . . .

Once outside the tent, the hugeness of the mountain overwhelmed us to stillness and silence. He and I stood, side by side, gazing at the dark purple giant, listening to birds calling from dark, shadowy trees.

After a few minutes, he turned to me and whispered, "Let's go!"

Mel ran in a crouch, Indian-style, so I had to run that way, too, hurrying behind him through the trees that scraped and scratched at my face, skin, and clothes. Being a boy, Mel didn't care about scraped skin and snagged clothes. My gender demanded a more acute sense of personal damage. Eventually, I would learn to worry about things like calories, suntans, and flyaway hair. But that early morning in the Blue Ridge Mountains, my only aim was to keep up with my most revered hero, who cared not one whit about the condition of my apparel or whether my arms were bleeding. Had I uttered even the slightest hint of a complaint, I would have been accused of being a *girl* (what could be worse?) and sent back to the tent.

Eventually, he found a path and we walked it beneath the soft moonlight. Mel warned me about bears, and when he heard me swallow hard, he reminded me that he was part Indian. It did not occur to me to suggest that, if he was part Indian, then I must also be part Indian. All I knew was that his declaration of kinship with the Cherokee tribe made him impervious to things like ax murderers, escapees from insane asylums who brandished hooks where their hands should be, bullies who liked to hurt little girls, and now, obviously, bears as well. If I stayed close to Mel, no evil could befall me, and my love for him made my chest hurt.

We found an outcropping of rocks, and in the near-total blackness, scrambled onto it and perched ourselves at the very edge. Thus situated, dangling straight out over the Shenandoah Valley, which slept peacefully thousands of feet directly beneath us, my brother and I watched the sun ease its way over the Blue Ridge.

Pale and delicate, the day seemed rather shy when it was new, stepping politely in our direction as if in proper greeting. A summer lady she was—a bashful, understated Southern belle cloaked in finery. She wore pink and the most demure shade of violet with an orange sash about her waist. Then, without warning, she tossed off her frail pinks and violets and flung herself at us all wrapped in daring blue and red and purple. I laughed, and Mel laughed. He whistled between his fingers, and I clapped my hands as we both swung our legs energetically back and forth over the rocky, murderous drop into the valley.

Then the day threw off her colors and stood naked before us, wearing nothing but the sun, and she seemed not nearly so pretty without her lavish wardrobe. Mel and I lost interest in her and slumped wearily against each other. He would droop forward, then snap himself awake. Then I would sigh, crumple sleepily toward the tip of that rock, and come suddenly awake again.

In the end, he and I curled up together like two kittens and slept wrapped in each other for warmth. Mama found us well over an hour later, and we got into terrible trouble, Mel worse than me. Being part Indian didn't do him a bit of good when Mama was yelling things like, "You are older than she is! I don't expect you to act like that! I expect you to take care of her!"

If you have never been spanked with a wooden spoon, it is useless trying to describe it. Let me assure you, however, that the impact of a small, slender piece of wood on a quivering set of buttocks is something one remembers clear into adulthood.

Then Mama turned to me. She was angry beyond angry and demanded to know what I had learned from this experience. I answered right away, for I had been paying close attention and knew full well what had been shown to me.

"I am like daytime, Mama," I told her. "I am scared at first, but if I know you like me, I will show you all my colors. And if I am sure you love me, I will take off all my clothes and dance!"

She stared at me, speechless, so I figured I could go and hurried off toward camp before she remembered what she'd intended to do. As I passed my brother, I heard him mutter, "Dance with no clothes on? What a dumb-ass thing to say. Who the hell would look at you anyway?"

But I was too happy, and he could not make me mad. Mel could be part Indian if he wanted to be. I was part Dawn and that was much, much better.

—*Camille Moffat*

The Salvation of Jan and Kurt

L ucy Hobbs had recently lost her husband and now, in her seventies, found herself living on a Social Security pittance inadequate to sustain her basic expenses. She could have moved in with her daughter in Galveston, but she wasn't ready for that yet. Surely, she was still needed somewhere! The advertisement posted on the bulletin board at Stanton's General Store in Alvin, Texas, seemed the perfect answer: "Widower needs housekeeper to cook, clean, and take care of two boys, ten and five years old—room, board, and a small salary."

The door of the ramshackle farmhouse opened, and Mrs. Hobbs introduced herself to a family in a desperate situation. The father, Gus, had lost his wife to cancer in 1943, when Jan Arthur was six years old and Kurt Rolf was only one. A few days before his wife's death, Gus's father, a seaman with Gulf Oil, had been killed when his oil tanker collided with a ship. Gus's mother had moved in with him and helped care for his boys; but just one year later, she had died of cancer. Shortly after his mother's death, Gus discovered he had colon cancer and subsequently had a colostomy. By the time Lucy Hobbs stepped through their doorway in 1947, Gus had begun to crumble, along with the family finances and the house.

Mrs. Hobbs, gray-haired and grandmotherly plump, peered at Jan and Kurt through round wire-rim glasses that perched on her nose like a small silver bird. The boys were sunburned, bare-chested, and barefoot. From their heads to their toes, they were ragged, skinny, and mosquito-bitten. She knew immediately that she was needed there and took the job.

The unruly boys had driven off every other housekeeper their father had hired. Some of them left in tears after enduring only one day of Jan's deliberate defiance and disobedience. The boys were often left alone and hungry, subsisting on jelly sandwiches. They were uncivilized barbarians—that is, until Lucy Hobbs came into their lives.

The moment Mrs. Hobbs finished moving her few possessions into the drafty farmhouse, Jan began his usual tactics. He pedaled his bike down the driveway and onto the shell road that led to town, several miles from their farm on a busy highway. Mrs. Hobbs lumbered diagonally across the uncut yard, cockleburs and nettles nipping at her ankles, caught his handlebars and told him not to leave the farm.

"You're not my mother, and I don't have to mind you," Jan spit out angrily.

With surprising strength, she dragged him into the house and plopped him down on a chair. She emphatically told the boys, "I will not put up with any disobedience. If you want homemade biscuits and gravy for dinner, you'd better behave for the rest of the day!" The salvation of Jan and Kurt had begun.

Armed only with the force of her willpower and the promise of regular meals, Mrs. Hobbs brought stability to the boys' chaotic lives. She began the transformation process by insisting on cleanliness and good manners. "Cleanliness is next to Godliness," she told them. She assigned chores to Jan and Kurt and insisted they do a good job. "Anything worth doing is worth doing well," was an adage the boys heard often.

She took them shopping at Stanton's General Store, where they picked out patterned chicken feed sacks, and then she bargained with them, "I'll make shirts for you out of the sacks you pick, but you have to take good care of the chickens." She made sure that the boys fed and watered the chickens, kept the nest boxes filled with clean hay, and gathered the eggs daily. Their rewards were new shirts for school and bacon and eggs for breakfast.

Mrs. Hobbs used Tom Sawyer's tactics to get the boys to plant a garden. "I'd plant it myself, but I want you boys to have some of the fun. And won't you be proud of yourselves when you see those nice straight rows of vegetables sprouting up? And just think how delicious they'll taste." She encouraged them through the preparation and planting, and when the dog days of the project came around, she required they keep the garden weeded and watered. Their reward was a lesson in perseverance and fresh vegetables for dinner: beans, corn, squash, and tomatoes.

She asked them to chop down the weeds in the yard and make a path for her to the clothesline. "I just can't stand thrashing through these weeds to get to the clothesline. I'm afraid I can't do the washing anymore if you boys don't chop me a path." When they complained that they didn't have a lawnmower, she recited one of her favorite principles: "Where there's a will, there's a way," and insisted they do the job with a hoe. Their reward was a yard they could run across without getting stickers in their bare feet, and line-dried clothes and linens.

Mrs. Hobbs kept clean sheets on the bed the boys shared. At first, they rebelled at going to sleep at a decent hour, but she insisted, telling them, "Pretend you're going to Mary White's party." Then she tucked them in and made sure they said their prayers. It didn't take long for them to figure out that Mary White's party was a good night's rest between clean white sheets.

The farmhouse was not insulated. It was cooled by fans in the hot Gulf Coast summers, and warmed in the winter by a Dearborn butane space heater located in the kitchen. Tin can lids were tacked over holes in the floor to keep warm air inside and to keep cold wind and mice outside.

During the intensely hot summer afternoons, Mrs. Hobbs called the boys into the house. "You boys come in here and rest awhile before that sun turns you into lobsters." At first they rebelled, but they soon enjoyed resting and listening to the radio: the King of Swing, Bob Wills and the Light Crust Doughboys from Burris Mills, out of Fort Worth.

On frigid winter mornings, Mrs. Hobbs lit the Dearborn and started breakfast before she woke the boys. Drawn by the smell of bacon frying, they shivered all the way to the kitchen, the only warm room in the house, where they dressed for school.

Lucy Hobbs was not opposed to using dessert as an incentive to good manners, hard work, and compliance with her rules. When they had accomplished a particularly obnoxious task, such as cleaning out the pig pen or chopping weeds with the hoe, she would treat them to homemade doughnuts rolled in sugar or their favorite, rice pudding.

With the structure of regular meals and bedtimes, Jan and Kurt began to blossom. They were occasionally tempted to defy Mrs. Hobbs and go skinny-dipping in snake-ridden rice canals, but drawn by the delicious smell of fried chicken and mashed potatoes and gravy wafting through the kitchen window, they resisted the urge to run away.

The boys' father continued his downward spiral, drinking more and more heavily, coming home less and less often. Mrs. Hobbs and the boys were often stuck in the country, miles from town, with no transportation. Gus was no longer able to pay her, but Mrs. Hobbs stayed on in spite of having to use her Social Security check to buy butane and food. She was petrified at what would happen to Jan and Kurt if she left. When they told her they were afraid she would leave, she reassured them: "God gave me a mission to save you boys, and I'm going to stay as long as I can."

But after five years with them, her health and eyesight began to fail. In spite of her fears, she couldn't keep up with the job of raising them. Mrs. Hobbs told them many times that she would have to leave soon. At first Jan and Kurt panicked and begged her to stay. But after having heard her expressing her need to leave over and over, they no longer took it seriously. One day while the boys were at school, she packed everything she owned into one suitcase and went to live with her daughter in Galveston. Now in her eighties, she had given all she had to give. She had no way of knowing the great loss they experienced at her leaving or the traumas they endured without her presence in their home.

Several years later, her daughter brought her to Alvin to see Jan and Kurt. She was growing deaf and nearly blind. They were happy to see her, but as teenage boys, they were not adept at expressing tender emotions. She never told them she loved them, but she did. They never told her they loved her, but they did.

Lucy Hobbs could not have realized how well she had accomplished her mission. Her lessons had soaked into their souls, and they grew like oak trees, strong and beautiful. Although she never knew the result of her sacrifices, I have benefited from them. I married Jan.

On a frosty December dawn, I flick a switch, and the house begins to warm; another switch, and the coffee perks. I sit at the kitchen table and watch the outline of bare oak branches appear as the first gray strokes of light brush across the black sky. My prayer for the soul of Lucy Hobbs rises with the steam from my coffee. If she were here today I would tell her about a family that she never knew belonged to her. I would spread before her a meal of her own making: the meat and potatoes of our lives—a marriage of more than forty years, four children, and eight grandchildren. I would see to her comfort, cover her shoulders with a warm shawl, keep her coffee cup filled to the brim. And at last, reward her with the rice pudding of words not said to her in time: They love you. You are the mother they remember.

—*Nancy Gustafson*

 Clown School

I lay in bed aching for a mental health day. I'd call the school secretary and croak out the words "strep throat." Thirty minutes later, she'd hiss into the intercom, "Listen up, speech students. No speech therapy today." The cruel news would not be welcome. At Thomas Jefferson Elementary School, speech was an exclusive club with very stringent membership requirements. My absence would especially upset James, the most zealous of my club members. James had coined the club slogan, "We Wove Peech!"

Picturing James' dejected face when the announcement of my demise was blatted over the intercom system, I reluctantly dragged myself out of bed. My morose sigh scattered flakes of cherry Pop-Tart across the mirror. Reasoning that rosy cheeks would clash with my blue funk, I skipped the makeup ritual and went straight to my closet. I pulled on gray slacks and an off-gray blouse—an ensemble that highlighted my Quaker gray, two-inch roots. Even my sterling silver earrings refused to shine. The mirror confirmed that my outward appearance was a precise reflection of my despondent soul.

Maybe a gaudy scarf would disguise my melancholy. In two minutes, a scarf with vast pink, purple, and teal psychedelic solar systems orbited my neck. I tied it into a flamboyant, 1980s-fashionable bow. Unfortunately, the ruse was useless. I still looked and felt abysmal. I jerked on my fleece parka, wool cap, and fur-lined mittens; spent ten minutes scraping the ice from my windshield; and cursed every irritating red light (six) between my house and Jefferson School.

James, red cheeked and runny nosed, greeted me at the door. "Where you been, Miss Smiff? You wate."

Oh, why, oh, why had I come to school?

"I'm not late, James. You're early. Go back to your classroom."

"Nah. Miss Tim's wate too."

"James, Miss Kim is not late. I'm not late. You're early. Go eat breakfast."

"Nah."

He trailed me down the hall and into my classroom. The radiator pipes clanged. I dropped my overloaded satchel onto the floor; opened the closet door; and jerked off my coat, hat, and mittens.

"James, I need a cup of coffee. You'll have to go somewhere else."

"Nah. I just dough wif you."

"James"—I whirled around—"I'm not in the mood for early-morning visitors. You'll have to . . ."

"Wow! You wook pwetty, Miss Smiff."

"What?"

"You wook pwetty, Miss Smiff."

"Well," I stuttered, "Thank you, James."

"I wike a pwetty bow." His face lit up with a contagious smile.

I fluffed the harlequin bow and beamed a smile at him. "Really, James? I look pretty?"

"Weawwy pwetty, Miss Smiff."

"Well, thank you, James." Instantaneously, I felt better. Maybe I would get my mental health day, after all.

"You wook weal pwetty, Miss Smiff. You wook wike a cwown."

"What?"

"You wook wike a cwown, Miss Smiff! You weawwy do!"

I bit my tongue in an effort not to laugh. Tears rolled down my cheeks. When I could no longer hold it in, my laughter exploded with an unattractive snort.

James was puzzled. "What's wong, Miss Smiff?"

I knelt down beside him. "You make me so happy. Guess what, James? I've been acting like a clown, too." (I should have said fool instead of clown.)

I still have my blue-funk days. Still occasionally feel the need to make a deathbed call to the school secretary. Still think of James, crawl out of bed, look in the mirror, and tell myself, "You wook wike a cwown, Miss Smiff."

For me, a mental health day is just a laughing matter.

—*K. Anne Smith*

My Sister, the Mother

It was late afternoon, I remember, and Ethan was home from his first round of chemo, a day or so before he would be a full six months old. It was after the tears had stopped—after the piercing diagnosis, the slur of first days, the nights that had crackled with terror—and I had spent the day with my sister, playing at normality, working harder than we'd ever had to work at make-believe. I had just finished buttoning my coat, had turned back toward the kitchen to say goodbye, and there she was, my sister—who paled and looked away whenever a doctor pricked her finger—placing a syringe in her baby's "central line" to force back the blood that had started to seep. My sister, the mother, I thought, and those words still caption my memory of that moment.

My memories of moments not long before that one are like snapshots filled with color and light: My sister, standing sideways, her head back in laughter, her swollen middle silhouetted against the hues of July. Ethan, in the delivery room, swaddled in powder blue, raising a fist in salute to the father he'd just met. The three of them, where there had been two: Ethan nestled in my sister's arms, her husband leaning in for a closer look—realizing they'd just reinvented the world. And my sister again, weaving the buggy through Michigan Avenue's crowds—a balloon tied to its handle, Ethan's booties kicking in the air, the giraffes and zebras on the mobile above him dancing and whirling. I'd been standing across the street that morning when I'd looked up and suddenly seen them, and I remember thinking that they were a parade unto themselves.

But then—overnight—the snapshots changed to black and white.

In one, Ethan's parents, grandparents, and I are gathered in a circle around him, on the day when he awoke with one of his eyes protruding. "It's an infection," we told ourselves, or, "He's bumped himself on a toy." "Look how he's smiling and cooing and playing," we said—and said again, too loud, too urgent—"and eating; he's eating so well." "The doctor will laugh at us for worrying," we laughed—to prove that it was true—as we zipped him into his bunting and tied his hat beneath his chin. By that night he was sleeping in a crib in the Four West wing of Children's Memorial.

When my sister and I were growing up—less than two years and rarely more than three feet apart—we tried on motherhood every time we draped ourselves in our dress-up clothes. But nowhere we had ever imagined pushing our babies in our high-heeled wanderings had prepared us for the realities that awaited us in Four West. A mere elevator ride away from the state of denial the lucky inhabit—where it's possible to believe that bad things happen only to other, faceless people—Four West is a place where the unthinkable is routine and what was once routine is no longer thinkable. Where every door opens to reveal a family frozen in flight, battling gravity. Where children ride on the bases of IV poles down the halls instead of on bicycles down the street, their teddy bears swinging from the hooks above them, their every giggle and wave and shout a more defiant thumb in death's eye than no-handed wheelies could ever be. And adults leave it to their glances to speak the words their lips will not.

The images within my memories of my first visit there are tilted at drunken angles, as though my internal camera was jarred each time it clicked. From within the pea-green haze that envelops what I remember of that day emerge slanted walls and crooked doorways, floors that slope and windows that list, lights that spew a neon snarl of jagged edges. There is one image, though, that is more discernible than the others. It is of the three of them again, Ethan and his parents, clustered by his crib—deportees from the state of denial, looking lost. That image lingers as an ache every time I recall it.

Early in my life, before I was certain of much else, I was certain that I was to be my sister's protector—that, although I was the younger, the quieter, the less outgoing, and although she was gifted with brightness and beauty, she was more vulnerable than I to the blows of a bruising world. There I am at three, in the album of family remembrances, hurling myself headlong into the belly of the six-year-old bully who'd punched her. And at five, marching up to the teacher who'd forgotten to give her her skating race ribbon. "That," I am announcing, thrusting an indignant mitten, "belongs to *my sister.*" And at ten, outside her cabin during our first stay at overnight camp, shrinking from the Minnesota darkness and the cries of distant loons, waiting for her to answer my knock and lean out the window—so I can whisper goodnight to her. It was the closest I could come to tucking her in.

On that first day in Four West, I began to understand that the darkest night we'd ever known had fallen and I couldn't tuck her in. Every time a nurse took Ethan from my sister's arms and carried him off—for blood tests and blood typing, for a bone scan and a CT scan, for an MRI, an X-ray, a bone marrow aspirate—I wanted to snatch him back and hiss, "He belongs to *my sister*." But instead, I had to watch him go and to watch her watch him go, and when he would finally reappear, he would be limp and sedated and pale. Those days assaulted like a siren keening.

Then, in the next days, after Ethan went home for the short time before treatment, the instant of numbness that follows a breath-sucking impact evaporated, leaving his family rocking in pain. In every memory I gathered of my sister then, she is weeping. The night before Ethan's return to the hospital, I found her crumpled in the bathroom, sobbing, "I can't do this. I can't go through this. I'm just so scared." And instantly, I envisioned a moment we'd lived years before, during the summer when I was six and she was eight, when she climbed the ladder of the highest diving board at the city pool, inched her way to the edge of the swaying plank—and froze. Thirty feet below, I felt her terror. "You don't have to do this," I screamed up to her, not caring who heard. In the end, my sister inched her way back to the steps and climbed down to solid ground.

This time, as Ethan's mother, she leapt.

When she surfaced, back in Four West, the world as she had known it had been replaced by another, and I saw homesickness in her eyes. When I think of her then, it's as though she were groping her way through this alien landscape, where "bed" was a chair next to Ethan's crib. Where dinner was gulped, standing, between crises and cries. Where people who'd known her all her life weren't certain what to say to her and those she'd met just moments before—those whose children lay nearby—could speak with her as though they'd known her all her life.

I can see her standing by the window of Room 486 late on that first morning, knowing that her baby, whom she'd always protected—from startling noises and glaring lights and icy gusts of wind, from smoky rooms and jutting corners and bee stings and germs, from strangers and from pain, from sadness—was now lying inert on an operating table with steel slicing his skin to insert a "central line" through which toxic substances would flow. In that snapshot, I see her recognizing that, in this world where she now resided, she was expected to view such brutality as protection. On her face, that recognition looks like the imprint of a slap.

But then, there she is, later that day, bent over the tubes sprouting from a plastic torso, learning to inject and draw, to flush and swab, to clamp. And there she is the next morning, *mooing* and *oinking* to the tune of "Old Macdonald"—verse after verse, until Ethan laughs, another verse, then another, until he squeals—while chemotherapy drips into his veins. And there she is, masked and gloved, holding him still, despite his wails, while a nurse changes the dressing covering his surgical wounds. And there, sweeping the sheets of his crib, gathering clumps of the hair he'd just grown, and then talking to the doctors in a language still foreign to her. *Carboplatin*, she is saying, and *neutropenic. Growth colony stimulating factor* and *hyperalimentation. Nasogastric tube* and *absolute neutrophil count. Anti-emetic.* And that's my sister, too, her back and shoulders steeled, her eyes sending flashes of warning, telling the resident who's predicted this treatment's failure that if he wants to practice doom-and-gloom medicine, he can find somewhere else to do it, because this baby, her baby—Ethan—is going to recover.

I remember that, toward the end of the last day of that first round of chemo, at just about the time when Ethan would have been playing on the kitchen floor, with twilight pressing against the windows and soft jazz drifting through the room, when he would have been watching his parents shed the workday and settle into the evening—chatting with each other, preparing for his bath, putting pasta to boil on the stove—when he would have been waiting for that moment when his father would scoop him up and toss him in the air and his mother would pretend he was a jet plane, dipping and soaring to the changing table, a nurse came in to say he needed one more test. For an instant, I saw my sister flinch and her eyes begin to fill, but then, pushing her headband firmly back on her hair, she stood up. And they started slowly down the hall, a parade unto themselves.

In that snapshot, Ethan is peering over his father's shoulder, trailing a jumble of wires and tubes. The nurse is behind them, pushing the IV pole. And a few feet back, bringing up the rear, with a pacifier in one hand and an emesis basin in the other, with a Barney doll stuck in her pocket and a tube clamp hanging from her belt, with her eyes a shade too bright, but a determined tilt to her chin, is my sister—making faces at Ethan until he squeals.

—*Laura S. Distelheim*

A version of this story was published in *Whetstone*, Volume 13, 1996.

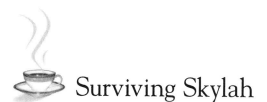 Surviving Skylah

I spent most of my early childhood in my room. It wasn't that I was a particularly naughty child whose punishment was being confined to her room. I was merely a child who needed to protect her stuff.

Skylah was the problem. She was the bane of my existence. With her curly yellow hair and pudgy, rose-colored cheeks, she could have been the model for one of those cherubs Michelangelo painted on the ceiling of the Sistine Chapel. Everybody but I thought she was utterly delightful. I tried to warn our parents about the evil lurking behind those innocent, China blue eyes, but nobody would listen.

I repeatedly told our parents how Skylah would sneak into my room and steal my best toys. How she would leave a terrible mess all over the place and sometimes break things. I begged them to put a lock on my bedroom door, but they wouldn't hear of it. Instead, I was told to "make allowances" because she was younger. I wasn't all that sure what allowances were, but I knew I didn't want to make them. I was left with little choice but to spend most of my time in my room, standing guard over my things. It was a lonely existence.

Of course, I had to come out sometimes. Mealtimes were the main problem. I didn't eat a lot in those days, because I had to get back to my bedroom before Skylah finished her food. Fortunately, Skylah possessed a healthy appetite, so it usually wasn't a problem. Not until the day my favorite chocolate cake appeared on the table, a cake so tantalizing in its rich, dark decadence that I couldn't resist a second slice. That cake was my downfall.

She couldn't have gotten there more than two or three minutes before I did. But it was time enough. My beautiful new porcelain doll lay broken on the floor—head smashed into a thousand pieces, her silk kimono scrunched and smeared with sticky chocolate from Skylah's grubby little hands. One sad glassy gray eye stared out at me accusingly from beneath the dresser, where it had rolled.

Well, what would you have done? I smacked her smug little face, of course. And then I smacked her again, quite hard. At her screech of protest, Mother came hurrying into the room. She surveyed the wreckage with a grim expression. I thought I was in big trouble for sure, because I wasn't supposed to hit my sister—ever. But justice prevailed, that time, at least. Mother told Skylah that she deserved the slap. She didn't know there had been more than one.

I decided to push home my advantage.

"She needs to buy me a new doll."

"Yes, she certainly does," agreed Mother.

Skylah was forced to empty her piggy bank of every last coin. She'd been saving for a new gerbil and a cage to keep it in. She'd had almost enough saved, and now there she was, counting out her last pennies to give to her spiteful sister.

Skylah sobbed brokenheartedly about it all being "only an accident." I relished every clink of change as it hit the floor.

Life is most unfair sometimes, for I had little time to enjoy my victory.

That very evening saw Skylah in the hospital with a raging fever and a sore throat. I was left with Mrs. Nichols next door while my parents took Skylah to the hospital. I didn't understand what was going on. When our mother and father didn't return home that night, I was afraid something really bad had happened to my sister.

The next day, my dad returned home and explained that Skylah's tonsils had been removed that morning and she was going to be fine. I didn't believe him. I thought she was dying and it was my fault because I'd made her cry. I didn't tell anybody how I felt; I couldn't get the words to come out. I spent the whole day with a really sick feeling in my tummy, sitting quietly in Mrs. Nichols's musty blue velveteen chair, pretending to read. Mrs. Nichols thought I was the best little girl in the world. I hated her.

Skylah came home two days later. I forgot my concern for her as soon as I found out she'd gotten to eat nothing but ice cream for two whole days. Things returned to normal, and soon I was wishing there was a second pair of tonsils they could take out of my sister.

Now, why am I thinking of all this some fifty years later? Well, Skylah was recently in the hospital again, this time to remove her gallbladder. I sat by her bed while she was still a little groggy from the anesthetic.

"Jane, do you remember when I broke that china doll of yours and you made me pay to get you a new one?" she asked.

"You never did pay," I said. "I gave you the money back. I also bought you a gerbil out of my own pocket money. It was waiting for you when you got home from having your tonsils out."

"Yeah, well . . . I broke that doll on purpose. I wanted to pay you back for being such a mean sister and not letting me play with your toys. I was a rotten little thing, wasn't I? I sometimes wonder how you put up with me." Her giggle was a bit groggy.

She probably didn't notice my gritted teeth as I said sweetly, "Do you have any more organs that could be removed while you're here?"

Sometimes I wonder why the two of us are such good friends.

—*Margaret B. Davidson*

A version of this story was published as "Sisters" in *Hodgepodge Sunny Edition*, fall 2001.

These Small Things

My mother reads the newspaper in bed at night. Propped up on pillows and reading glasses perched on the end of her nose, she makes a pleasant rustle with the turning of pages, the folding of sections, in the quiet of her bedroom at home. I think this has been her ritual forever, but I can't be sure.

Tonight, she is sleeping in my house, borrowing my son's bed, reading my newspaper, which is different from hers. She finds this interesting and tears out an article from the health and fitness section about the power of cranberries to fight bad bacteria in the digestive tract.

While she reads, I walk into and out of the room, making more trips than necessary to my son's dresser for fresh underwear and library books as I ready the children for bed. Truth be told, I just want to hear that rustle, to see her pink satiny slippers with the little bows sitting on the floor by her suitcase, to smell her creamy ready-for-bed scent, so oddly out of context in a bedroom decor of homerun hitters and dinosaurs.

She has come to give me a dose of comfort and companionship in the middle of a five-day stretch in which my husband is traveling on business, and I am grateful for it down to my bones.

I'm grateful as I rise for the umpteenth time from our supper, a supper she has prepared, to fetch some critical item for my three-year-old daughter—catsup, the polka-dotted fork, no, the other polka-dotted fork, more apple juice.

I'm grateful as she loads the dishwasher while I take a call from my husband in Chicago, who is kind enough not to mention the piano bar he and his hard-working colleagues are preparing to visit after dinner at a good restaurant. (I learn of these things only after he is home and only if I ask—wise man.)

I am grateful when she graciously agrees to four quick games of Clue Junior with my seven-year-old son after supper, and when she discreetly busies herself with some small thing in her room while I attempt to handle my red-haired daughter's fatigue-induced tantrum. (Whose fatigue induced the tantrum, I wonder as I write this, my daughter's or mine?)

"These are precious years for you, but they can wear you out in a hurry, can't they?" she sympathizes when we finally have a moment to talk. I am lying next to her in bed for a little while, being a daughter instead of a mom.

"You managed with four," I say in wonderment, staring at the ceiling.

"Oh, but they were spread out more. I had help from the older kids."

This is only partially true. My siblings were seven, eight, and twelve years old when I was born. And when Dad was working all day and earning his degree at night on the G.I. Bill, they were busy toddlers. (She once told me that for four years she ironed two white dress shirts each day for my dad: one for work and one for night school.)

She is just being kind.

I rearrange the Goosebumps pillow under my head and think about what I always think about when my husband travels and I am managing the household and the family alone: single parents, and how they manage to do it every day, every night, every weekend.

"I'm glad you're here tonight," I say, and squeeze her hand.

"I love to be here," she squeezes back.

In the morning I bring a steaming cup of coffee to her bedside. She relishes it like nectar from the gods.

"Do you know how long it's been since someone brought me a cup of coffee in bed?" She sighs, taking her first sip with obvious pleasure.

"I thought Dad always brought you coffee in bed," I say, surprised.

"No, he doesn't know how to operate the new coffeemaker."

I make a face. "This is the same man who in his early seventies learned how to operate his own computer, modem and all."

We shake our heads and giggle in the gray morning light. Then I'm off to answer my daughter's call from the steps, where she is stretching and singing "Old McDonald."

The next day my mom and I talk on the phone. She's back home, planting tulip bulbs and making chicken-vegetable soup. I give her a play-by-play of my day. She "mm-hmms" and "tsks" in all the right places.

"Thanks for coming up for the night, Mom," I say again before we hang up.

"Thanks for bringing me coffee in bed," she says, and means it.

—*Marsha McGregor*

Walk Softly, Children Working

The early morning rush hour has begun. Buses, motorcycles, and cars crowd a busy street in Guatemala City. Men in business suits and women in the latest fashions stride purposefully to work. Along the sidewalk, shoeshine boys wait hopefully for customers.

Roberto's torn jeans are tied at the ankles with strings. One string has slipped and is cutting into his flesh. His bare feet are pushed into worn cotton shoes. A customer sits on Roberto's rough-hewn wooden chair. His knees already throbbing as they push into the uneven sidewalk, Roberto places the man's foot on a small stool and snaps the plastic protector around the customer's ankle, guarding the cuff of the man's slacks. He scoops up the black polish with his fingers and quickly applies it to the man's scuffed shoes, as the shoeshine boy next to Roberto calls out, "*Tsch! Tsch!*" trying to attract businessmen to his chair. As Roberto pulls the cloth back and forth to bring up the shine, he hears his little sister crying. His grandmother is pulling the little girl back onto the sidewalk.

A bus, belching a cloud of exhaust, pulls away from the curb to join the four lanes of traffic. Roberto's grandmother returns to her juice stand. She deftly peels oranges and squeezes them in her metal handpress. Two large glasses of juice, covered with plastic, stand ready for thirsty customers. The carton of eggs on her table is for those who prefer a raw egg in their morning juice. Roberto's little sister, clutching her grandma's skirt, is weeping. A raw red cut beside her eye is swelling rapidly.

Antonio, wearing a colorful shirt and a handwoven jacket, stops near the little girl. He gently touches her head.

"She was playing on those metal poles and fell into the street," the grandmother calls to Antonio over the traffic din.

Antonio nods. He puts down his briefcase and looks around for Roberto. The two exchange a silent grin. While Roberto's customer pays him, Antonio opens his briefcase. It is filled with pencils, crayons, papers, and articles. Roberto shakes his head "no" to another prospective customer. Antonio squats down on a bench as Roberto hoists himself into his shoeshine chair. Antonio hands Roberto an article to read, about pollution in Guatemala City. Roberto holds the paper, momentarily focusing his thoughts. Then he begins to read, mouthing the words silently. When he has read the article three times, Antonio gives him a paper and some pencils and crayons.

The teacher and student exchange a few words. Roberto bends over the paper for ten to fifteen minutes and then hands it to Antonio.

"Write your name and grade," says Antonio.

When Roberto hands the paper back to his teacher, Antonio shows it to me. A slow smile of pride crosses his face. On the paper, a huge cloud of exhaust almost hides the cars and buses and, on the street, a small boy, thin and shivering, is having trouble breathing.

"He got the main idea," says Antonio, and with utmost respect, he puts the paper into his briefcase. He shakes hands with Roberto, saying, "I'll see you tomorrow at the same time."

Antonio teaches some of the thousands of working children on the streets of Guatemala. He is allowing me, a teacher on leave from my job in Canada, to follow him for a few days as he teaches. Last week, I walked in the main garbage dump of this huge city. I saw lovers stealing kisses among the stench of rotting refuse, the only home those young people have ever known. I went to large markets and saw many other young children who work ten hours a day, six days a week, selling fruit, begging, peddling cheap jewelry. And, tucked away in unused corners, I saw teachers, like Antonio, gathering these children together for an hour a day, or twenty minutes a day, giving them a chance at literacy, at an education.

We move on. Antonio walks half a block. Behind a small peanut stand are a girl, about thirteen, and her father. Antonio shakes hands with both and speaks briefly with the parent. Then he turns to the girl. "We'll start classes today."

"Now?"

"Right."

The girl pulls out two plastic containers from under her table, stacks them one on top of the other, and sits on them.

"She's in year three," says Antonio.

Her writing assignment is: *Think about one thing that is really difficult in your work. What can you do to change it? What have you done? Did it work? Why or why not? Do you need the help of someone else? Who? What could that person do?*

A short time later, we move on down the street. At the next corner, an extended family has two stands, one of fresh fruits cut and packaged in plastic bags and another of electronic equipment. The three boys here are more rambunctious.

"We're starting today? Where do we sit?"

"Today, we'll do a dictation."

The single chair becomes a table, and the boys quiet down as they kneel around the chair and labor to write. . . .

Today is January 12. Most schools began today. I looked out of my window this morning and I saw many children getting ready and walking to school. They seemed happy. I got up early too. But I got ready to go to work. I also have a right to happiness. I also have a right to an education. Today, I, too, will start classes.

Antonio moves on. We walk into a tire repair shop. Through the back door I can see a boy of eleven, stacking old tires. The owner calls to the young boy. He and Antonio sit on the bench in front of the counter. The boy has never held a pencil, has never been in a classroom. Antonio hands him an 8½-by-11-inch line drawing of a tree and asks him to trace it, first with his finger.

"Which hand will you use?" Antonio asks.

The boy looks down at his hands. "The right one, I think."

Antonio hands him a yellow crayon. "Now, follow the outline without lifting the crayon from the paper."

Next, he does the same thing with a red crayon and then a green crayon. Finally, Antonio produces another paper. On it is a cartoon face—an outline that swirls off into the word "yo" ("I"). Tiny drops of perspiration form on the boy's nose as he carefully follows the loops and curves that will later lead him to print letters and words. Conversations in the shop quiet down. After twenty-five minutes of intense work, the boy goes back to his job of stacking tires. He shakes the stiffness out of his wrist and grins slightly. The owner looks at the boy with pride and, as the boy passes, he puts an arm around his shoulder.

This deceptively simple program is giving thousands of working children in Guatemala a chance at literacy and empowerment. When the everyday challenges of my job and the difficult circumstances facing some of my students threaten to overwhelm me, I think of Antonio and the street children of Guatemala. I remember the poverty and their struggle. I remember the makeshift classrooms and impromptu lessons. I remember the students' thirst for knowledge and joy of learning. I remember their parents' pride and perseverance. I remember the ingenuity and dedication of their teachers. And I am humbled and inspired.

—*Madeleine Enns*

 Summer Solstice

The answering machine's blinking light is the first thing I see as I enter my home. The apartment is small, and I can see the light as soon as I open the door. Buffy, my blond cocker spaniel, hurls herself from the overstuffed couch and dances at my feet. I let her lick me until she is sated, and then she returns to her still-warm nest.

I stare at the answering machine. I'm still not sure how I feel about it. While I don't want to be reminded of my obligation for the night, the promise of a familiar voice seems like tonic to my lonely soul.

I throw my overburdened key ring onto the counter. It lands with a loud slap before sliding to its resting place in the corner. There are small scratches in the blue Formica from years of what I like to call key bowling. Sometimes Michael and I would take turns, earning a point for perfectly wedged keys. I can still hear him say, "You're the man, Mom!"

I wonder if they know today is his birthday.

I glance again at the blinking red light. It draws me like a beacon.

I push the play button, and a soft, tentative voice fills the room.

"Hi, Melanie. Call me when you get in."

The caller didn't leave her name; she didn't have to. She knew that I'd know it was Chessie, sweet, copper-haired Chessie with the perfect smile and the large blue eyes. Chessie, who tonight at the bar will appear aloof until maybe her third drink, after which she will lure even the lowest life forms to our table just for fun.

I smile. I love Chessie. And I love April, Rita, and Debra, too. But today is Michael's birthday. It would be wrong to join them.

The next message is from Rita, glib, honey-voiced Rita, whose heart is bigger than her body. "Hi, sweetie. Call me when you get a chance."

Then April. She hasn't bothered to turn down the music, and Janis Joplin competes and wins over her message.

I wonder why there isn't one from Debra.

The girls. We still refer to ourselves that way, although we are women now.

I close my eyes and remember the day I returned home from the maternity hospital to my cramped, second-floor apartment with the rickety staircase. Michael was wrapped in a thick blue blanket, and I cradled him protectively. After two days of round-the-clock nurses and visiting relatives, I ached to have him all to myself. I had just put on my slippers when the doorbell rang. If it had been anyone else, I would have resented the intrusion. I opened the door, and there they were. My heart rose like a balloon.

They aren't company; they're closer than family. They are an extension of me.

Chessie, generous Chessie, brought me a box of white knit baby clothes that I know she was saving for herself but insisted I keep.

Rita, maternal Rita who dreams of having five children, took Michael from my arms and refused to part with him for almost an hour. She shut herself in his small yellow nursery, and when I stood at the door I could hear her singing. This made me cry a little, and I said a prayer that I would be as good to Michael as Rita would be to her children.

April, perpetual gypsy April, glanced at the infant, cooing, "Oh you beautiful darling!" in her adopted southern accent as she poured the wine. "I guess we're all gonna have to smoke on the balcony," she said.

Rita, serious Rita, finally emerged from the nursery and whispered, "He's asleep." She accepted the wine from April but didn't drink it, not until she'd put fresh sheets on my bed, filled the diaper stacker, and made iced tea.

And Debra, effervescent Debra who was still in high school, came later bearing a homemade book of coupons for babysitting, story reading, and diaper changing.

The phone rings again, pulling me roughly from the comfort of my memories.

I do not answer, but instead watch until the red light flashes. I know it must be Debra.

I walk to my bedroom and remove a worn scrapbook from the nightstand. On its cover *The Girls* is written in red nail polish. I lay on my stomach, and my feet hang over the bed.

The first picture is of Chessie and me, round-bellied toddlers wearing identical pink bikinis and standing in front of a wading pool.

Chessie and me at five, six, ten, twelve.

Then it's Chessie, April, and me, looking gangly and awkward. April's blond bangs are cut too short, and she seductively juts her hip while smoking a candy cigarette. Chessie and I make the peace sign. I remember that after this photo was taken, we shared a Winston Gold that April had pinched from her grandmother.

A wrapper from a Three Musketeers bar is wedged between the pages. It's still sticky.

Then, a small school photo of Rita. Her thick, dark hair is styled into frizzy curls, and it's obvious that her mother has given her a perm. Under it are the words *New Girl,* in letters clipped with pinking shears from magazines. There is a snapshot of Rita in her candy striper uniform. Her sister Debra is dressed in a pink corduroy jumper and wears pigtails.

As we grow older, we grow closer.

Junior year homecoming . . . I didn't want to go, because I was doubling with Chessie and she was golden in her satin strapless and I was dull in my pale lace. I felt plain next to Chessie. My mother said Elizabeth Taylor would feel plain next to Chessie, and then the doorbell rang and she pushed me toward the door. The boys pinned on our corsages, and Chessie's came out of a clear plastic tube and mine out of a large white box from the florist. Hers was small and wilted, and mine was a tight cluster of fragrant pink roses, and then everything was okay. The next day my stomach knotted with guilt at having felt jealous of Chessie. I made a small bouquet with my roses and brought it to her.

Senior year. April didn't have a prom date, but she told us she didn't want to go anyway. I told her that she was my date, and Chessie brought Rita. Although Debra was only a freshman, she went with a handsome football player. But she was not one of us yet, so we ignored her.

The shrill ring of the phone makes me jump, and this time I answer.

It is Chessie.

"Hi," she says. I know she means, "Are you coming?"

"Hi," I say, and she knows I mean, "I'm not sure."

An unusual silence falls between us.

"April is flying in from Boston. Debra can't make the restaurant, but she's coming later. Rita finally got a sitter," she says.

I'm torn. I've spent the first Friday of summer with the girls for the last eight years—our own solstice. Our night. We always drive out to the Jersey shore for an early dinner, pick a seedy bar to nest in, and then walk the beach carrying silver-tipped sparklers until the sun comes up.

We've been doing it since the summer we turned twenty-one. Debra was there, too, using a copy of Rita's ID. If anyone thought it strange that both dark-haired girls were named Rita Ginardo, they never said.

Chessie says, "It won't be the same without you." Her voice is soft and liquid.

Guilt hits me like a fist, and I wonder how I could have thought even for a moment that they wouldn't know that tonight's summer solstice falls on what would have been Michael's ninth birthday.

Chessie, fragile Chessie, who cried so hard when she drove me home from the hospital that even through my grief I wondered how she could see the road.

Rita, hollow-eyed Rita, who lost so much weight from her grief she had to buy new clothes.

Debra, strong Debra, who told me she'd had a fight with her husband, the same football player from senior prom, and could she crash on my couch. I saw through the ruse, but lonely and scared, I said, "Sure." She stayed for two months.

And April, unconventional April, who gave me a puppy, as if a puppy could replace a dead son. She was so earnest, and I knew she would gladly have taken my pain and made it hers, and I held the puppy to my chest until it was wet with my tears.

I realize that Chessie has stopped talking and is covering the phone with her hand. I can hear her small gulping noises, and then I'm crying, too. We weep almost silently into the phone and not for the first time I think of her as my lifeline.

Buffy pads into the room but does not join me on the bed. Instead she looks at me mournfully with her deep brown eyes, and I wonder how she always knows when it's six o'clock.

"I have to feed Buffy," I say, breaking the silence.

"We don't have to go out," she says. "We could come to your apartment, drink some wine . . ."

"No," I say. "I need to take a shower, but I'll be ready soon."

I wait for her to break the connection before I put down the phone.

I follow Buffy into the kitchen. She holds her silky tail high and wags it, as if she's leading a parade.

I sit with her on the floor and watch her eat. I talk to her, but I'm really talking to myself.

"Buffy," I say, "I'm not forgetting that summer solstice falls on Michael's birthday. Or that my life is lying in scraps at my feet. But right now, what matters is that they're insisting I be there, because the night truly won't be the same without me."

And it won't.

She looks up briefly from her bowl and licks my face. I think she understands.

—Christine M. Caldwell

Six Summers Ago

Six summers ago my mother, my sisters, and I lived on sweet pickles and granny smiths. Mom sang to us of the importance of apples, crooning they were food for our brains. To me, then, summertime meant playtime—three glorious months of doing cartwheels in the sun, munching on sweet pickles, and feeding my brain granny smiths, oblivious to the changes going on in my body and within myself. Carried weightlessly on the carefree days of my twelfth summer, I never once stopped to look back or forward. Racing toward and crashing through the unyielding forces of adolescence at undeviating speed, I basked in my naive happiness. Looking back now, I sometimes wish I could return, if only for a few moments, to that freewheeling summer of six years ago.

The blazing heat kept us perpetually in our bathing suits. Although the news (according to Mom) warned to stay out of the sun, that its evil UV rays would char and shrivel us up like bacon, we had our way with the sun. Mom had stockpiled sunscreen and she tried to slather it on my back, as she'd done for eleven summers before—as if I'd still let her. I usually managed to escape her sunscreen attack by mouthing off and showing her that I'd already liberally applied it myself, thank you very much. Then I'd dash to the bathroom and wipe the greasy lotion from my ashen skin and cover myself head to toe with even greasier baby oil. I was determined to get a tan by the first day of seventh grade, even if it meant branding my skin with blisters and pink pillowy scars. Six summers ago, I felt impervious to deadly UV rays and the need for SPF 30, 25, 15, or whatever.

That summer, Mom made a killing from our annual, weeklong garage sale. My sisters and I took turns as cashiers, positioned tall and lanky behind the Nike shoe/cash box. I took pride in my ability to shuffle through tens and twenties, counting out loud and smirking smugly as I dished out change, repeating religiously, "Thank you very much. Have a nice day," while our costumers looked on smiling and my sisters took it all in enviously. My sisters, both younger than I am, thought of me as their garage-sale mentor; next summer, maybe, just maybe, they too could deal money like a blackjack dealer.

But the queen bee of our garage sale was Mom. She buzzed in and out of our house every other hour, bringing out piles of old tennis shoes, hangers dripping with worn dresses, and tattered furniture from the basement. Her arms strained as she lugged out chairs, tables, stereos, books, and myriad neglected belongings. I'd turn righteously toward my sisters and wisely advise them, "Go help Mom before she breaks her back." They'd bow their heads obediently and trot off to help, while I expertly made change from a fifty-dollar bill.

By the last Sunday of our sale six summers ago, Mom was running ragged. She had cleared out almost every possible unused and overlooked item from our wardrobes, cupboards, closets, basement, and various nooks and crannies of the house. Then it happened: I can still see with crystal clarity the image of my favorite Barbie—which, although I hadn't played with her in ages and probably never would bother with again, I had always assumed would always be there—being handed over to a bubblegum-chewing girl I was sure would merely toss my doll into her growing heap of garage-sale Barbies. I excused myself from the TV-tray cum cashier-counter, announcing curtly that if my mother wished to sell my cherished Barbies, I wasn't going to be her checkout lady.

My sisters and I then and there decided it was a perfect time to end the garage sale. We reasoned with Mom that it was Sunday, we'd made a good profit, and there was really nothing left to sell. That's when she dove off the deep end. We watched dumbfounded as our mother ripped through the house. We heard her footsteps pound clear through the kitchen, up the stairs, across the carpet, and into her bedroom. As she thundered through her closets, my sisters and I stared holes into the ceiling, fearing she would break through the floor and fall right on us. Five minutes of thumping and bumping later, she hustled down the stairs, nearly missing one of them, clutching to her chest her most treasured childhood memento, her prized piece of American culture, her hunka-hunka burnin love: her beloved velvet Elvis. We braced ourselves for the incredible scene unfolding before us, standing silently before our garage-sale-maddened mother as she spoke.

"We have too much stuff in this house. It's time to move on, to make space for bigger and better things," she said as she whisked by us and toward the garage. "If I could sell your Barbie, I can . . ."

She paused, looked my way, and gave me her biggest, warmest, I-understand-just-how-you-feel Mom smile.

"I mean . . . it's just an old picture. Not really worth anything. No big deal. One last sale, that's all, girls."

We nodded robotically. We wouldn't stand in her way. Uh-uh. No way.

"Why are you all looking at me like I'm a crazy person? Keep moving on to bigger better things. Remember that, girls."

Yeah, Mom, but Elvis is the king of rock and roll. Elvis is your hero.

Six summers ago, my dad delighted the family with a swimming pool, a used aboveground job he bought from a guy across town. Daddy laid the foundation, poured the gravel, bought a solar cover, and invested in mass amounts of chlorine. We smothered him with hugs and thank yous for his gift of a swimming pool in our own backyard "for his girls," which, of course, included Mom.

While Dad worked his butt off Monday through Friday, my sisters and I bathed in the holy water of our pool. Mom made us her special iced tea, the only kind worth drinking, her secret ingredient hidden deep inside her sacred, gingham-clad recipe book. The deck of the pool served as our sleeping bay, reading nook, and a stage reserved for the talented few who were daring enough to belt out Boyz II Men songs to our adoring audience: Mom, who rewarded our off-key renditions with an exuberant round of applause and a standing ovation.

In mid-August, the meteorologists gave the go ahead to go out in the sun, as long as you wore SPF 30. Mom began to dangle the remainder of summer in our faces, preaching of its impending end.

"Enjoy it while you can, girls. Summer is almost o-v-e-r."

By then we had turned our attentions to school clothes and daytime soap operas, having filled up on the sun, pool escapades, sweet pickles, and granny smiths during June and July. Meanwhile, I'd taken to heart the beauty advice in my teenybopper magazine and, following the latest tress trend of the season, had my Mom chop off my hair. I'd also outgrown K-mart and discovered the mystique of the mall. I couldn't understand why Mom didn't understand that acid-washed jeans weren't cool anymore. I was ready for seventh grade, ready to play soccer, ready to go to concerts with my girl-friends, and ready to kiss a boy.

Oh, once in a while during the lazy last days of that summer six years ago, I'd venture outside, squinting my eyes to keep the shards of sunlight from piercing my eyes as I peered at the grapes to see if they'd ripened yet. At least, that's what I told my mom. Actually, I was peeking at a new boy with a nice smile and a great laugh who tied vines in the fields behind my house. My teenybopper magazine had told me to go for him, to make the first move, that guys were into aggressive girls then, six summers ago. In the month it took me to get up the nerve and figure out a way to approach him, he'd finished tying all the grapes and was gone, leaving me with my unsung preteen rhapsody.

Though the yellow sun crept up our backs, chasing the fall chill from the air, I was convinced my summer was over. I'd already left it and my childhood behind, and was poised to burst through the autumn leaves as an adult. Hadn't Mom said to move on to bigger and better things? Hadn't she sold her velvet Elvis so she could move on? Hadn't I sold my childhood to summer, starting with my favorite Barbie, so I could move on?

Six summers later, I reflect on all the bigger and better ways in which my sisters and I and even our parents have moved on. I now realize there is no such thing as "bigger and better." Who we are and what we have are good enough, often better than we realize, just as they were then, six summers ago, just as they are now and at any given moment in our lives.

Six summers ago, in my twelve-year-old innocence, I didn't question myself or the world around me. It was just another summer, and I readily accepted its gifts of sweet pickles and granny smiths, Mom's iced tea, and Dad's swimming pool. I never once considered how hard he'd worked to buy it and install it himself, so that his girls could have a wet haven to cool them in the summer sun. As summer came to an end, I hurled myself toward adulthood, intent on growing up, unaware the process had already begun with the manning of the TV stand at the garage sale. Only later, only recently, did I realize that on that last Sunday of our garage sale six summers ago, my mom sold her velvet Elvis not to move on to bigger and better things, but to cool the sting of her daughter's growing pains after selling her favorite Barbie.

Six summers ago, the sun singed my shoulders pink, but no sunburn scars mark the transition to bigger and better things during that last summer of my childhood. All that remains are memories of the biggest and best thing of all . . . love.

—*Heidi Kurpiela*

Grieving the F

Jason slumped at his desk, chin on fist, staring at the paper in front of him. Several minutes earlier, I had given all the students computer printouts of their assignments and grades for the past month. The printouts, which detailed each student's cumulative performance in my sophomore English class, contained no surprises; all graded papers had been returned previously. The students accepted the records of their work with little comment, and when the bell rang they escaped in a burst of high spirits to lunch. Everyone, except Jason. As his friends headed out the door, they asked Jason if he was joining them. He just shook his head.

I looked at him, legs sprawled in the aisle, lock of long, auburn hair streaked with purple falling across one cheek, eyes downcast. *What about his printout could be troubling him?* He was a straight-A student. He articulated original interpretations of the literature in class discussions and wrote with clarity and depth. He is one of those young people who light up the room and make me glad I teach. Jason shifted his weight, picked up the paper, set it down. He didn't look angry, just sad.

"What's wrong?" I asked. "Is there a mistake?"

"Only my mistake," he said. "I'm grieving my F. I didn't do a homework assignment."

It was hard to see him so unhappy. "Could you maybe celebrate the As?" I asked. "There are at least ten of them."

"No," he said simply. "Not yet. I have to grieve my F first."

He sat there a while longer. At last the sadness drained from his face, he nodded to me, smiled, and left.

Most students would say, "Hey, one assignment. No big deal." Not Jason. He went through a dark space before he could forgive himself.

A teacher to the core, I see a lesson in everything. Turning that incident over in my mind for days, I sensed this time the lesson was for me. But I hadn't a clue what it was and the image of Jason slumped at his desk faded.

Now, a decade later, I've been filling my luxurious days of retirement with ballroom dance. Last week I actually performed with a group of five couples. It wasn't a competitive event; we were just a little show at the intermission of a party for other dancers. Still, it was my first dance performance and I worried about it for a month. I wanted to wear black so the audience would notice me least among the ten dancers, but we were doing a Latin number and the women had to wear bright colors. *What if my mind went blank and I stood there in my sunflower yellow dress looking like a complete fool?*

We entered the room arm in arm with our partners. The audience, seated at tables along three walls, clapped. The music started. To my surprise, I smiled a genuine smile, danced with more style than I'd ever had, reveled in the spontaneous applause of the audience when we did an intricate step. I could do this. We got to the part of the dance where we changed partners. My second partner and I had never come together quite right, and I was a little afraid of him, besides.

Step-point, step-point, kick. Roll-through, cha-cha-cha, spot turn, pivot turn. And there I was, exactly in front of him. We started the next part of the routine. *Knee flex, syncopated cross-over.* I'd never dreamed I would do so well—until, abruptly, I had no idea where in the routine I was. My smile stayed pasted on my face, but my feet shuffled frantically. My partner strong-armed me through the next few moves, and eventually I found my place. I nailed the steps again. I snapped my head in the right places. We ended with a flourish and a deep bow.

Afterward, friends and strangers rushed to compliment the group, me included. I could hardly talk to them. *Hadn't my mistakes glowed in neon?* I talked to the other performers. Most of them had stumbled in at least one place, but they didn't care. They said there had been five couples to watch, so no one would notice one person's misstep. We'd been a grand success, and they'd had a good time. I tried to believe them and push away the ache of disappointment, to pretend I'd had fun, too.

But through the night, when I should have been sleeping, I mentally went over and over the place I hadn't done well, the music and the routine forming a continuous loop in my head. *I must not have practiced enough,* I scolded myself. *Or maybe I overpracticed.* Sometime in the early dawn, I remembered Jason—and got the lesson. I had rated my performance one F and ten As, and I hadn't yet grieved my F. I got up, made a cup of warm milk, and attended to the pain of regret.

When I allowed myself to go down into it, my racing mind finally slowed. A memory of our sweeping entry and the audience's burst of applause flitted through my mind. *But you goofed,* my inner critic reminded me. *Yes, I certainly did,* I agreed. On the other hand, there was that friend's smile when I executed a snappy syncopation, the excellent transition. And the way I kept smiling when I lost my place till I got back on track. There was even the possibility I'd done better than I thought. Although my mind had quit working temporarily, my feet might have kept up with most of the steps. Over the next few days, I thought now and then of the place I had messed up. But more and more, I remembered that most of the dance had gone very well.

If I blank again next time I perform, I hope I will find a quiet place afterward to be with my disappointment. Feelings are like little children who can be hushed only so long before they throw a tantrum. Then, perhaps in minutes, instead of hours, or at least hours, instead of days, I will be able to find pleasure in what I've done. I will first grieve my Fs, and then I will celebrate my As.

—*Samantha Ducloux*

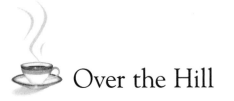 Over the Hill

"You are unemployable," the young woman said, reaching across her desk to return my resume.

Stunned, I stared at her. The expression on her face seemed smug, reflecting security in her own position. She rose, terminating my interview.

Getting shakily to my feet, I ducked my head to hide hot tears threatening to spill. I crammed my carefully prepared resume into my purse. With what dignity I could muster, I mumbled "Thanks," turned, and hurried out of the employment agency.

Climbing unsteadily into my car, I leaned my head on the steering wheel and let the tears flow. *Help me, God,* I prayed.

At forty-four years old, recently divorced, unexpectedly alone with teenage children and myself to support, out of the job market for eighteen years, I had four months of job hunting behind me.

At first, I had not worried. Although lacking a college degree (I had married and left university my junior year), I was widely read. I had been a secretary before the children came. Though I typed with only four fingers in my own hit-and-hope method,

I was accurate and fast. My shorthand was minimal, but in most offices, it was no longer needed. Word processors were, by then, common, and I felt confident I could learn to use one. But I needed a job now to put food on the table, and I could not wait for extensive training. Given a chance, I felt sure that I could be of use somewhere. But those words, "You are unemployable," rang in my ears and frightened me to the core.

It was a hot summer afternoon. Reluctant to go home and tell my children of this latest failed interview, I drove down Main Street and back, and parked in the only shady space. I slumped down in my seat.

I had called on the major companies in town. I had answered newspaper advertisements. I had asked everyone I knew to tell me of any openings they learned of. Health problems ruled out factory work. My only experience, years before, was in office work.

In more than thirty interviews, I had been told I was unqualified and "over the hill," despite recent laws forbidding age discrimination. Trying a high-fee employment agency seemed the last option. Yet, even there, the youthful counselor had refused to accept my application and resume.

Unemployable, she had said. What if I was? What if I couldn't find a job before my money ran out? What would happen to us? Please, God, show me what to do, I pleaded silently.

It was almost five o'clock. Shops were closing. Blotting my tears, I saw that I was parked in front of a shabby building. A sign over a small door between two stores read "Temp Services."

In near desperation I left the car and walked toward the sign. Following a faded arrow, I stepped inside and climbed steep stairs.

I half expected the temporary employment service to be closed. Instead an "open" sign was tacked on the door. I walked into a plainly furnished office. A dark-haired woman about my age sat at an old wooden desk. Without interrupting her telephone conversation, she waved me toward a lumpy-cushioned couch. A bulletin board behind her held job listings for day labor and factory work.

When she finished her call, the woman smiled and said, "I always have a cup of tea before I close shop. Would you like one?"

"Yes, please," I answered.

I watched as she dropped tea bags into chipped mugs and added water from an electric kettle. She brought me a mug, sat down beside me, and put her feet up on the low table in front of us.

"I don't know why but hot tea makes me feel better, even in summer. My name is Mary. How can I help you?" she asked.

Suddenly, words tumbled out. I told Mary my story from the day I got divorced and we moved to this southern town to start a new life, to my shock when the employment counselor had pronounced me "unemployable."

I heard my voice grow shrill. Yet, Mary listened quietly. Then she asked about my life as wife, mother, homemaker. She was sympathetic. She asked if I had done volunteer work. I fished out my crumpled resume and handed it to her. As we sipped our tea, she read it.

"May I keep this?" she asked at last.

"Of course."

"What do you think you could do best in an office?" she inquired.

"I'm told I write great letters. I'm good at organizing. I learn fast," I told her.

Minutes passed. She finished her tea. Then she looked me squarely in the eyes and said, "My dear, you have the most important qualifications an employer looks for. You're honest, you need work, and you will show up every day to put in a full day's work. You know how to juggle several tasks at once. It takes a good coordinator to manage a family and home. There is a place for you, and we'll find it!"

Could this be true? Mary believed in me! She did not see me as over the hill and unemployable.

She rose, and I followed. She told me not to worry. She gave me a typing test, which I passed. With an encouraging hand on my arm, she walked me to the door and added, "I promise I'll call you soon."

With renewed hope in my heart, I nearly ran down the stairs and hurried home.

Two days passed. Then another. My confidence waned. Would Mary truly call as she had promised?

Each time the telephone rang, I jumped. I was afraid to leave the house in case I might miss Mary's call. Nearly a week later, I sat watching the telephone, willing it to ring. At last it did.

"Hello!" Mary's voice was cheery. "A man has called who needs *you* for two weeks. He's starting a fishing tackle company and wants someone who writes good letters and can work unsupervised. If you get along, this could become permanent. Can you start tomorrow morning at eight?"

Could I!

"I know nothing about fishing," I warned her.

"Doesn't matter. This gentleman wants an honest worker who is mature and can be left on her own a lot," Mary said. "It's perfect for you."

"Mary, you don't know what this means!" I blurted out along with my thanks.

The pay for two weeks would be meager, but it was a beginning. A chance!

After Mary rang off, I sat staring at the telephone, thinking back over the week. If I had not felt so devastated by the first interviewer that fateful day, I would not have lingered downtown. Or parked in that one space along Main Street that was a haven of shade and found a haven of another sort. Coincidence? I think not.

On the brink of despair, I had reluctantly climbed those worn stairs and found a compassionate woman of vision who had said, "There is a place for you, and we'll find it."

A prayer answered. A promise made and kept. So began the first step in a positive direction . . . over the hill . . . where my future was very bright, indeed.

—*Marcia E. Brown*

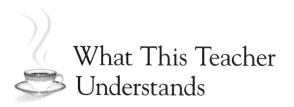

What This Teacher Understands

What this teacher understands is that our son's learning disabilities and attention deficit hyperactivity disorder (ADHD) are legitimate disabilities.

What this teacher understands is that our son takes an amphetamine medication, a form of "speed." This medication helps him to focus on what's being taught in class and also diminishes some of the excess energy created by ADHD.

What this teacher understands is that when our son is on this medication, he doesn't eat, feels dazed, is nauseous, has constant headaches, and the neck tic caused by use of this medication gets worse.

What this teacher understands is that without this amphetamine medication, our son will have a harder time controlling his moods (like a bike racing downhill with no brakes) and keeping quiet.

What this teacher understands is the strength and courage our son must have in order to endure the sometimes horrible side effects of the medication he takes and of the various medication combinations he's tried, so that he can be more compliant in school.

What this teacher understands is that there will be times when we, as parents, will grant our son the opportunity to come to school unmedicated so that he can feel less sedated.

What this teacher understands is the tremendous amount of frustration our son deals with every day because of his learning disabilities, as he struggles to keep pace with his classmates, to comprehend the material he is presented, and to communicate his thoughts on paper.

What this teacher understands is the bravery our son shows and the hurt he shoulders as he walks the halls of his middle school, ignoring the taunts of peers who refer to him as a "sped" (special education student).

What this teacher understands is that we, as parents, readily acknowledge and own our son's imperfections, do not condone his inappropriate behavior, and work hard to teach him the importance of taking responsibility for his actions.

What this teacher understands is the level of resilience our son must possess each day in order to go to school and be told that something wasn't done; or that something wasn't done correctly; or that something was answered correctly but because he wrote in green pen rather than pencil, his grade has been dropped from 100 to 80—and yet feel good about himself when he gets on the bus most mornings.

What this teacher understands is that if our son remembers his assignments two days more than he did the week before, it's progress, an *effort*. And that when he asks for help, he is acknowledging that he doesn't understand, which also means he is listening more and making more of an *effort* to understand.

What this teacher understands is that in taking our son to a tutor outside of school, we are not questioning his teachers' abilities; we are merely trying to augment what he is learning in school, so that he can catch up with his peers.

What this teacher understands is that with all the negative feedback our son hears throughout the day—"Why didn't you do this?" or "Why didn't you follow the instructions?" or "Why didn't you pay attention?"—we spend our time with him after school and on weekends focusing on the good things he has done (and can do), so he will stay motivated in trying to see beyond his limitations.

What this teacher understands is the gratitude our son and we, his parents, feel when she sends us emails acknowledging when our son has done something well or accomplished something good.

Because of this teacher's understanding—and because of her kindness, extraordinary efforts, acceptance of his imperfections, and sincere belief in our son—he has finally started to believe in himself. We have been so fortunate to have her in our lives.

—*Carol L. F. Kampf*

 # Stopping Traffic

This is a story about my best friend. Actually, it's not just about my best friend; it's also about my husband, who happens to be the same person. But that's beside the point.

Perhaps I also ought to mention that this is only one of many amazing stories I tell about him, because he is, in truth, an amazing person. But that, too, is beside the point.

Here is the point: This is a heartwarming story about an amazing man. And it goes like this:

One blustery, wintry day, at around 4:00 in the afternoon, my friend and I were driving peacefully along in the right lane of the Garden State Parkway in New Jersey. The Garden State Parkway at some points has five lanes of speeding traffic. During almost any season, most of the cars are heading madly toward the New Jersey shore in the misguided hope that they will find peace and quiet at the water's edge. Somewhere in my soul I am convinced that if they would drive less madly on the way to serenity, they would find it sooner. But I digress.

On this particular day, at this particular hour, we noticed that the traffic was developing a very peculiar pattern. It was racing along in the second, fourth, and fifth lanes, but the right and middle lanes were considerably slower. Perplexed, we moved to the second lane and prayed it was not an accident (which could keep us there for hours). Construction was the roadblock of choice.

Pretty soon we noticed a car pulled over on the shoulder. Standing near it was a rather attractive girl of perhaps twenty-five or so, frantically waving her hands. And there, in the right lane, was something fairly large, which we figured was screwing up traffic. We pulled over to where the girl was parked and got out of our car. She was practically in tears, but didn't have to tell us that the article in the right lane was a mattress or that a box spring was in the third lane of traffic, getting hit occasionally by cars.

Still holding back tears, she explained that she'd just bought the set, which had been tied on top of the car by the salesperson. But the wind had knocked them off her car and onto the parkway. Panicked, she'd pulled over and had been trying to get someone to help her. She didn't have a cell phone, and, when you really need them, police cars stay away in droves. So she'd been standing there in the bitter cold with her hands up for almost fifteen minutes.

She was there for almost fifteen minutes, and nobody—nobody—had stopped. Until us.

Where are the Good Samaritans of this world? Where are those caring Americans who help each other out in a pinch? If this had been a car accident, at least one other car would have stopped. Out of curiosity.

Never mind. You need only one, and we were it.

We listened to her story sympathetically. Then, without

any hesitation, my friend stepped out into the highway and stopped traffic!

I swear! He put up his hand and walked across the highway, stopping traffic! Stopping speeding cars swerving to avoid an annoying obstacle. Stopping cars hell bent on getting to a peaceful spot. Never thinking they might swerve into him! Fearlessly he stepped to the third lane and pulled the damaged box spring over to the side of the road. He then walked to lane one and saved the mattress. Then he waved the traffic on.

He waved the traffic on.

The girl was dumbstruck. I was frozen to the spot. My friend was not at all disturbed. In fact, he didn't notice our concern at all. There was more to be done. He had to figure out how to tie the mattress set back on the car safely.

Impossible. Her car was too small to start with, which is probably why she got into this predicament. So our car, which was a sight larger, would substitute. But how? Never mind how to tie it. First we had to get it up there. Two frail women (I am five-feet-two-inches and not very strong) and a sixty-four-year-old man (did I mention we are in our sixties?) would have to hoist first the box spring and then the mattress up on our car.

That was the plan: She and I would take one end, and he would take the other. Easily said if you've never lifted a queen-size box spring and mattress in a gusty February wind, on a highway with speeding cars, to the top of a car that's taller than you.

The first mishap was me. I tripped and dropped my end and fell onto my knee, which immediately started gushing blood all over her box spring. Great. And the scar will be there forever.

Tying a handkerchief around my throbbing knee, we

began again. This time successfully.

Resting for a moment before hoisting the mattress on top of the box spring, my friend advised the girl, who was still terribly upset, that she would, of course, get her money back or a new set in exchange, because the salesperson was at fault, not she. We suggested driving back to the store with the set, but when we called on our cell phone, the store was closed. The problem of returning it would be hers or theirs. If she did not get satisfaction, she could call us, and we would help. My friend is, after all, a lawyer. No, no, no. Not *that* kind of lawyer. He is an intellectual property lawyer. You know, the kind that deals with copyrights and trademarks. Again, I digress.

Not without further difficulty, we succeeded in hoisting the mattress on top of the box spring. Now we had to secure them. My friend's plan was to utilize whatever we had at hand. This included the torn string that was left from the original tie-up, some bungees we had in our car, a few T-shirts that he knotted together, and God knows what else. To make sure of no further mishap, he and the girl would sit in the front seats with the windows open, holding on to the set as he drove . . . very slowly. I would drive her car, following them to her house, which was a few miles away.

Oh, yes. Just as we were ready to leave, the highway authority drove up. A nice man, but a little too late. He did help us get safely back on the highway, though, and assured us that we could drive slowly.

When we arrived at the girl's home, she jumped out of the car, ran over to me, and gave me a big hug. It seems that while driving, she and my friend exchanged bits of information. She had once been a dancer. So had I, when I was young. She presently worked for a legal magazine that my friend subscribes to. And she had been a secretary at a law firm that my friend knew quite well. Small world.

Before parting we shared once more the unbelievable horror of her plight and received a hundred tearful thank-yous and hugs. We promised to keep in touch.

A final digression . . .

I often wonder. If that girl on the side of the road had been a white girl, would someone have stopped to help her sooner? I forgot to mention: she is black; we are not. I know how she must feel. I was looking for a cab in New York City not two months before on a snowy, frigid night. I had on black gloves, a black scarf around my face to help keep out the cold, and a black hat. Not one cab stopped for me, though a number of them were looking for fares. Finally, a black cabbie pulled over, and as I got in, I removed the scarf from my face. He looked at me confused. I was white! He could not understand why all those other cabs hadn't stopped for me. Couldn't he see that for a moment, at least, I was black?

My story has a happy ending. Our new friend was given a brand new mattress set with apologies from the store.

Would you like to hear about the time my husband saved a forest from a catastrophic fire? Single-handedly he braved the elements, fighting the persistent flames with just the shirt off his back . . . and got a terrible case of poison ivy, which lasted all summer.

He was only a little younger then.

—*Gila Zalon*

No Uncomfortable Silences

It has become a benign ritual sitting here at dusk, swatting mosquitoes and percolating yesterday's shadows through our thoughts. I imagine we do it to excavate our lost senses, to keep us vital in this passage of age we've entered. Wilfred's hat hides his drowsy eyes as he sways on the porch swing. He's tired, but he won't admit it. He's in the habit of playing Scrabble with Roy Kelly till late in the morning hours, always working to build his already abundant vocabulary. I tell him we're both in our seventies, and the words won't stick anyway. He sighs and drops his chin, peering at me through the reflection in his glasses.

"*Ambulate*," he says.

"I prefer to *walk*."

"*Interpolate*."

"I wish to *interpolate* the notion that you, with much affectation, are engaged in a foolish discourse you cannot win."

"That has *verisimilitude*."

"*Verily*."

The sun begins its drop behind the trees, and we sit in a silence that is shared by two people who have known each other all their lives. There are no uncomfortable silences, just a respect warranted by time, like two brothers aging across decades of life.

It was time for what Wilfred likes to call the "raconteur hour" of our evening, and I watch, waiting, knowing that like clockwork, he'll start up.

"Elliot, do you recall the whispering pines?" he asks.

Of course I remembered.

"The Smoky Mountains, winter of thirty-four," he continues.

I stare at him, at those little gray eyes I've known most of my seventy-four years, like I've forgotten the entire thing. It irks him to no end.

"Tell me how old we were again, so I can do the math," I say.

"You were twelve. In dog years, seven years older than me."

We'd both been in Boy Scouts then, long before the war stole our innocence. We had a good troop here in the Carolinas. Our leaders, using the weekend camps as subterfuge from their domestic lives, showed us how to cook stew in tin foil and how to carve sticks.

We were off on just such a weekend camping trip in the Smoky Mountains. It was winter, and a thick powdery snow hugged the ground. The trees wore white velvet; their branches looked like thin pins holding a foot of white snow against the blue sky. On the way up, our troop leader, a retired plumber named Lloyd Johnson, enlightened us about the whispering pines.

"And you believed it," says my friend. "The entire time." He laughs.

"And you didn't. Sure, you didn't," I say. "We all believed it, and not a one of us questioned it for fifteen years."

Then my memory plays back Lloyd Johnson talking about the psychology of the whispering pines.

Only in these mountains can you find the whispering pines. They're rare, very rare indeed. You see, these here pines are sensitive to human touch and emotions; they pick up on them. If you approach them very silently and take the needles of a branch in your hand and gently stroke them.

With that, Lloyd held one of his big plumber hands palmup and caressed it with his other hand like a baby, a smirk on his thin lips.

Well, that whispering pine will respond by swaying back and forth in the moonlight like it knows you. And if you listen real careful-like (here, he whispered deep in his throat) *you can hear the whisper it makes as it sways.*

I recall shooting a surprised grin at Wilfred and him shaking his head at me like he didn't believe it. But he did, later.

"Not at first," says Wilfred, squinting into the setting sun, before turning his face to me and lifting his eyebrows. "I had my doubts. You know I analyze everything. Besides—Lloyd Johnson, the plumber? He was good at whittling sticks and cooking stew and fixing leaky faucets. But he was no horticulturist!"

No, Wilfred did not believe old Lloyd Johnson. Not right then.

Two nights later, we went to find the whispering pines. A heavy snow had fallen that evening, and Lloyd Johnson gathered all fifteen of us into the cabin living room. He was a heavy man with a thick turkey neck that shook when he spoke, burying his chin in folds of skin whenever his mouth opened. His tiny mouth was no match for his bulky form; in fact we often joked that God had stuck it on by mistake. He leaned on a cane he'd just finished whittling that, like all his other sticks, had a spiral handle that spun around into a ball at the top.

Boys, we are about to go searching for the whispering pines, a most mysterious tree here in the Smoky Mountains. We all will have flashlights, but once we get to the area, everyone must be silent and turn off all the lights, or we'll frighten them.

Across the room, Wilfred raised a brow at me as he spun his flashlight in his hands.

The other scout leaders are already out there trying to locate the pines. Stay together!

We walked through those silent woods on padded snow. The snow-laden trees formed a thick cottony fortress, their branches bent low to the ground. Our flashlights flickered over every object and into each others' faces. As the muffled sounds of our low whispered conversations hung in the frigid air, our breaths formed clouds of steam. We must have resembled a sloppy train trudging slowly through the forest, the steam-breath trailing behind us and twisting up to the bright night sky. When our voices got too loud, Lloyd Johnson was quick to turn his chubby face to us and quiet us by waving his gloved hands toward the ground.

Finally, after a thirty-minute hike, we stopped and huddled around the plumber. In front of us a gorge dipped into blackness, the other side lit by the moon, and the great pines cut a jagged horizon line. Lloyd hushed us, and when our chatter stopped the silence was powerful. You could hear clumps of snow falling from trees twenty miles away.

The plumber stood at the foot of an enormous pine, its needles coated with thick snow all the way to the top. The branches drooped heavily, the lower ones actually kissing the ground and forming a solid base.

This, Lloyd began in a whisper, steam rolling out of his mouth, *is a whispering pine. We must keep quiet, because they are very sensitive to sound.*

We looked at each other, and I recall those faces were set in frozen amazement, afraid to blink or move. Lloyd had us all. Including Wilfred.

Lloyd stood before us like Paul Bunyan, his fat Eskimo gloves gesturing, sweeping us in, and we the followers, the innocent students, the ensemble of idiots, watched as he lifted an arm and gently took a bough in his hand. With his other hand he stroked that branch and let fly with epithets of baby talk:

Nice tree . . . ah-huh . . . such a nice tree . . . yes you are . . . mmm-hmmm.

And then, that tree moved. It swayed a little as if from the wind at first, and as he continued to coo and pet, it swayed back and forth like a great pendulum. Lloyd turned his proud face to his disciples.

See? He grinned. *They are very sensitive to human touch.* He turned back to the tree and gurgled some more.

We took turns then, one after the other, under the careful guidance of Lloyd Johnson, stroking that tree's branches, talking to it like a baby cradled in our arms. It swayed so much that the snow fell from the top in a sprinkling of magical white dust onto our heads. Lloyd stood there with the other scout leaders, chortling like he knew something we did not.

After an hour of standing on that cold mountainside talking to a pine tree, we finally made the trip back to the camp. The group reverberated with an excited energy, as if we'd discovered an ancient secret that would forever change the course of boy scouting. The fifteen of us walked in leaps, chattering away about the way that tree swayed in the night sky as we stroked its needles. We stayed up late that night, whispering about making the cover of *Boy's Life,* as our flash-lights bouncing off the cabin walls in a blackness filled with the bearlike snores of Lloyd the plumber and the other scout leaders. When we did finally sleep, we dreamt of wandering through the forest over a cottony white ground lit by the moon, surrounded by whispering pines that bent low as we passed, gentle giants watching over us in their world.

"Really had us, didn't they?" I say to Wilfred, as I watch him sip the last of his coffee. The setting sun lights the sky a bright crimson red.

"Until 1949, right before old Lloyd Johnson died," he says.

I look at him forgetful-like and say nothing, goading him to tell it again. Works every time. Here he goes.

"Yep. It was fifteen years later, guess I was twenty-five. I was back in Asheville for a family reunion, and there was Lloyd at the gathering, all hunched over on his cane. Time hadn't been at all kind to him. I sat next to him in the corner under a big pine tree. He looked at me and said, 'Wilfred Beems. You still pick your nose?' I asked him if he still carved sticks like a crazy fool. He held up his cane, and it had that curl handle that ended in a ball at the top. 'Last one I carved. Stroke,' he said. Then we sat there in silence, like there was nothing left to say. I glanced up at those pine branches.

"'Think it's a whispering pine?' I asked him. His face kind of turned to the branches, and then back at me; his mouth twisted into a crooked grin, and he let out a raspy, phlegm-filled laugh. Sounded like he was having a heart attack and couldn't breathe. Still laughing, he said, 'Could be, if you go get a thin yacht rope and tie it to the top, then go hide over there and get a group of Boy Scouts interested in talking to a tree.'

"I kind of froze then, just staring at his lined face, and for a moment I felt like a part of my childhood had been stolen. Then I said, 'Lloyd Johnson, you old son of a gun,' and laughed with him. We laughed so hard, everybody stared at us like we'd lost our minds. When I stood to go, he handed me his cane and said, 'I won't need this anymore.' He up and died two weeks later."

Wilfred looks over at me. I sit with my feet up on the railing and feign sleep. He shifts in his chair, annoyed, until I open my eyes and grin at him. And the silence continues like that while the cicadas buzz in the trees, and then they, too, fall silent, respecting the space where nothing is said.

—*Timothy A. Agnew*

An Unexpected Truth

"You can use my big new glove, Mommy," the little boy said in short, excited breaths as he searched the room for his glove. He ran into the TV and apologized, "Oh, excuse me. Ha!" looking quickly to make sure his mother still stood in the door waiting. He must not lose her. He found the glove under his bed and handed it to her, noting that she held it the way she always held his things, as if she expected to hand it back to him right away. But she wouldn't hand it back. Not today. Today, she was finally going to pitch to him.

As he ran to the closet to get his ball and bat, the bat fell to the floor with an oafish *thump, thump, thump,* and he grunted in agitation, bending to pick it up. He had so wanted everything to be quiet for his mother—no loud noises to cause her to flit away like a bird. He looked to her, and she smiled faintly, seeming somewhat amused by his excitement.

Danny Keith was his real name, but his mother had started calling him Keefer when he was just a baby, premature and brought home weighing four pounds. All his little friends had called him Keefer, too, until he started school and the teacher had called out his name off the roll like a trumpet blaring. By now, in second grade, about the only person to call him Keefer was his mother, and there was something warm about it that made him feel closer to her. He needed that desperately sometimes—the closeness—for his mother "wrote things" and always seemed just out of his reach. Even now as he held open the back door for her, she seemed not to notice, walking past him with a fixed gaze, holding the glove as though it were something that might spill.

Once outside, he took some practice swings with the bat, while his mother read the trees and the sky like a new book and breathed in the air deeply, closing her eyes. Sometimes he felt that she belonged more to the earth and sky than to him or to his father or to anything else—that if left to the elements long enough, she would dissolve into them without a trace. And she was always searching for what she called "Truths." She once said there were moments when she seemed about to know all Truths, only to have them slip away. He hadn't quite understood what she meant, but it had caused him to want to be truthful with her.

The late September sun was just warm enough to make his scalp draw up and crawl like a caterpillar, and he leaned on the bat waiting for his mother, enjoying it. She had put him off all summer with vague promises, which he'd thought she'd never keep, but here they were together, about to play ball, and he cherished every moment, even the waiting.

"Ready, Keefer?"

His mother's voice startled him, a voice that sounded strange out there in the sun, like it belonged to someone besides his mother. No, he wasn't ready! Yes he was! Oh, it didn't matter, for he would hit the ball hard and long for her, and then go bring it back so she wouldn't have to run after it. He didn't want her to tire of the game too quickly and go inside.

He ground himself into his stance, gripping the bat fiercely. She smiled at him and threw the ball like real pitchers she'd seen, bringing her right leg around and following through, only to have the ball go streaming over his head and to the right of him.

"That's okay, Mommy." He laughed and ran to get the errant ball. He would explain that throwing the ball wasn't easy when you hadn't practiced. He didn't want her to be discouraged. But when he came back with the ball, she was listening attentively to the dying leaves in the wind as they spoke of the fall or of the coming winter, or of some Truth that she strained to hear.

"You can pitch underhand if you want to, Mommy."

She brought herself back to him at the sound of his voice, and when he threw the ball to her, she forgot to close her glove on it, so that it dropped at her feet heavily. He ran to pick it up for her, but she bent to get it herself, and he hurried back to his batting spot, feeling somewhat confused. Then before he had set himself to swing, she lobbed the ball past him, and he saw her turn away with searching eyes. He ran quickly on his short legs to pick up the ball before she could attach herself to something else.

"I'm sorry, Keefer. I'm just no good at this."

"No! It's okay, Mommy, really." He just had to hit the next one for her.

He threw the ball back to her, and she caught it with both hands, causing her to hurt one of the fingers on her ungloved hand. He ran to her. "You all right, Mommy? Let me see."

"I'm all right." She showed him the finger, and he bent to kiss it shyly before turning in a circle and dancing back to his spot with his mother's warm smile still on him.

This time he set himself to hit the ball out of sight, and he concentrated so hard on it that it blurred as it came toward him, and he cut the air with a mighty swing that took him off his feet. He sat on the ground in a pool of embarrassment, wondering if she were disgusted with him to the point of quitting.

"I'll get it this time, honey." She ran past him and reached down to brush his head with her hand as she went. He reached up to touch that spot and thought how strange it was to see his mother run like that. She ran funny, and he loved her for it.

"I'll just bet you hit it this time," she encouraged, seeming to know how badly he needed to hit it for her.

He readied himself, and this time he could feel all the muscles in his body strain toward the ball as it cracked against his bat and sailed out of the yard and into the pine thicket across the road. He threw down the bat and caught his mother's proud smile as he called back to her, "I'll get it, Mommy. You wait there!" Knowing even as he said it, that he would lose her—knowing.

And when he returned with the ball, red-faced and heart racing, his mother stood twirling a leaf she had plucked from the box elder, and she seemed to be looking at something far away that only she could see.

"Mommy, could I hit just one more for you? Just one more?" He waited, looking up at her with his brown eyes. "Mommy?"

"Umm?" Her eyes sought his, but brushed past them without taking hold. "Another day, Keefer. Mommy will pitch to you another day, I promise. You're doing fine, just fine." And the leaf twirled in her hand, soaking up the energy, allowing her mind to go elsewhere.

He reached into his pocket and pulled out two sparkling rocks to give her. "Here, Mommy. These are for you for playing ball with me. You sure are a nice mother to do that. Do you think those're real diamonds in the rocks? They're for you, Mommy."

She let the twirling leaf slip through her fingers and bent to take the rocks from him. Then looking at him tenderly with shining eyes—brighter than diamonds—she dropped to her knees and pulled him to her, swaying back and forth like the trees in the September wind.

With his face held against his mother's soft hair, the little boy didn't understand. He had only wanted to make her happy—to thank her for playing ball with him. He hadn't meant to make her cry.

—*Betty Peterson*

This story was first published as "An Unspoken Truth" in *Bluegrass Woman*, August-September 1980.

 Angel Wings

I answer the ringing phone. "Hello?"

"Hi, darlin, it's Patty. Haven't seen you in a while. How're you doing?"

It's not a rhetorical question. Patty knows I've been struggling recently with mood swings and insomnia as my hormones adjust to the approach of menopause.

"Pretty good today," I answer. "How about you?"

"Fine, as ever. Can you come over tomorrow around noon and change a phone number for me?"

"Sure."

She closes our conversation with her signature phrase: "Angel wings around you!"

Patty's friends number in the hundreds, and she keeps tabs on all of them. She's part of an interdenominational prayer circle that covers a great swath of western Washington. Just let slip one word about an ailment or a child having a crisis, and you know your name will get added to the list of folks needing mention in prayer.

As I walk down the block to Patty's house the next day, I feel a twinge of guilt. It should be me calling up to check on her, I tell myself. But life gets so hectic, and every day finds me rushing about to get all the needful things done.

Patty doesn't do any rushing around, although I joke with her about bundling her up in bubble wrap, sitting her on a skateboard, and pushing her down the street just to get some fresh air.

I walk into her room. Angels, wings spread, cover all the walls, beaming down on visitors. Angel paintings, angel sculptures, even a teddy bear with wings: Beneath one of the angels is a framed certificate citing Patty's counseling credentials.

"Hi, darlin!" she says from her hospital bed. She's in her usual semireclining position.

I turn off her television.

"First, can you straighten out my right hand?" Patty asks.

I uncurl her fingers and tuck her hand back into place. The humming pump at the foot of the bed keeps the air mattress inflated.

"Now, raise the tray just a bit."

I circle around to her left side and adjust the control on the tray's support post. On the tray sit the tools of Patty's life: a Bible; two phone books crammed with names and numbers of family, friends, and acquaintances; and a specialized telephone.

"See the slip of paper on the big black phone book?" she says. "That number needs to go in position five."

The telephone holds twenty programmed numbers. Patty can turn the phone on by blowing on a puffer switch positioned by her mouth. Then she waits until the blinking light cycles to the phone number she wants. Another puff on the switch and the phone dials out automatically. One of the programmed numbers summons the operator for calls to people not on the list.

I dig the telephone's instruction manual out of the drawer, find the right page, and punch the sequence of buttons to change the number for Patty's grown daughter, Jenny. Jenny's family has just moved to Boise, Idaho, where the job prospects are better and the cost of living lower than in the Seattle area.

"Jenny says there's a Mormon church on every corner. She says, 'Mom, the Mormons are gonna get me!'"

I laugh. Patty knows I'm Mormon. She and Jenny are Lutheran, and Patty's husband and young son are Catholic, but we have all the most important precepts in common. We all believe in God and angels and the power of prayer.

The phone rings. "Hello, hello!" Patty says. Her phone recognizes the command and turns on the speaker. A sad voice pipes up, and Patty goes into counselor mode. Who better to advise and comfort newly diagnosed multiple sclerosis patients than someone who knows the disease inside and out?

I look at family portraits on the bureau, while Patty talks with an acquaintance in distress. In one sense her world has shrunk to the four walls of her room, yet in another Patty's touch has spread to anyplace a telephone can reach. Anyplace in our town, in our state, in our country.

"Angel wings around you!" she says at last and puffs to disconnect the phone.

"Would you check the calendar for me?" Patty asks.

I detach the calendar from its clip on the refrigerator and bring it back to Patty's side.

"What birthdays are left this month?"

"Linda on the twenty-fifth," I say.

"Already done."

Another friend comes over regularly to address birthday

cards. You can guess what greeting gets inscribed in each and every card!

"Matt on the twenty-seventh."

"Already done."

Someone else keeps Patty stocked up on greeting cards. Another friend does her Christmas shopping. Each person who renders Patty some small service finds the deed a small thing in comparison to the ministration of love and care she gives in return. I often leave feeling humbled. If Patty can bear her trials with such grace and strength, how petty am I to complain over lesser problems?

"Gerene on the twenty-ninth."

"Already done."

Patty doesn't need the calendar off the fridge. She's got a better one in her head. Birthdays, anniversaries, names of children, details of the trials of family and close friends—she remembers them all. Her memory is nearly photographic.

Sure, she'd like the use of her arms and legs again. But since multiple sclerosis has shut down most of her body, Patty makes good use of what she has left: her voice, her mind, her heart.

I put the calendar back in place, and we chat for a while about my two grown daughters. When it's time to go, I turn on her television and say good-bye.

"Angel wings around you!" she calls after me.

Angel wings . . . invisible, unseen. As I close the door and walk outside, I feel them around me already. And I know that angel's name.

—*Joyce Holt*

 Gordon

I was eleven when I first met Gordon. My mother and father had been divorced only a matter of days, so I wasn't a prime candidate for meeting Mother's new beau. I treated him rudely despite the gifts he brought to me. I didn't want anything to do with anyone who might stand in the way of what I knew would be an imminent reconciliation between my parents.

At fourteen I gained a stepfather. Gordon and my mother married after a three-year, turbulent courtship. By that time I had come to realize I was gaining an ally right in my own home. Gordon didn't always agree with my mother's method of discipline. He, in fact, believed that children were interesting smaller versions of adults, and regarded their feelings and thoughts with an honesty and respect that I had never known.

Learning to accept him into my home and my heart brought me experiences I would have forgone otherwise. Gordon was understanding and appreciative of my love of the theater, and he carted me back and forth to rehearsals, productions, and cast parties. He even let me have a cast party at our house. He cooked for two days, set up an elaborate feast, and stayed upstairs while my friends and I indulged in sheer delight. When they went home, Gordon came back downstairs and cleaned the mess himself, sending me to bed.

"You worked hard," he said, referring to my part in the school play. "You need to go to bed."

He encouraged my friendships, and was one of those parents who constantly chauffeured groups of kids to dances and ball games. We'd pile into the back of his beat-up Datsun pickup truck, covered with blankets, as he delivered all of my friends to their homes.

After enduring a childhood full of conflict with my mother, I reached a point one spring when I decided I'd prefer to go live with my biological father. Knowing I would meet staunch opposition from my mother, I instead approached Gordon with my plan.

"I hate to see you go," he said. "But your happiness is what's important here."

As it turned out, my father wasn't able to have me come and live with him. Sadly, this caused a rift in my relationship with him. I was truly disappointed but at the same time bolstered by the fact that Gordon had put my wishes and needs ahead of anyone else's, including his own. This concept was new to me, but one I came to accept throughout my years with him.

When I married young and found myself in a dire financial situation, he loaned me money but never made me feel like I'd imposed. He became "Grandpa Gordon" to my children. When my marriage failed, he encouraged and stood by me, and never once said "I told you so."

Years later—and since divorced from my mother—Gordon walked me down the aisle a second time, and welcomed more grandchildren. All the while he remained my rock and my strongest parental guide. He met and married Carol, a wonderful woman, and they've since spent many happy years together.

Gordon has never once in more than three decades said a negative word about my "real" father. In fact, he consistently encouraged our visits and praised his efforts. When my sister got married, both Gordon and Dad walked her down the aisle. With Gordon's blessing, both my sister and I have re-established our relationships with our father.

Throughout history, countless philosophers have contended that "blood runs thicker than water." I beg to differ. Although I love my natural father dearly, I have another father not of my blood and no longer through marriage who has stood by me through thick and thin. He has taught me some of life's most valuable lessons. He remains my confidante and true friend. And he is my closest "relative."

From petulant preteen years through adulthood, I have had the honor of learning from this brilliant psychologist and professor. Yet none of the knowledge I've acquired from Gordon touches on his profession. I gained, instead, insight into what really matters in this life, and I learned that families are there to help us live it.

What did Gordon learn from all of this? That's hard to say. If I was to fathom a guess, it would go something like a quote I've seen on greeting cards and wall hangings. It reads, "A hundred years from now it won't matter what kind of car I drove or how much money was in my bank account. What will matter is that I was important in the life of a child."

I was that child.

—*Kimberly Ripley*

 Leaving

The first time I left my mother, I was five years old. She told me I couldn't go out to play until I picked up my toys. Who could tolerate such treatment?

"I'm running away," I announced.

"Oh, dear, I'll miss you," she said, shaking her head, "But if you really want to go, I guess I shouldn't stop you."

Mother got my red coat from the closet and tucked my white mittens in a pocket. "You'd better wear these," she said, "It's just mid-afternoon, and it's already chilly out there. It will get really cold tonight."

She walked me to the porch, kissed me good-bye, and closed the door behind me. I heard the deadbolt slide into place.

Off I stomped. As I passed the house next door, my footsteps slowed. It struck me for the first time that I had no idea where I was headed, and after a moment, I turned around. Plopping down on our front steps, I began to consider my immediate future. But as the afternoon wore on, I didn't stir from my spot.

Mrs. Ford, our neighbor, took out her trash and called, "Hi, honey. How you doing?"

"I'm running away," I said, and my lips started to tremble.

"You are? Well, I won't disturb you then," she said, and went back inside.

As darkness fell, I decided to be generous. I knocked on the door, and when Mother opened it, I strolled past her.

"I'm giving you another chance," I said, as she wrapped me in a warm hug.

"May I have a kiss then?" she asked.

Not yet totally forgiving, I replied, "My kisses haven't come in today."

"I love you," she said, "Come on, the meatloaf's already on the table."

After supper, I climbed into her lap and covered her face with kisses.

"They just came in," I explained.

"I'm so glad," she said, "Now, go pick up your toys."

I never ran away again.

But I left, and that's different. First, I left for the first grade. I didn't have far to go, because our house was just across the street from my school. On the first day, I ran home at lunch, barely able to contain my excitement. "Mom! You'll never guess what happened. I can read, 'I can run'!" I shouted.

She enveloped me in a hug. "That's wonderful!" she said, "I can't wait to see what you'll learn this afternoon."

I hurried back to school. I couldn't wait to find out either.

Next, I left for college. She waved until my train pulled out of sight. She had helped me pack my bag, and when I got to my destination, I found a note she had tucked among my sweaters that read, "We're so proud of you!"

Though I was beginning to grow up, to break away, when I was lonely, I could phone to hear her voice. Our conversations always ended with, "I love you." The mail brought boxes of peanut butter cookies she had baked, clothes she had made for me, letters full of news from home.

When I married, I left again and moved far away. She remained my touchstone. At first, I phoned to ask trivial things: "Mom, how do you bake that chocolate cake with fudge icing?" She wrote out the recipe and sent it.

Then, I phoned to sob out the news that broke my heart: "Mom, I lost the baby."

She came the next day.

Finally, I phoned with words I dreaded to say: "Mom, my marriage is over."

She didn't pry, assigned no blame. She simply said, "I love you." I went home to my parents and got well inside.

Each time I left, she sent me off with a smile and words of encouragement. She never clung, though sometimes she couldn't hide the tears in her eyes.

I always felt her by my side.

Years went by, and in my thirties, I began law school. Then the day came when it was time to leave again. In the past, leaving had been a matter of choice, a part of getting on with our lives. Not this time. Before, we'd always known we'd see each other again soon. Not this time. I had always been the one who left. Not this time.

Mother died ten days after she was diagnosed with cancer.

It was not an easy death, but in the midst of pain, she managed to tell me one more time, "I love you."

I went on living, because that's what people do. Each morning, I got out of bed and did whatever was necessary. I returned to law school classes, with the bittersweet knowledge that, though I would soon become an attorney, my mother would not be there to share the day when my dream came true. Friends helped. Work helped. But I moved mechanically through my routines. For the first time in my life, I could not sense my mother by my side.

One evening, as I was going through her things, I found a quotation she had written in the margin of a book: "Love is a very agreeable passion, and sometimes it is stronger than death." She believed that, and I had the feeling she wrote it for me to find one day, after she'd gone. She believed what she had written, and I realized her words were true.

Mother had never really left. The way she'd lived her life remains as my moral compass.

Born to privilege, she didn't complain when her fortunes changed, but simply dug in and found ways to keep her family happy and secure. During the Great Depression, she tried to stretch our food each day, to save a little for tomorrow. Yet, when those with no food came to our door, she made sandwiches for them. With grace, she played the hand that was dealt her. Poverty, war, the loss of my dad, and cancer, she faced them all and managed to find joy, despite them. Her faith never wavered.

I see her smile in my memory. I hear the echo of her thoughts in my own. I find her love when I love others. I feel Mother always by my side. And I know this: Love is a very agreeable passion, and sometimes it is stronger than death.

—*Ramona John*

 Contributors

Ellen Jensen Abbott ("Monday Morning") lives in West Chester, Pennsylvania, with her husband, Ferg, and children, William and Janie. In the predawn hours when the house is quiet, she writes middle-grade and young-adult novels.

Timothy A. Agnew ("No Uncomfortable Silences") runs a part-time sports medicine practice by day and writes whenever he can. He free-lances for several publications and is currently working on a collection of short stories. He lives with his wife, Suzanne, in Sarasota, Florida.

Dawn Allcot ("A Plane Ticket, a Phone Call, and a Country Song") lives on Long Island, New York, with her husband and three cats. A freelance writer, she is a regular contributor to several magazines and Web sites, including *Church Production Sound, Sound & Communications, Paintball Sports International,* and N2Arts.com.

Beth Ambler ("A Bike with Pink Ribbons") began her writing career when she ended her career as an executive and started a new life as someone with multiple sclerosis. She resides in New Jersey with her beloved husband, Chuck, whose rivals for her attentions are Butkus, her Labrador retriever, and Syco, her 160-pound rottweiler puppy.

Teresa Ambord ("A Christmas to Remember") lives in Anderson, California, with her teenage son and her best friend and faithful pooch, Annie. Freelance writing is a growing part of her life. She writes in many genres, but is happiest when writing humor pieces.

Maureen Anderson ("Lessons from a Four-Year-Old"), of Detroit Lakes, Minnesota, hosts the syndicated radio program "The Career Clinic," which is broadcasted worldwide. She is also the coauthor, with Dick Beardsley, of *Staying the Course: A Runner's Toughest Choice.*

Joyce Lance Barnett ("Little Big Woman") has lived her entire life on the farm where she was born in Mills River, North Carolina. There, she and her husband, Carl, raised their two daughters in a medley of horses, hard work, and mountain grandeur. An artist and writer, her work includes both word and pastel portraits of the people, the animals, and her three grandchildren who now enjoy these magnificent mountains.

B. J. Bateman ("The Comforter") shares an A-frame in Gresham, Oregon, with her newly retired husband. Since her own retirement, B. J. has focused primarily on her family, dancing, and writing. She has published several pieces, both fiction and nonfiction, won two writing awards, and completed a novel.

Maura Bedloe ("Something More") writes from her seaside home in a small village in southeastern Tasmania, Australia, where she lives with her husband and two small children. Her work has been published within Australia, the United Kingdom, and the United States. Through her storytelling, she seeks to unearth and bring to light the wonderful and miraculous tales that lie buried in the lives of ordinary human beings.

Sande Boritz Berger ("Ninety-Day Wonder") lives in Manhattan and Bridgehampton, New York, with her husband and has two daughters.

After nearly two decades as a script writer and video/film producer, she returned to her first passion, writing fiction and nonfiction. Her award-winning short stories, poetry, and essays have been published in numerous anthologies and literary journals.

Marcia E. Brown ("Over the Hill") is an Austin, Texas, senior citizen whose writing has appeared in magazines, newspapers, and anthologies. Specializing in humor, she has completed a book of her funniest family stories. Marcia is a member of the National League of American Pen Women and the Texas Writers' League.

Renie Burghardt ("My Enemy, My Friend") was born in Hungary and immigrated to the United States in 1951. She lives in the country, where she enjoys nature, reading, and family activities. Her writing has been published in numerous magazines and anthologies, including *Whispers from Heaven; Listening to the Animals;* and *A Cup of Comfort: Stories That Warm Your Heart, Lift Your Spirit, and Enrich Your Life.*

Christy A. Caballero ("Leaning into the Harness") is a freelance writer and photographer who lives a couple of deer trails off the beaten track in Oregon. The woods, the sound of the river, or the sight of the ocean can all put a smile on her face. Her work has earned national awards, including the National Federation of Press Women Communications Contest and the Dog Writer's Association of America "Maxwell" Award. Christy has contributed stories to other volumes of the *A Cup of Comfort* series.

Christine M. Caldwell ("Summer Solstice") recently completed her first novel, *The Complete Lily Lansing*. A graduate of Rutgers University, Camden, she works as a purchasing agent for an electronics manufacturer. Caldwell lives in New Jersey with her husband, Mark, and her daughters, Brooke and Jillian.

Talia Carner ("Walking into the Wind") lives in Long Island, New York, with her husband and four children. Her personal essays have been published in *The New York Times*, anthologies, and magazines. Her novel, *Puppet Child*, was released in July 2002, and two others will follow soon. Before becoming a full-time writer, she was a marketing consultant to *Fortune* 500 companies and the publisher of *Savvy Woman* magazine.

P. Avice Carr ("Sister Power") is a human tumbleweed. She has rolled through twenty-nine towns in North America, living and collecting stories. Today, she divides her time between her husband's farm in Pennsylvania and her family in Ontario, Canada. She is the mother of five daughters and the grandmother of eleven children.

Candace Carteen ("A Long Way from Anywhere") resides in Battle Ground, Washington. She's a stay-at-home mom, homeschool teacher, and published author. She and her husband, George Blakeslee, have an adopted son and hope to adopt a sister for him.

Mary Chandler ("The Beaded Bag") lives in Rancho, Santa Fe, California. Her work has been widely published in national magazines, anthologies, newspapers, literary journals, and on the Internet. She loves to travel (especially if opera is on the agenda), enjoys visiting with family and friends, and is never without a good book.

Cinda Williams Chima ("An American Christmas Story") changed college majors fifteen times, exiting with a degree in philosophy. Today she is a dietitian who writes frequently on health and family issues. Married and the mother of two sons, she lives in Strongville, Ohio.

Rebecca Christensen ("The Favor") and her husband, Jeff, after having moved twenty-seven times between Maryland, California, and New York, finally settled on beautiful Bainbridge Island, Washington, where they make their home. This is her first published story.

Charmian Christie ("Wet and Naked") is a writer from Guelph, Ontario, Canada. Her writing career spans instruction manuals, plays, training videos, essays, magazine articles, and short stories (fiction). In her spare time, Charmian does community theater, where she takes comfort in knowing she isn't as crazy as the character portrays.

Bobbie Christmas ("I'll Give You a Dime") is the founder of Zebra Communications, a publishing consulting firm. She is the compiler of *Purge Your Prose of Problems*, coauthor of *The Legend of Codfish and Potatoes* with Parliament member Dale Butler, and past president of the Georgia Writers Association. Her writing credits include hundreds of articles and stories in more than forty publications. She resides in Atlanta, Georgia.

Nan B. Clark ("Steady as She Rises") lives in Beverly, Massachusetts, with her husband, Tom, whom she met when they were both rookie newspaper reporters. A special needs tutor, she knows how courageous children can be.

Harriet Cooper ("A Five-Dollar Bill") is a freelance humorist and essayist living in Toronto, Ontario, Canada. Her stories, poems, articles, and anecdotes have appeared in a wide range of newspapers, magazines, anthologies, and Web sites. When not writing, she teaches English as a second language, practices yoga, and hides from her three cats.

Pat Curtis ("Love Lessons") works part-time in the Christian bookstore Great Expectations. A mother and grandmother, she lives in Joplin, Missouri, with her husband, Max, and their two Yorkies.

Barbara Davey ("Home Is Where the Hearth Is") is a health care administrator at a major teaching hospital by day. After hours, she celebrates her Celtic heritage with storytelling, paying homage to those ancient souls who were "walkers-between-the-worlds." Nearly a dozen of her inspirational essays have been published in literary magazines and anthologies. She and her husband, Reinhold Becker, live in Verona, New Jersey.

Margaret B. Davidson ("Surviving Skylah"), born and raised in England, now lives in Fairport, New York, with her husband and cat. Retired from a paying job, she devotes her time to improving her writing, playing tennis and golf, and traveling. She and her sister chat daily by e-mail.

Laura S. Distelheim ("My Sister, the Mother") received her J.D. degree from Harvard Law School. Her literary nonfiction has appeared in numerous journals and anthologies and has been nominated for Best American Essays and the Pushcart Prize. She lives in Highland Park, Illinois, not far from her sister and her nephew, Ethan, who is now a nine-year-old bundle of energy.

Samantha Ducloux ("Grieving the F"), a lifelong teacher and student of many things, including languages, family relationships, writing, and dance, has published fiction and nonfiction under the names Samellyn Wood and Samantha Ducloux. She lives with her husband in Portland, Oregon, where she is learning to grieve the Fs and celebrate the As.

Madeleine Enns ("Walk Softly, Children Working"), a retired teacher, lives in Winnipeg, Canada. Her stories have been published in several magazines, including *Rhubarb* and *Sophia*.

Kathleen Ewing ("A Pair of Nothings") was an aerospace manufacturing engineer when the world tilted on its axis on September 11, 2001. Now an office coordinator, she resides in Arizona's central mountains, where she enjoys horseback riding, target shooting, and four-wheeling the back country in her Dodge pickup truck.

Patricia Fish ("My Funny Mother") hails from Pasadena, Maryland. An accountant by training, she now writes full-time. She published her first book, *Everything You Need to Know about Being a Woman Can Be Learned in the Garden*, in 1999.

Kristl Volk Franklin ("A Dittle Code") was born in Celle, Germany. Since becoming a United States citizen, she has lived in six different states but considers the South her home. She writes screenplays and has published award-winning fiction and nonfiction in the inspirational and psychological-thriller genres.

Brenda Fritsvold ("Incidental Kin") lives in Seattle, Washington, with her husband and two young sons.

Mona Gable ("Girly Girl") is a writer whose articles and essays have appeared in numerous publications, including the *Los Angeles Times Magazine*, *Health*, the *Wall Street Journal*, and *Salon*. She lives in Los Angeles with her husband and two children.

Elaine C. Gast ("Placid Drive"), a freelance writer and yoga teacher based in Haiku, Hawaii, holds a master's degree in writing from Towson University. She has authored books for nonprofit organizations and published articles in national magazines and newsletters, and she currently writes for local newspapers on Maui.

John Gaudet ("Dad's Belt") lives in Prince Albert, Saskatchewan, Canada. A freelance writer whose articles and essays have been published in several print and online publications, he is presently working on a novel. He enjoys reading, writing, and spending time with his wife, Chantalle, and their daughter, Charisa.

Cheryl Glowacki ("Reverse Psychology") resides in Berrien Springs, Michigan, with her supportive husband, Rick. She thanks her son, Scott

Strzyzykowski, for being the star of her first published essay, her daughter Shannon for introducing her to the *Cup of Comfort* book series, and her daughters Stephanie and Sarah for encouraging her to write.

Dawn Goldsmith ("Snow Angel"), newspaper reporter, bibliophile, and Illinois resident, freelances full-time and has published essays and articles in a variety of publications and online sites, including *Christian Science Monitor, Skirt! Magazine, Quilt World,* and several anthologies. She also reviews books for *Publishers Weekly* and *Crescent Blues E'magazine.*

Tanya Ward Goodman ("Moving Grandma West") is a freelance writer and full-time mother. She lives in Los Angeles, California, with her husband, David, and son, Theodore Roscoe. She is currently working on a memoir chronicling her experience with her father and his Alzheimer's disease.

Christine Goold ("Dear Mom") is a college instructor and writer. Her magazine articles have appeared in numerous regional and national publications. Her two published gothic romance novels are set in her native Colorado, where she lives with her husband, Gary. Jana, her daughter, is now a theater student at the University of Evansville, Indiana.

Whitney L. Grady ("Why I Teach") resides in Kinston, North Carolina, with her husband, James, and their dog, Shug, where she teaches seventh and eighth grade at Arendell Parott Academy. She gains inspiration for her writing from her students, friends, family, and weekends at the beach. This is her first published story.

Nancy Gustafson ("The Salvation of Jan and Kurt") has published poetry, short fiction, essays, and articles in several anthologies and journals. She is retired from Sam Houston State University, where she worked as a program coordinator for the Correctional Management Institute of Texas. She lives with her husband, Jan, in Huntsville, Texas.

Kira Hardison ("Rockn Da Nose") lives in Colorado. She is a homeschooling mother of three boys. When not retrieving things from their noses, she writes.

Maureen O. Hayden ("A Midwest Miracle") is a reporter at the Evansville (Indiana) *Courier & Press*, where she covers the religion beat. A journalist of twenty years, she's written about an array of issues, from family matters to civic affairs. She lives in Evansville with her husband, Daniel, and their three children, Emily, Elliot and John Michael.

Joyce Holt ("Angel Wings"), a native and resident of Seattle, Washington, wrote the script for the city of Renton's centennial pageant, a two-hour musical chronicle of local history. She likes to weave, draw caricatures, perform ventriloquism, volunteer in church children's programs, and write science fiction and historical-fantasy novels.

Molly Hulett ("Daughter of the Bride") is a freelance writer for a variety of magazines and corporate clients. She lives with her husband along the South Carolina coast.

Ramona John ("Leaving"), a retired judge, is the published author of two books and numerous magazine and newspaper articles. She lives with her husband, Dick, and their dog, Greta, in Crowley, Texas.

Carol L. F. Kampf ("What This Teacher Understands") holds two master's degrees, one in counseling, and is the owner of a human resources consulting firm. She lives with her husband and two sons in Alpharetta, Georgia. Her writing has appeared in several publications, including *Attention Magazine,* the *Harrisburg Patriot News,* and ParentToParent.com.

Sandy Keefe ("What Dreams Are Made Of") lives in El Dorado Hills, California, with her husband and two daughters, Allie and Shannon. Her older son, Burt, lives in Santa Cruz, California. Sandy is a registered nurse who provides case-management for children with severe disabilities. She enjoys freelance writing for consumer and professional publications.

Marla Kiley ("Till Death Do Us Part") lives in Denver, Colorado, with her husband and two sons. Her articles have appeared in numerous magazines and newspapers. When not at the computer or changing diapers, you can find her airing out her brain on a long walk.

Heidi Kurpiela ("Six Summers Ago"), of North Collins, New York, majors in journalism at Buffalo State College. She writes for two newspapers and works in a bookstore.

Inez Hollander Lake ("Caroline's Prince") lives in the San Francisco Bay Area with her husband, son, and her highness, Princess Caroline. When she is not checking her daughter's formalwear and invitations to royal dinners, she writes, edits, translates, teaches, and enjoys the riches of full-time motherhood.

Charles Langley ("Reglar Feller") returned to writing after a fifty-nine-year hiatus and at age eighty-six has published more than 100 stories, poems, articles, and columns for e-zines, print magazines, and books. He recently compiled an anthology of the writings of members of the Creative Writing Group, which he moderates.

b.j. lawry ("Pink Organdy") was a former reporter, feature writer, editor, and publisher of magazines and newspapers for thirty-six years. Retired now in the Arkansas hill country, she continues to write and has authored two published books, *Desert Heat*, a romance novel, and *The Piper of Featherly*, a mystery.

Penny J. Leisch ("Like a Rock") is an award-winning poet and photographer residing in Chandler, Arizona. In addition to writing instructional materials, book and film reviews, travel features, essays, articles, and a family activities column, she teaches writing and photography.

Nancy Massand ("Time Out") is a teacher at an independent school in Queens, New York. She and her husband have raised three delightful daughters and recently added two sons-in-law to the family. Nancy's stories have appeared in numerous publications.

Marsha McGregor ("These Small Things") is a freelance writer who lives with her husband, two children, and three cats in Hudson, Ohio. Her essays and articles have frequently appeared in *The Plain Dealer Sunday Magazine*. She also writes corporate and marketing communications for regional and national companies. Marsha is a member of the International Women's Writing Guild.

Kathleen McNamara ("Pass it On") is a fourth-generation Californian who lives in the San Francisco Bay Area. She is a health writer who dabbles in fiber arts and calligraphy. Though no competition for Martha Stewart, she also restores antiques, grows an herb garden, and can't resist hunting for great finds at craft shows, flea markets, and eBay.

Jennifer Meyer ("Tender Is the Night") is a freelance writer living in Eugene, Oregon. Her first novel, *Missing Pieces*, is awaiting publication, and she is working on a second. She has two sons, ages twenty and sixteen. She and her wife, Kate, were recently wed after twenty-two years together.

Camille Moffat ("The Rising of the Sun") lives in the south and writes from her home on the side of a mountain overlooking the Shenandoah Valley. About her writing, she says, "I've always been grateful that I can write. After all, everyone needs a gift of some kind, and I'm a lousy cook."

Janet L. Oakley ("Sons and Streams") is the educational curator at a county museum in Washington State. She also writes social studies curricula for schools and historical organizations as well as novels and essays. Her future husband took her fishing for the first time four months after they met.

Betty Peterson ("An Unexpected Truth") is currently a professor of English at Somerset Community College in Somerset, Kentucky. She writes in all genres and has published in *English Journal, Seventeen,* and *Appalachian Heritage,* to name a few, in addition to having had several plays produced. She was recently commissioned through a grant from the NEA to adapt Harriette Arnow's novel *The Dollmaker* for stage.

Kimberly Ripley ("Gordon") makes her home in New Hampshire with her husband, Roland, and five children. She is the author of five books, including *Freelancing Later in Life,* and conducts writing workshops around the country. Her writing has been published in magazines and anthologies, including several volumes of the *A Cup of Comfort* series.

Julia Horst Schuster ("Ah, Fruitcake!") is a columnist and book reviewer. Her stories have appeared in consumer and literary magazines. She is president of Emerald Coast Writers in Destin, Florida, and editor of the nonprofit group's annual literary journal, *SandScript: A Journal of Contemporary Writing.*

Bluma Schwarz ("Pure and Simple") is a semiretired mental health counselor and freelance writer, residing in Florida. At age sixty-nine, she published her first story in *Iowa Woman.* Her stories have since appeared in *Potpourri, Potomac Review, AIM,* other volumes of the *A Cup of Comfort* series, and elsewhere.

Alaina Smith ("Grandma and Grandpa and Karen") has a passion for writing. Her inspirational true stories have been published in anthologies, and she has completed a novel. She lives near Portland, Oregon, with her husband, Frank.

K. Anne Smith ("Clown School") is a retired speech/language pathologist who currently teaches public speaking at the college level. Her short stories, poems, and articles have appeared in numerous magazines, including *BlueRidge Country, GreenPrints,* and *Family Fun.*

Thomas Smith ("Innocence and the Divine") has a wife he is crazy about and two dogs that are (mostly) housebroken. He is an award-winning writer, reporter, TV news producer, playwright, and pretty fair banjo picker. He divides his time between Raleigh and Topsail Island, North Carolina.

Sigrid Stark ("My Jar of Self-Esteem") once considered a career as a funeral singer. She now lives in Edmonton, Alberta, Canada, where she juggles being the mother of four teenagers, a pastor's wife, and the manager of marketing and fund development for a local nonprofit. Faith and friendship continue to inspire her writing.

Mary Helen Straker ("King David") lives six months in Zanesville, Ohio, and six months in Bonita Springs, Florida. A graduate of DePauw University, she has worked for a Zanesville newspaper and *The Seattle Times.* She is the mother of four children and grandmother of six.

Annemarieke Tazelaar ("A Little Child Shall Lead Them"), after years of teaching, now owns her own business and spends her spare time writing. Several of her stories have been published in *A Cup of Comfort* books.

Susan B. Townsend ("The First Day") is a writer and stay-at-home mother. Transplanted from the west coast of Canada six years ago, she now makes her home on a 300-acre farm in southeastern Virginia with her husband, five children, and a zoo full of animals. Her nonfiction work has appeared in several anthologies, including other volumes of *A Cup of Comfort*, and her fiction can be found in numerous e-zines.

Kathryn O. Umbarger ("The Last, Best Gift") discovered the joy of writing at age fifty and since then has earned thirty-seven writing awards. She has been published in fiction, essays, poetry, and allegory, but her passion is writing for children. She lives with her husband on the Snake River in southeastern Washington, where she enjoys grandchildren, camping, and kayaking.

Jeanette Valentine ("Marching Orders"), a freelance writer in the San Francisco Bay area, has been obsessed with her craft since first grade, when she won a writing contest by penning thirty-eight stories. (The second runner-up wrote seven.) With her son, Lamont, in college 3,000 miles away, she now applies her expert nurturing skills to Mimi, a gray-and-white tabby cat.

Peggy Vincent ("All Creatures Great and Small") is the author of *Baby Catcher: Chronicles of a Modern Midwife* (Scribner 2002), a memoir of her years as a home birth midwife. Peggy's writing has appeared in *Reader's Digest, The Christian Science Monitor, Skirt!,* and various other publications, including *A Cup of Comfort*. She lives in Oakland, California, with her husband and teenage son, and two adult children live nearby.

Bonnie L. Walker ("The Educated Dude") is the author of several language arts textbooks. Her articles have appeared in the *Washington Post* and other publications. She enjoys yoga, tennis, and playing games with her grandchildren. Her most significant years were spent as a middle school teacher.

Linda C. Wisniewski ("Little Black Cat") has worked as a librarian, newspaper reporter, and freelance writer. She lives with her family in southeastern Pennsylvania and teaches memoir writing at Bucks County Community College. She enjoys reading mystery novels, practicing yoga, and watching her retired scientist husband cook fabulous gourmet meals.

Robin E. Woods ("Christmas Is Delicious!") is a former early childhood art, music, and movement teacher living in Montclair, New Jersey. A frequent contributor to parenting publications, she hopes that her writing, which chronicles the innocent and sometimes humorous impressions of her children, will someday thrill and embarrass them.

Gila Zalon ("Stopping Traffic"), the mother of three grown children, divides her time managing her husband's law office, writing, and acting in local theatre groups. When her children were young, she wrote two plays for school fundraisers in which she also performed, and more recently she wrote two short screenplays that were produced by a local film company. With "Stopping Traffic," Gila is thrilled to have entered the world of books.